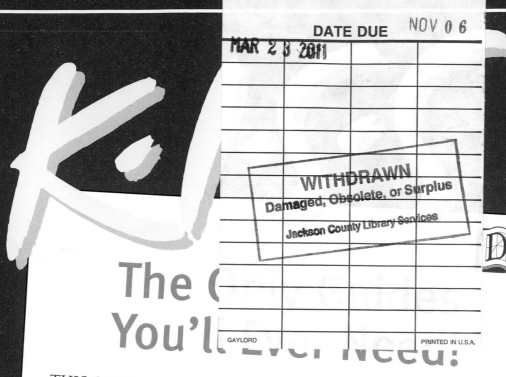

The Guides You'll Ever Need:

THIS SERIES IS YOUR TRUSTED GUIDE through all of life's stages and situations. Want to learn how to surf the Internet or care for your new dog? Or maybe you'd like to become a wine connoisseur or an expert gardener? The solution is simple: Just pick up a K.I.S.S. Guide and turn to the first page.

Expert authors will walk you through the subject from start to finish, using simple blocks of knowledge to build your skills one step at a time. Build upon these learning blocks and by the end of the book, you'll be an expert yourself! Or, if you are familiar with the topic but want to learn more, it's easy to dive in and pick up where you left off.

The K.I.S.S. Guides deliver what they promise: simple access to all the information you'll need on one subject. Other titles you might want to check out include: Babycare, Sex, Pregnancy, Beauty, Yoga, Online Investing, Sailing, and many more to come.

GUIDE TO CARING FOR YOUR

Horse

MOIRA C. HARRIS
Foreword by David O'Connor
Olympic Gold Medalist

DK Publishing

**LONDON, NEW YORK, MUNICH,
MELBOURNE, DELHI**

DK Publishing, Inc.
Line and Copy Editor Ruth Strother
Senior Editor Jennifer Williams
Editorial Director Chuck Wills
Publisher Chuck Lang

Dorling Kindersley Limited
Project Editor Julian Gray
Project Art Editor Martin Dieguez
DTP Designer Mike Grigoletti

Managing Editor Maxine Lewis
Managing Art Editor Heather McCarry

Production Rita Sinha
Category Publisher Mary Thompson

Produced for Dorling Kindersley by

studio cactus Ⓒ

13 SOUTHGATE STREET   WINCHESTER   HAMPSHIRE   SO23 9DZ

Project Editors Jane Baldock, Laura Seber
Project Art Editors Laura Watson, Sharon Rudd
Editorial Assistance Kate Hayward

First American edition, 2003
03 04 05 10 9 8 7 6 5 4 3 2

Published in the United States by DK Publishing, Inc.
375 Hudson Street, New York, NY 10014

Library of Congress Cataloging-in-Publication data

Harris, Moira C.
    KISS guide to caring for your horse / author, Moira Harris.-- 1st American ed.
    p. cm.
  ISBN-13: 978-0-7894-9198-5
  ISBN-10: 0-7894-9198-2
    1. Horses.   I. Title
SF285.3 .H357 2003
636.1--dc21

                                                      2002073495

Color reproduction by Colourscan, Singapore
Printed and bound by Printer Portuguesa, Portugal

See our complete product line at
www.dk.com

Contents at a Glance

Foreword

HORSES HAVE BEEN a part of human life and development for over 6,000 years. Originally a source of food, they soon became invaluable to us: They have carried men into battle, helped us to explore new lands, and transformed our abilities in agriculture. In modern times, horses have continued to change people's lives, whether it be in sport, in one form or another, or just through plain companionship.

I have been lucky enough to have made my life in the horse world. Horses have taken me all over this planet and introduced me to situations and people I would never have had the opportunity to meet otherwise. From riding a horse from Maryland to Oregon when I was 11 years old to standing on the podium to receive three Olympic medals, horses have taken me beyond my wildest expectations.

Lance Armstrong has a very good book out called It's Not About the Bike. Well, let me tell you that it is about the horse. At times, horses have been my most cherished companions, soul mates, and partners, without whom it would have been impossible to achieve my dreams. There is never a day that I do not want to be around them and feel their unique curiosity, or share their practical view of the world. They make me a better person and I hope that The KISS Guide to Caring for Your Horse will give you, too, an insight into their world and what they can do for you.

There is a saying that there is nothing better for the inside of a man than the outside of a horse. I believe that communication between horses and humans fosters human health and social development at a cheap price. Horses are social beings, and they gain strength from being with those they can trust. For doing the tasks that we ask of them, our self-proclaimed promise to our horses must be to give safety and comfort in return. That gives us, as humans, a huge responsibility – the personal care and trust of another species.

In this book you will find myriad interesting facts, thoughts, and useful tips to enrich both your first-time and ongoing relationship with horses. Whether as an experienced horse owner or as a person who can enjoy horses only occasionally, this book will open doors, provoke new questions, and enhance your knowledge of all aspects of the horse's world.

DAVID O'CONNOR

Introduction

LIKE MANY YOUNG GIRLS, I was completely horse crazy. My walls were covered with horse posters, my desk at school was a sea of penciled galloping equines, and my thoughts raced all day toward those beautiful creatures. Even my bookshelves were crammed with paperbacks on horse health care, grooming, riding, and competing. I read them voraciously, gleaning as much as I could in hopes that one day I'd be a full-fledged horse owner. Those books were certainly cherished, and their information came in handy when I, as an adult, finally realized my horse-owning dream.

It's my hope that you can use this book the way the way I referred to my small equine library all those years ago. No matter what your skill or your interest level, there's always more to learn when it comes to horses. You've already taken a good step forward, however, just by picking up this book. By using the knowledge I have acquired as an equine journalist over many years, I have been able to provide you with the latest information on all that is involved in riding and horse keeping. More importantly, as a horse owner, I have related my own experiences to your needs; after all, I've been there. Hopefully, after reading through this book and using it to reference items from time to time, you will gain insight into the fun, responsibility, and the rewards of keeping a horse.

And what could be better than allowing a horse to share your life? For me, horses have a multi-faceted purpose. They're my chosen activity, my sport, if you will. Riding is part of my fitness regimen, and it not only helps keep me in shape, it challenges me to stay that way. Horses also serve as great therapy: even after a difficult day in the office, I can leave it all behind and escape to the world of a perfectly timed jump, an exhilarating canter, and a friendly whinny. Being a horse owner has also made me more responsible, and I have more empathy for all creatures - even people. In short, being a horse owner has brought me joy on many levels.

Before you make a commitment, though, remember that horses are indeed a huge responsibility. A horse is not a recreational vehicle that you can ride just when you want to. He requires special food, housing, health care, routine maintenance, and exercise – requirements that other domestic animals don't have. Horses are expensive, too – both in time and money. Having a horse in your life is not only a big commitment, it's a lifestyle change. Equestrians work very hard to be dedicated caretakers, as well as being adept at riding (a skill that must be mastered if one wants a fulfilling equine experience). If you believe you have the enthusiasm and dependable nature that it takes to be around horses, you're in for a life-changing experience.

The KISS Guide to Caring for Your Horse is organized so that you can find information easily and quickly. While you can (and hopefully will) read it from cover to cover, it is also set up as a reference tool so that you can open it up at any time and go straight to the material you need.

So, you're all set to start learning. But also keep in mind that horses are great teachers. They can give us confidence – yet occasionally teach us how to be humble. They show us how to love, how to respect another being, and how to live in harmony. These things make the time, money, and effort we spend as horsemen and horsewomen more than worthwhile.

MOIRA C. HARRIS

What's Inside?

THE INFORMATION in the K.I.S.S. Guide to Caring for your Horse *is carefully arranged so that even if you've never sat in a saddle before, you can find out just what keeping a horse will mean for you.*

Part One

In Part One, I'll discuss the unique relationship that we have with the horse, and how our two histories have been entwined over centuries. I'll give you insight into what makes horses tick and share the most popular breeds of horses from around the world with you.

Part Two

Read Part Two if you're thinking about buying a horse – it will show you what is involved in ownership. I'll help you find the best ways to start riding, then give you advice on how to search for your ideal horse. Since horses take special equipment and housing, you can read about all the gear you'll need to keep your horse happy and healthy.

Part Three

In Part Three, you'll read about the particular health care and nutrition needs a horse has. You'll discover situations where a horse might need special attention. This section covers not only routine maintenance, but also first aid.

Part Four

In Part Four, I'll let you in on one of the most rewarding aspects of horse riding: competition. You'll discover a host of ways in which to participate in equine sporting events. I'll even help you prepare for your first horse show so that you will have a positive experience in the show ring.

Part Five

In Part Five, you will read about the importance of proper training and how you can work with your horse so that he is a willing riding partner. I'll also discuss the pros and cons of raising a baby horse, as well as what to expect from a horse at any age – including the older horse.

The Extras

THROUGHOUT THE BOOK, you will notice a number of boxes and symbols. They are there to emphasize certain points we want you to pay special attention to, because they'll help you understand horses better. You'll find:

Very Important Point

This symbol points out topic information that deserves your undivided attention. Don't skip these points!

Complete No-No

This is a red flag. It either emphasizes something that you should avoid doing, or it is a general warning.

Getting Technical

This is material that delves deeper into the subject or is of a complex nature.

Inside Scoop

These symbols highlight a particular experience or a bit of extra knowledge I've gained through my years in the horse industry.

In addition, you will find boxes that will provide you with information that is significant, practical, or amusing.

Trivia...

I've included a few bits of trivia to provide you with a little extra material that is interesting or not widely known.

DEFINITION

*I'll use boxes to **define** and explain any unfamiliar horse terms or jargon. You'll also find a glossary at the back of the book with all the horse terminology.*

INTERNET

www.dk.com

These give specific addresses on the World Wide Web. The Internet can be a useful tool for horse lovers — just be careful where you find your information.

PART ONE

Selecting the Horse for You

THE HORSE IS AN IMMENSELY versatile animal, and each breed has something unique to offer us. With all this talent just waiting to be "harnessed," you'll have plenty of options while discovering the perfect horse for you.

Chapter 1

A Mutual Partnership

Horses and humans have gone together since the dawn of civilization. We have forged a connection with the horse that is unlike any other. But our partnership is one that must be built on mutual understanding of each other's strengths and weaknesses. Whether toiling in the field, galloping down the back stretch, or, best of all, trotting up to whinny a hello, the animal that has inspired myth and legend is also flesh and bone – forever changing those lives he touches.

In this chapter...

- ✓ **A useful partner**
- ✓ **A horse is not a dog**
- ✓ **The benefits of horses**
- ✓ **The drawbacks**
- ✓ **Is there a horse in your future?**

A useful partner

BACK IN THE CAVEMAN ERA, a horse, like any other wild animal, was looked at as a source of food. But horses quickly (and thankfully) became something that was of better use to humankind. Being mounted gave early humans perspective on their surroundings and a new understanding of how they fitted into the whole scheme of things.

The development of civilization is linked arm in arm, or rather, "arm in hoof," to our relationship with the horse. Because of their partnership with horses, humans were able to travel over greater distances in search of food, and also had an advantage when hunting prey because they were able to get much closer, faster.

HELLENISTIC STATUE

The Greeks were the first to depict the horse frequently in literature and art – the figure of the horse was found in pottery, sculpture, and on walls.

During Egypt's rise to power (around 2000 BC), horse-drawn chariots were used to conquer other empires. From the earliest records, the horse played a huge part in our ancestors going to battle, exploring the world, and colonizing new lands. Xenophon, an Athenian soldier, is known to nearly every serious equestrian as the first true horseman. His book *On the Art of Horsemanship* is still a valid study of how to train and treat horses.

Different roles

Over the centuries, humans have enjoyed the fact that horses are powerful animals that can be trained to do pretty much whatever they are asked. Today, horses are our other half in a variety of sporting events, from racing to Olympic competition. Their willing nature also makes them ideal to help people with disabilities find their feet in a way that no mere machine can. Finally, horses are good for our souls, allowing us to share in a unique friendship that has its own language.

■ **Horses are transported** *all around the world to compete in events such as the Olympic Games.*

A horse is not a dog

A NEIGHBOR OF MINE used to boast, "My horse acts just like a big puppy. He practically wants to sit in my lap! He recognizes my car when I drive up and he whinnies." She was lamenting this statement a few weeks later, after an unfamiliar goat wandered on to her property and her horse reared and ran away, leaving her dumped off in the dust.

While a lot of people might claim that their horse acts just like a big dog, nothing could be further from the truth. Horses are complex animals. Although they are domesticated, they still have a lot of instincts that emerge when they are frightened or angry.

Horses don't respond in the same way that dogs do – they don't come when they are called or enjoy lavish attention. In fact, a lot of horses would prefer the company of their own kind, rather than that of their owner.

The hunter versus the hunted

The canine species is designed to hunt – and in days gone by, the horse was probably a favorite on their menu. Wolves and their kind know how to map territory, how to hunt, and where to find prey. Their sharp teeth and claws, coupled with the strength, speed, and mentality of the pack, were created for their main job: to kill prey. As a prey animal, on the other hand, the horse is designed to preserve itself. Horses in the wild have an amazing sense of smell and can detect an enemy before actually seeing it. Meanwhile, their eyes are positioned on the sides of their heads, so that they can observe what is around them while they're grazing. Their fast legs and flinty hooves, along with their vast lung and heart capacity, are designed to get the jump on any potential hunters.

■ **Horses use their ears** *to constantly funnel information to the brain. Any foreign sounds can send a herd dashing to safety.*

Canine friends

Today, many horses and dogs seem to get along well in domesticated life. In fact, there are breeds of dogs, such as the Pembroke Welsh corgi, the Jack Russell terrier, and the Australian cattle dog, which are considered to be breeds that horse people most enjoy.

Don't assume that your dog will take to your horse, and vice versa. If introductions are not made very gently, a dog can traumatize a horse. Some horses never get over their fear of dogs if they suffer an attack.

But if a dog is particularly aggressive around a horse that hasn't been socialized with canines, you can expect the horse's behavior to revert back to what it is in the wild. It may give a good protective kick or even gallop away.

■ **Even if your horse** *is comfortable with a canine, avoid accidents by making sure that the dog does not get under the horse's feet – never leave them in a confined space together.*

Herbivore nature

Horses are vegetarians. If you put a hamburger in front of your horse, he would only eat the bun (if he didn't mind the ketchup and mustard of course). They are grazers, which means that they forage from the ground and they eat mostly grasses. This is different from other animal vegetarians, such as deer or goats, which are browsers, eating leaves from bushes and trees.

Often several members of the herd will sleep while one horse stays awake and alert to danger. Horses can doze while standing up, so that they are able to move at the first sign of a predator.

In the wild, horses spend up to 20 hours a day grazing. In order to cover enough ground, a herd will walk for many miles each day. Newborn horses, therefore, have to be on their feet and ready to move with the herd in a matter of hours – this is crucial for their survival.

The benefits of horses

IF YOU ASKED THE TYPICAL PERSON what the benefits of horses are, they might say, "well, they can plow the field." And they'd be both right and wrong. I mean, yes, they are good beasts of burden, but do you really know many people who have 40 acres that they're planning on harvesting soon?

Hobby horses

Horses are not just a link to our past, when they were used to transport people and goods. They still work at various jobs and provide us with joy today. Nowadays, most people do "something" with their horses. They take them on trail rides, and they learn a new skill – riding – on them. Equestrians spend most of their free time, money, and energy on their horse-riding passion. It's something that opens into a brand new world, full of its own lingo, equipment, and personalities.

INTERNET

www.newrider.com

This is a British-based site with basic information for the beginning rider.

Competition cohorts

Taken to the next level, you can match your riding skills against others in a range of events and competitions. Horses and riders compete in a variety of ways, from western rodeos, to Olympic events. Horses are involved in many professional sporting events, such as thoroughbred racing and international show jumping. You'll also find kids taking their ponies to nearby shows to display their riding skills and perhaps come back with ribbons.

Friendship for all time

Even though horses aren't like dogs, it doesn't mean that you can't have a relationship with them. A horse can quickly learn to recognize his owner. Horses don't bark a greeting, but some may whinny for you. They like consistency, and when you visit a horse on a regular basis, he looks forward to your arrival. A friend of mine has a horse who actually sidles up to the fence and waits for her to hop on his back for a ride. They both share a mutual respect for one another, and they enjoy each other's company.

■ **Competing** *can boost your self confidence, and will also give you the opportunity to meet other horse lovers and their equine friends.*

The drawbacks

LIKE EVERYTHING, THERE ARE PROS and cons to having horses in your life. They aren't like pets that live with you in your house. They have specific requirements in order to flourish, and just because you have space on your property to keep one it doesn't mean you should hop over to the nearest farm and drag a horse home.

Last year, a guy I know who lives in an area zoned for horses was given a free horse. Yes there is such a thing – but that horse did come with a price. This man had no idea what was involved in actually looking after a horse. He thought it would be fun to take the horse for trail rides, to show off his new acquisition to his buddies, to try something new. What he didn't realize was what an incredible burden he had taken on and set up home for in his backyard.

Do not think about buying your own horse if you cannot commit to a long term partnership. Finding a new owner for your horse may prove more difficult than you think.

The time costs were one thing, but the responsibility and the money involved turned out to be too much. In less than 12 months, he was looking for a way out from this "gift horse."

Horses are a BIG responsibility

A horse is like a 2-year-old child in a lot of ways. He depends on you for everything, but his needs are basic. He needs proper shelter from the elements, which means you can't just stick him in the spare bedroom or park him in the garage. He requires food that isn't found at the supermarket – or even at the pet store – and he needs to be fed on a regular schedule or his health may suffer. He needs a constant supply of fresh water (up to 13 gallons a day), and he needs exercise. If he is to be ridden he will need well-fitted tack.

He needs a special veterinarian who concentrates on large animals, so you won't be able to take him down to the cat-and-dog clinic around the corner. He needs his feet looked after frequently by a *farrier*. Finally, he needs space.

DEFINITION

*A **farrier** is different from a blacksmith. Both work over a forge and work metal. A farrier exclusively shoes horses, while a blacksmith works metal for various other reasons. Some blacksmiths may also be farriers.*

Keeping a horse

A horse does best when he is around other horses, since horses are herd animals and can suffer psychologically if they don't have a buddy to hang out with. Equestrian centers and boarding stables can provide your horse with a home and buddies, as well as a place for you to ride.

It is not only the amount of land but the quality of grass that is important for horses. There should not be any stagnant water or hazards like broken fences.

INTERNET

www.haynet.net

This site has everything under the sun that has to do with horses, plus links to a host of other sites.

However, if you are able to keep your horse on your property, you have to have ample, usable land for him. The hill with a 45-degree angle is probably not suitable for anything other than mountain goats.

Mucking out

You need to clean up after a horse, whether he is on your property or residing at a boarding stable. You need to remove your horse's manure, not only because of the smell but because of the swarms of flies and other parasites that can develop if you leave it.

Horses take time to care for – so if you have a busy schedule, perhaps riding occasionally at your local horse rental center would be better for you than having the responsibility and commitment of owning your own horse.

■ **Your horse's stall** *should be mucked out at least once a day. Droppings and soiled straw should be removed, the floor should be swept, and the bed shaken up. Fresh straw can be added to the bedding.*

An expensive pastime

There's a saying that "a boat is a hole in the water that you throw money in." Well, to alter that slightly, a horse is a hole in the pasture. Horses are a luxury, since a saddle horse doesn't really have any purpose in the modern world other than to be your riding companion. And you have to weigh up the expense of owning a horse against how much free time you actually have to get out riding in an average week.

It is a good idea to consider insurance for your horse to cover him in case of injury or illness. It's also wise to insure yourself as well.

Their tack (riding equipment) is expensive, as a well-made saddle can cost from $500 to $2,000. And horses need bridles, halters, saddle pads, girths, lead ropes, and more. Not only is there the initial outlay on these, they'll need to be replaced when they're faulty. You'll need barn equipment (that's not even counting the cost of the barn!), your own riding gear, and if you get really serious, you'll need to buy your show apparel and pay for your competition fees.

■ **A snaffle** *is the most common type of bridle.*

Horses' feet grow like our fingernails, so they need to be trimmed and shoes nailed on regardless of whether or not you ever ride the horse at all. They have special ailments that require a regular vaccination program. And horses are somewhat fragile creatures, so you have to be prepared to handle veterinary emergencies with a fund set up for that purpose.

■ **Horses need to be shod** *by a professional farrier every 4 to 6 weeks. Good shoeing is time consuming, and is a highly skilled job that requires specialized equipment.*

Size matters

If you don't own horse property, you've got to find a place to keep your horse. The animals are big individuals and are considered livestock. If your land is not zoned for horses, you will have to find a place that is. You can't have a casual attitude about a horse. He's not like a recreational vehicle that you can just take out whenever you like. If a horse is prevented from getting out and exercising, expending some of that cooped-up energy, he can go stir-crazy and develop some bad habits.

The average horse weighs about 1000 lbs (450 kg) and is very powerful. A horse can really be intimidating if he decides to throw his weight around, especially if you are nervous around large animals.

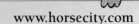

INTERNET

www.horsecity.com

This site has news and information on horse topics, updated daily.

■ **Horses need an adequate** *outside area to relax and move around in. Not only is this important for their physical health and circulation, but it's important for their mental health, too.*

SHORT QUIZ

Here's a short quiz to see if owning a horse is really an option for you:

1 The aroma of a stable:
a) is a delightful mix of hay, warm hides, fly repellent, and, yes, even manure. It's all good.
b) reminds me of the camel house at the zoo on a hot day. Bleah!

2 After I pet several horses, I:
a) don't mind going out to lunch.
b) must get to the restroom to wash the dirt off my hands as soon as I can.

3 I like spending my money on my:
a) hobbies, because they really give me fulfillment in life.
b) wardrobe, because I can't miss a sale – ever!

4 My obligations outside of work:
a) are very few, so I'm looking for a long-term commitment to something new.
b) are so many that my head is spinning. What day is it?

5 Financially speaking:
a) I've got a good cushion to work with, so I can afford a couple of luxuries for myself.
b) I'm a 50¢ cab ride from bankruptcy. If I could find 50¢.

6 When I've done something athletic, I:
a) feel invigorated, as I pride myself on keeping in shape.
b) feel as though I'm going to go into cardiac arrest. Who knew stairs were so tough?

7 Being up off the ground:
a) gives me perspective on the world. I'd love to view it between two fuzzy ears.
b) gives me the willies. I think I'm afraid of heights.

8 I live in an area where:
a) there are several opportunities for a person to keep horses.
b) the only thing that is horsey is that long-faced girl in the carpool lane next to me.

Mostly a's

If you answered mostly (a) to the questions, you would probably thrive in an equine environment. You're not afraid to get a little dusty on the trail, and you've got enough resources to cope.

Mostly b's

If you answered mostly (b) to the questions, please go out and buy a bike instead!

Is there a horse in your future?

SO IS IT WORTH IT? Can you see yourself riding off into the sunset with your favorite equine partner? If you can take the responsibility, and if you can make the commitment to care for him, then you're on your way to a great relationship.

Make your dream a reality

So many people dream of actually owning their own horse, but not so many are actually lucky enough to make that dream a reality. If you have assessed all the aspects of horse ownership, and are fully aware of the commitment and time it entails, then there's no reason why it should be an impossible goal to reach.

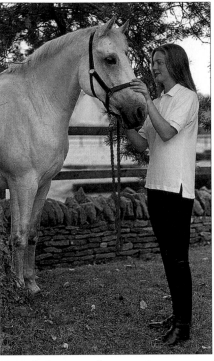

■ **Both horse and owner** *derive great satisfaction from their mutual friendship.*

A simple summary

✓ Horse and human history has been entwined for thousands of years.

✓ A horse differs from a dog in many ways. He is very different from other domestic animals.

✓ Horses can be companions, partners in work, and good therapy for the soul.

✓ Horse and rider can enjoy a special relationship.

✓ Horses are a huge responsibility and a long-term commitment. They are expensive to look after and need a lot of space.

✓ A horse can be in your future if you consider all that he needs to be healthy and happy.

Chapter 2

The History of the Horse

To APPRECIATE HORSES, it's a good idea to see where they came from so that you can understand where they are going. Although contemporary society is light years away from the horse-and-plow days, horses can still be found working and playing side by side with us. As a domestic animal unlike any other, horses play a vital role in today's world, and you'll find folks who adamantly claim they can't get along without them in their lives.

In this chapter...

✓ **Dawn Horse versus modern *Equus***

✓ **Wild versus domestic life**

✓ **How a horse is built**

✓ **All horses can do**

THE HERD INSTINCT IS STRONG IN BOTH WILD AND DOMESTIC HORSES

Dawn Horse versus modern *Equus*

THE FIRST HORSE HAD MORE IN COMMON *with a tiny deer than it did with Seattle Slew. Its name was* Eohippus, *and it walked the earth more than 50 million years ago. Known as "the Dawn Horse," it was probably the size of a fox, and it had three toes on its hind feet and four on the front. It was small enough to hide in the bushes for protection, rather than run from its predators as modern horses do. It browsed on the leaves of bushes.*

Some equines today have characteristics that reflect their wild ancestors, and there are several giveaways: stripes on areas such as legs and down the spine, thick coats, and bushy manes and tails.

Trivia...

Horses, asses, onagers, and zebras all belong to the Equidae family. Their different features have evolved as a result of the various environments they live in.

Through the centuries, the little deerlike horse evolved, adapting to its changing environment. When grasslands formed in North America (its area of origin), the animal developed larger teeth to crop grass. As it evolved, its legs grew longer to give it greater speed, and it began to travel mostly on its middle toe. Its back went from a convex shape to a sloping build. About a million years ago, the side toes disappeared, and an animal with strong teeth, a sloping neck, and strong hooves emerged. This animal was known as *Equus*, and it is the species that we know today as the horse.

About 15,000 years ago, humans arrived in the Americas. At about the same time, the horse disappeared from these lands, possibly due to hunting, but possibly due to the changing environment after the Ice Age. Whatever happened, the horse was thriving in Eurasia and Africa, having migrated over an ancient land bridge. Five thousand years later, horse met human in the Ukraine, and the tribes caught and tamed these horses, bringing about the first domesticated *Equus*.

■ **The modern horse evolved** *from* Eohippus, *which existed over 50 million years ago. The body size grew larger, the legs grew longer, and the shape of the jaw and the size of the teeth changed.*

Wild versus domestic life

EVEN THOUGH THE TAME PALOMINO that you see decked out in silver and trotting down Colorado Boulevard in the Rose Parade doesn't seem to have much in common with the stripy zebra, both have similar instincts working for them, some of which have to do with being herd animals.

Herd life

Being a herd animal means living in a group. There is safety in numbers, especially where horses are concerned. "The survival of the fittest" was certainly the case for wild horses, with the weakest or oldest ones becoming supper for predators. Because of this, generations of horses had to become tougher, faster, and stronger for the species to continue. Horses survived because they are able to run away from their predators. If necessary they can also protect themselves with a well-aimed kick. A horse's kick has enough force to kill its enemy.

Horses are fully active soon after they are born. This is extremely important for their survival in the wild. Unlike wolf or lion cubs, which are helpless for the first few days of life, the foal is on its feet and bonding with its mother soon after birth.

Trivia...
In some parts of the world, horses continue to live in wild herds. For example, there are an estimated 50,000 mustangs roaming the Western range.

■ **The foal always** *stays close to its mother, so that it is ready to follow her and the rest of the herd if there is any sign of danger.*

Animal instincts

Domestic horses still have a lot of these traits. The "fight or flight" trait is one where a horse will run from what she sees as danger, but if cornered will struggle and bite and kick if she feels she can't escape. No human can be a match for an extremely frightened horse.

But training and desensitizing a horse to the chaos of modern life enables her to overcome her instincts and learn to trust her handlers. You'll see riders encouraging their horses to walk calmly past vehicles. You also see international competition horses that are able to jump a course of 5 ft (1.5 m) fences, with crowds roaring in their ears and flash bulbs popping in their eyes.

If a horse spots another horse in a tense, excited posture, she will interpret this as a sign of danger. Tense looking people will also, therefore, make the horse nervous and want to take flight. It is best to approach horses in a relaxed, unfearful way.

■ **Police horses are trained** *to be desensitized to loud noises, obstacles, and crowds of people, so that they can help with riot control and demonstrations without panicking.*

Today's modern horse still enjoys being part of a herd. Domestic horses can suffer great separation anxiety if their buddies are taken from them, and some horses don't do well as solitary creatures. They whinny and pace until their equine friend has returned. Also, some horses can be quite obstinate about leaving their horse friends to go out on their own. These horses can be very *spooky* out on the trail alone, but they relax more when traveling with another horse.

DEFINITION

A horse that is easily startled by things in its environment and overreacts by bolting, shying, or whirling around is considered to be **spooky**.

Feeding habits

Wild horses forage all day long. They walk for a dozen miles or more daily in search of the best food and water. Their bodies are designed to process food constantly (usually most of their waking hours), so the ideal natural diet for them is a forage that has good roughage.

One solution to the feeding dilemma is to give a horse enough free-choice hay to chew on during the day.

The domestic horse's diet, however, is very different. A horse that is out on pasture, eating for most of the day, is probably in her most natural state, but a good deal of horse owners don't have hundreds of acres of grassland. Instead, most domestic horses are fed large portions of dried hay twice a day (this makes up at least half of their overall diet). On top of that, people add grains to their feed program. Now, as long as the horse is getting ample exercise to burn off this fuel, it's a good mix, but if she is just standing around in her stall most of the day and night, her system will be stressed.

GOOD QUALITY HAY

Herd behavior

The stereotype that a horse herd is made up of a bunch of mares and led by one stallion is only partially true. Herds are indeed made up of mares and their foals. Their pecking order keeps the band in check, with a dominant mare at the top making the decisions about where to graze, rest, and find shelter. This mare might not be the fleetest and strongest, but she's the mare who's been around the block and knows a thing or two. Her experience and wisdom controls the movement of the other members of the herd.

■ **All the horses** *in a herd are alert to the movements and reactions of their companions. The herd instinct is very strong, and even domesticated horses feel much more comfortable and noticeably calmer in the company of other horses.*

How a horse is built

A HORSE HAS WONDERFUL TRAITS that are wrapped up in an amazingly beautiful and versatile package. Starting from the top, the horse has a large head and a long neck that can bend all the way around to her ribcage. She carries a lot of weight up front, so to counterbalance this she possesses a sloping shoulder, a strong back, and powerful hindquarters.

The horse has no muscles below her knees and hocks – instead she has a complex series of tendons and ligaments that run down those leg bones. She has a "stay apparatus" that locks her joints in place so that she can, in effect, sleep while standing up. The horse's back is built like a suspension bridge, which enables her to take a rider's weight and still move with minimal effort.

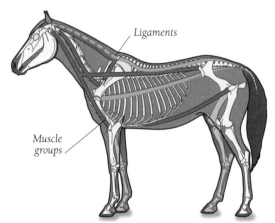

Ligaments

Muscle groups

■ **This diagram shows** *the position of the main muscles and ligaments in a horse's body.*

■ **Horse senses** *are very acute. Horses move their ears to pick up sound from all directions, and they roll their lips back to distinguish smells more clearly.*

Horse senses

A horse's senses are different from ours. The ears can pick up sounds from all around. The eyes, placed high up on the horse's head, allow the horse to see everywhere except for directly in front and directly behind her. Her sense of smell allows her to identify her food, her enemy, and her friend. The horse's sense of touch is valuable to her eating and survival. She uses her lips and whiskers to help feel around. She is sensitive enough to feel a fly and then zing it off her hide with a swish of her tail.

The best foot forward

The hoof is a remarkable structure made of material similar to that of your fingernails on the outside and, yes, the hooves constantly grow. In the wild, a horse on the move wears her hooves down to the appropriate length but, because our domestic horses hardly have the opportunity to travel a dozen or so miles daily, we've got to do that for them by having their hooves trimmed regularly.

The horn of the hoof grows from the coronet (the hairline at the base of the leg) down. It can take up to a year for the hoof to grow out completely.

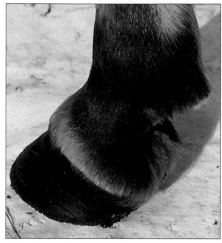

■ **Hooves are worn down** *from walking on roads and can be protected with shoes.*

COAT PATTERNS AND COLORS

In primitive times, a horse's coat helped camouflage her from predators. Today, a certain color horse can be the one of your dreams. Horses come in a variety of colors and patterns. Here are some of the most common:

- **Appaloosa:** Spotted like a Dalmatian or blanketed on the rump with spots
- **Bay:** A red-brown horse with black mane, tail, and points (muzzle and legs)
- **Black:** A true black horse must have dark eyes, muzzle, and flanks
- **Brown:** The coat may appear black, but muzzle and flanks are lighter
- **Buckskin:** Golden with black points and often a stripe along the spine

- **Chestnut:** Various shades of red, orange, or gold
- **Palomino:** A golden coat with a flaxen mane and tail
- **Pinto:** Large patches of color, as if the horse were splashed with paint
- **White or cream:** White hair with pink skin underneath
- **Gray:** A mix of white and black hairs on dark skin. Dapple gray has dark rings

All horses can do

WHAT GOOD IS A HORSE IN MODERN LIFE? Horses have great strength, but they also have agility and versatility. That's why the horse is seen doing so many different things. Can you name another animal that can work side by side with us, compete in sports, offer companionship, and provide us with a wonderful hobby?

Career paths for horses

Horses follow different career paths, depending on their build and temperament. For instance, you'd hardly take a Shire – a large workhorse that can weigh nearly a ton – to give pony rides to kids. Conversely, a Shetland pony wouldn't really be a big help plowing fields. That's why horses have been bred into so many types: Careful selection has enabled us to use horses for specific purposes, making the most of their particular qualities.

> ## Trivia...
> *Horsepower is an English unit of power, equal to 33,000 foot-pounds per minute (1 foot-pound is 1 pound lifted over a distance of 1 foot) or approximately 746 watts. The term horsepower originated with James Watt, who determined that a horse could do 33,000 foot-pounds of work a minute drawing coal from a coal pit.*

■ **Although heavy draft breeds** *play less of a role in agriculture in the Western world today, the breeds have not disappeared and are often on display at shows.*

Working horses

You may have observed horses pulling hansom cabs in the park. Well-matched teams are often seen pulling wagons to give hay rides. There are still places where it makes sense to use a horse or sturdy mule to pack into the backcountry, especially over hilly or mountainous terrain. And of course, who hasn't seen the famous Clydesdales pulling the beer wagon on television?

There are other types of working horses. A police horse must go through rigorous training to earn her badge and be put on the beat. Park ranger horses must be surefooted and have fantastic stamina to go through rugged terrain. Working cow horses rely on quick reflexes and intuition to round up cattle.

■ **Working cow horses** *have inborn savvy that allows them to "read" a cow's body language, and become vital members of cattle ranch operations.*

Therapeutic riding mounts help give children and adults who have physical or mental disabilities the chance for special rehabilitation. Even the lowly rental horse – you've probably ridden one at some point in your life – gives nonriders their first taste of what it would be like to be an equestrian.

Even recreational horses have jobs to do and have received specific training: show hunters and jumpers are taught to clear fences with ease; barrel racers exhibit lightning-fast speed riding a cloverleaf pattern; dressage mounts perform a delicate ballet with grace and precision; reiners slide and spin their way to glory; polo horses and riders play against each other in an exciting game; endurance horses can race up to 100 miles (160 km) in one day, sometimes galloping for hours at a stretch; and trail horses give their riders a view of nature from a perspective unlike any other.

A horse has to be conditioned and trained to do a particular job. Just because some horses can do a 100-mile (160-km) endurance ride does not mean that you can take any old horse and gallop her for hours.

A typical day for a modern horse

What's it like to be a horse? Let's take an average trail mount at an equestrian facility. She wakes up early and is given a flake of alfalfa hay for breakfast. This is a large section of compressed stems and blossoms, which will take her most of the morning to chew. The facility's workers clean her stall. Her owner arrives at midday and unlatches her stall door, puts her halter on, and leads her out. Her coat is brushed free of dust, her mane and tail are combed of tangles, and her feet are picked to get rid of mud. The rider fits the saddle and bridle, grabs a helmet, mounts up, and heads for the trail.

They have an enjoyable hour-long ride before returning home. The owner then dismounts, untacks, and leads the horse into a small corral filled with soft dirt, removes the halter, and closes the gate. The horse enjoys rolling in the dirt. She shakes off a layer of dust and has a little play. After a bit, her owner puts her halter back on, leads her out, and takes her over to the wash area where she is given a rinse. The horse dries off in the sun before being led to her stall for the afternoon. She touches noses with the horse next door, before cocking a back foot, relaxing, and drifting in and out of sleep. Soon her afternoon meal arrives at around 4:30 p.m. She alternates eating her dinner with several long drinks of water. It is now night, but she is still alert and observant. Finally, she catches some sleep, standing up. During her deepest sleep, however, she stretches out on her side and even makes a snoring noise. She's had a good day.

Off to the races

Horsey heroes usually take the form of racehorses. In the '70s, the media seemed to spotlight these champions: Secretariat, Ruffian, Seattle Slew, and Affirmed. Racehorses have a special place in horse lovers' hearts because they are so impressive to watch.

■ **Racehorses epitomize** *all that horses embody: incredible speed, heart, courage.*

Although evidence of racing can be found in ancient times, match races, where two horses are pitted against each other, didn't take shape until about the 16th century. Once races started gaining popularity, more horses were added to the mix and more formal racecourses developed. Since then, "The Sport of Kings" as it's sometimes called, has become established in nearly 50 countries.

Types of races

Horses race on dirt tracks or on the turf. There are races for "distance" horses, which range from 5 *furlongs* (1 km) to 2¼ miles (3.6 km), and also for sprinters, such as the Quarter Horse quarter-mile (400 m) races. In most races, competitors are equalized according to the horse's age, sex, and past performance and the weight of the jockey. Lead weights are added under the saddle if necessary.

> **DEFINITION**
>
> *A **furlong** is equal to 220 yards (200 m). There are 8 furlongs in a mile.*

Racehorses travel at speeds of up to 45 mph (72 kph). Steeplechasing involves jumping over fences. Harness racing combines the fastest trotters and pacers, which pull their drivers in small, lightweight two-wheel carts.

A simple summary

✔ Over a period of 50 million years, horses evolved from a small, timid deerlike creature into today's spirited and powerful *Equus*.

✔ Despite the fact that horses have been domesticated for at least 5,000 years, they still have many instincts of their wild ancestors.

✔ A horse is a herd animal and keeps a strict pecking order.

✔ Horses have been bred into many different shapes and sizes to perform different tasks.

✔ Horses are versatile and adaptable, working for us, as well as providing companionship and a partner in competition.

Chapter 3

The Mind of a Horse

PIGS ARE SMARTER THAN HORSES, you've heard some people say. Well, that may or may not be true, but the fact is, the horse is a highly intelligent creature and displays his smarts every day whether in the pasture or under saddle. Adjust your own way of thinking to get into the brain of the horse. Since horses can't speak English, you'll need to decipher their sign language to discover everything there is to know about them. By watching how horses relate to each other, you can also better understand how to relate to them yourself. Then, perhaps, you won't mind spending your day with both the Black Stallion and Babe.

In this chapter...

✓ **Equine nature**

✓ **Equine five senses**

✓ **Your horse's basic needs**

HORSES ARE ALWAYS ALERT TO THEIR SURROUNDINGS

Equine nature

I'VE HEARD IT SAID THAT HORSES are the dumbest animals in the barnyard. It's a popular belief that horses don't have the power of reasoning, but in reality the horse just thinks differently from the way humans do, and if you see things from the horse's point of view, he is indeed a very smart cookie.

Are horses smart?

Intelligence has nothing to do with how trainable an animal is. In fact, the more brainpower an animal has, the more likely it is to make its own decisions (sometimes that decision might not be the one that you want!). But while horses are extremely trainable, they are not automatons, there to do our bidding. Complex traits, such as willingness, courage, and trust are what allow the horse to be trained at all.

Horses are good problem solvers. When a horse is not successful at a task, he tries another tactic until he gets it right. His efforts are systematic rather than random, and once he completes the one task it becomes easier and quicker for him to do similar tasks.

Horses also possess insight. This is seen when a horse figures out how to open a latch to let himself into a forbidden pasture. Insight can help a horse figure out that there is food inside a trailer and climb aboard to get at the goods.

Have you heard of the horse Clever Hans? In 1913, Hans traveled all over Germany, and to the delight of crowds across the nation, he could correctly answer basic mathematical equations and complex verbal brainteasers. He'd paw out his answer with a front hoof. Everyone was mystified by the fact that this horse could actually think – he could reason better than some of the people in the crowd! The reality was that Hans had been taught by his owner a very subtle form of Morse code, and the horse was responding to this to deliver the right "answers." Hans couldn't really count, but he was clever enough to fool a lot of people!

INTERNET

nicholnl.wcp.muohio. edu/DingosBreakfast Club/IQ/EquineSmarts. html

Check out these social intelligence test results from the Journal of Animal Science.

Horse sense

Horses are extremely perceptive – they have to be if they don't want to end up as horseburgers for the local lion den. They are programmed to be constantly on the alert to danger and to react if they find it. Their responses are determined by how they react to the information delivered by their five senses. Some people might find it unsettling that the horse is so perceptive, as if they can sense something dangerous before actually seeing it.

Also essential to his survival, the horse has to be prepared to take off at a moment's notice. Be that as it may, the horse can learn quickly how to determine if something is really a threat, and if something is safe. He may at first be frightened at the sight of a herd of cattle if he's never seen one, but once he determines that cows are not going to kill him, he will get over it. A horse will remember that lesson. This is why it is quite easy to desensitize a horse to the chaos of traffic, tractors, barricades, buildings, and other oddities of modern life.

Memory of an elephant?

One of the horse's greatest traits (and one that can cause owners great chagrin) is his memory. Horses never forget a thing. They categorize all their experiences either as something to fear (and therefore run away from), or they make a mental note of things that are harmless. Once a horse has learned something, he doesn't really need much of a refresher course.

A horse will always remember mistreatment but will also be very forgiving if put into the right hands and trained properly.

Champion show horses are often given the winter off after a winning season. Come spring, however, all they need is a bit of physical conditioning to get back into shape. They don't need to rehearse their lessons under saddle. That's usually for the rider's benefit instead.

Horses can be taught a variety of things. If you've seen the Olympics, you've seen horses perform precise movements of dressage. But they can also be taught tricks like a dog. Using positive reinforcement (that is, rewards for desired behavior), a horse can be taught to bow, sit, lie down, and paw.

■ **Circus horses** *are often trained to perform a range of impressive tricks to entertain their audience, such as walking on their hind legs.*

Body language

It's been said that to think, you need to use language. Just because horses don't speak a language that we can hear doesn't mean they aren't talking to us all the time. Horses use subtle and unsubtle forms of communication to let their wants and needs be known. A horse will tell you that he will submit to you through his body language. Here are some of the ways a horse communicates with different parts of his body:

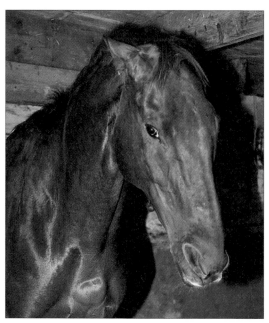

■ **Ears flattened against** *the horse's head means your horse is pretty ticked off. Be warned!*

a **Ears:** If a horse's ears are forward, he is concentrating on something ahead of him. An ear flicked back shows that he's aware of things going on behind him. If you're riding a horse and he has an ear twisted in your direction, it means that he's aware that you're on him and telling him what to do. "Airplane ears," which you'll see on some horses in competition, are denoted by their soft, floppy sideways stance. This is usually a sign that the horse is concentrating on the task ahead and is very focused and receptive.

b **Eyes:** A horse's eyes are generally soft in appearance. If you see the whites of a horse's eye, it means that the horse is startled or fearful.

HORSING AROUND

One of the world's greatest horsemen, John Lyons, reminds us that horses can be capable of a great deal more than we might think. He taught his horse, Dream, to stick out his tongue when John waved his fist, and John rewarded Dream with a lot of attention. What was most surprising is that Dream actually took that trick and taught it to Bright Zip, another horse in the stall next to him. John recalls coming into the barn and seeing both horses playing and sticking their tongues out at each other. It reaffirmed to him that horses are among the brightest creatures on the planet (as well among the creatures with the best sense of humor).

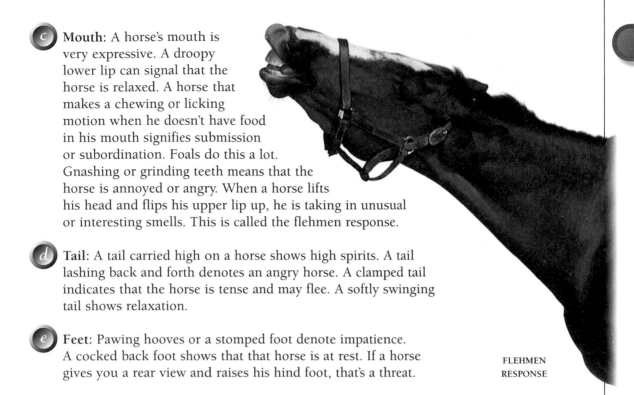

c **Mouth:** A horse's mouth is very expressive. A droopy lower lip can signal that the horse is relaxed. A horse that makes a chewing or licking motion when he doesn't have food in his mouth signifies submission or subordination. Foals do this a lot. Gnashing or grinding teeth means that the horse is annoyed or angry. When a horse lifts his head and flips his upper lip up, he is taking in unusual or interesting smells. This is called the flehmen response.

d **Tail:** A tail carried high on a horse shows high spirits. A tail lashing back and forth denotes an angry horse. A clamped tail indicates that the horse is tense and may flee. A softly swinging tail shows relaxation.

e **Feet:** Pawing hooves or a stomped foot denote impatience. A cocked back foot shows that that horse is at rest. If a horse gives you a rear view and raises his hind foot, that's a threat.

FLEHMEN RESPONSE

Steer clear of his rear – and more

A horse is a running machine, and his main defense is speed. Horses are extremely strong animals. They not only produce a powerful kick, but they also have excellent aim and a surprising range of motion. If a horse cannot flee from something he fears, he will defend himself. Add steel shoes to this and the recipient of a kick from a surprised horse that suddenly lashes out can be crippled for life.

The safest place to be is close by the hindquarters but not directly behind the horse. While a horse can kick out sideways, there is less impact if you are closer and he can't get full velocity behind his thrust.

In general, a horse will bite or kick only if provoked. Most horses nip with their lips if they are annoyed, but they won't bare their teeth. A few horses, however, have behavioral problems and will use their chompers on you.

Horses can get a little nippy if you constantly feed them treats by hand. A better way to reward your horse is to place the carrots or apples directly in his feed bucket.

INTERNET

www.erc.on.ca

Here's an interesting site that includes a Safety Around Horses fact sheet from the Equine Research Center at Guelph, in Canada.

Equine five senses

TO UNDERSTAND HOW A HORSE REACTS to situations, you'll need to see how he comprehends things through his senses. It is worth remembering that the world as a horse sees it is very different than the one we experience.

Sight

A horse has the largest eyes of any land mammal. Like most prey animals, a horse's eyes are situated on the side of his head so that he can have superb peripheral vision. Although he can't see directly ahead or behind himself, these blind spots do not prevent the horse from viewing objects located there. A horse will tilt his head or turn to see things that are not in focus. He may even back up to get a better look. If the object seems odd or scary, the horse will give it a very extreme head-tilt, and may even **shy away** from the object.

Horses can see well at night and are actually quite adept at getting around in the dark. However, if you introduce a light source (for instance, carrying a flashlight on the trail) it can actually inhibit the horse's ability to see in darkness.

Hearing

Horses' ears work as funnels, and their hearing is much more acute than human ears. They are able to discern sounds very accurately, and can tell the difference between the tractor that rakes the arena, and the one that brings the hay by. Horses can be voice-trained to recognize words and sounds. However, riders must be consistent in the way they deliver a message to their horse. A horse will stop responding if you try to use the one sound for different commands, for instance, "Whoa" to mean "stop" as well as "slow down."

■ **A frightened horse** *will shy away from something he has seen and decided he does not like.*

Taste

Horses generally like sweet food. But that doesn't mean that every horse adores sugar cubes. Horses in the wild have never tasted treats of carrots, apples, and sugar and will often refuse them. Racehorses are often brought up without food rewards and must be taught to eat them (of course, once they learn, they will never turn back!).

Horses have very picky palates. That old saying "you can lead a horse to water, but you can't make him drink" is somewhat true.

Horses can tell the difference between two water sources, which is a constant source of befuddlement for riders who take their horses to competitions and want to keep them hydrated. Equestrians often flavor their horse's water with powdered gelatin days before an event. Then during the show, the horse will drink the unfamiliar water because the taste has been masked.

Smell

Along with hearing, the horse's sense of smell is crucial to his survival. Like a dog's sense of smell, a horse's is extremely acute, and he can recognize danger and delights carried on the air. He relies on smell to identify other animals and people, and stallions can determine which mare is in heat this way. Horses can smell water from miles away, too.

Horses make mental maps of their surroundings and can often find the way home even when the rider is completely lost. One way the horse figures out where to go is to follow familiar smells until he reaches a trail he remembers from previous experience.

■ **Mares recognize** *their babies in the herd by smell. A foal will often go to the wrong mother (anything of the right size and shape will do!) and try to suckle from her, but will be turned away when she smells him and realizes that he doesn't belong to her.*

Touch

A horse uses the whole of his body to feel. The top dressage riders only need to make subtle shifts in their weight, tense their muscles, or change their balance, and a well-trained dressage horse will respond by performing all those beautiful dancing steps. Some people refute this sensitivity saying, "I've got to kick my horse hard to go, he's totally dead-sided". They don't have the whole picture. The horse is failing to react to the rider's leg because he's desensitized to it, not because he can't feel it.

Horses use their lips and teeth to locate choice grass in the pasture, ignoring the lesser weeds and stems in the process.

Horses use their noses and lips to feel. Their long whiskers, which are usually shaved off by us for beautification purposes, actually work as feelers. The upper lip often works around like a camel's, allowing the horse to do amazing things, such as separate his medicine from the food that you tried to hide it in.

Your horse's basic needs

EACH HORSE HAS DIFFERENT NEEDS. Often this will mean getting specialist training, equipment, or veterinary attention to meet those needs. But, at the very basic end, a horse has a short laundry list of wants.

Food and shelter

A horse needs to be fed on a regular schedule. Horses have delicate constitutions, so stomach upsets are best prevented by feeding hay and grain at generally the same time daily. A horse also requires water – up to 13 gallons (49 liters) a day. A horse needs shelter from the elements, too. A horse in the wild will seek out rock outcroppings, lowland areas, and trees in storms. He also grows a thick coat in the winter and a shaggy mane and tail to give extra warmth. Modern horse owners often shave off winter hair, so a horse will need a blanket and a roof over his head to protect him.

Trivia...

The term "pecking order" comes from studies on hens. The most aggressive hens would peck the others to get to the feed trough first. A similar thing can be found in horses, although the most aggressive horse is not necessarily the leader.

Companionship

Horses are gregarious animals and do not thrive when they are left alone. But they can also get along with other animals, too. An only horse benefits from the company of a goat, barn cat, or, in some weird cases, a chicken or rooster!

■ **Horses love their own kind**, *and even when establishing the pecking order they will usually welcome a newcomer into the herd.*

Exercise

A horse needs exercise. Many people think they are providing the best situation for a horse by keeping him in a luxurious stable with bedding up to his knees and all the hay he can eat. This would be the equivalent, however, of locking yourself, day in and day out, in your bathroom.

A horse is built to travel hefty distances daily, so if he doesn't get out of that – in essence – prison cell we call a stall, he may develop bad habits and go stir crazy. Regular exercise alleviates boredom and health problems.

A simple summary

✔ Horses are very intelligent and can be trained to solve problems and use their natural insight to complete tasks.

✔ You can learn to read what a horse is trying to communicate to you by observing his subtle body language.

✔ Be on the alert for a horse's defense mechanisms.

✔ A horse's senses are in some ways much more acute than ours.

✔ A horse has basic needs of food, water, shelter, companionship, and exercise.

Chapter 4

Horse Breeds From Around the World

PALOMINOS, PINTOS, AND CHESTNUTS gallop across your dreams, tails flagging and manes streaming. But there's more to horses than just their color. Horses come from all over the world, and there are breeds that are centuries old as well as new breeds devised for distinct purposes. Here, we look at the new and the ancient – how they came to be, and what they are best suited for.

In this chapter...

✓ **The right horse for you**

✓ **America's most popular breeds**

✓ **Exotics from the Far East and Africa**

✓ **British and Irish breeds**

✓ **The cream of Europe**

✓ **Spirit from South America**

THE QUARTER HORSE IS ONE OF THE MOST POPULAR BREEDS IN THE WORLD

The right horse for you

WHEN A HORSE GALLANTLY charges across the movie screen, it gives every horse lover chills. What kind of horse is that? The beautifully matched team pulling the stately carriage, the dozens used in western battle scenes, the fairy tale black charger, the wild desert stallion – all these horses are distinct in temperament, athletic ability, size, and build.

Finding the right horse

It's true that many breeds of horses are versatile and can do a variety of activities, but it's important to select the one that is perfect for you. For instance, an Arabian might be a gorgeous creature, but she may be a little spirited for you to handle if you've never sat on a horse before. Shetland ponies might look small and cute, but they're known for their clever, crafty nature. It's important to find the horse that meets your needs and then you'll be on to a good partnership.

Hot blood versus cold blood

These terms often lead to confusion, so let's get it straight. A hotblooded horse does not have hot blood coursing through her veins, nor does she have a bad temper. And a coldblooded horse is not reptilian.

Hotbloods are those breeds that are descended from horses found in desert climates, hence the hot reference. The thoroughbred, the Arabian, and the barb fall into this category.

Coldblooded horses are the opposite of their hot cousins. Speed and courage are notable traits of the hotblood. In contrast to the hotblood's excitable temperament, the generally heavier and larger coldblooded horse has a docile, willing temperament. These well-built breeds developed in the colder climates of northern Europe and are generally draft horses related to the mounts of medieval times.

■ **Thoroughbred horses** *are renowned for their grace and stamina.*

What is a warmblood?

If you think that a warmblood is simply a cross between a hotblood and a coldblood, guess again. In European countries such as Germany, Sweden, Switzerland, and Holland, careful breeding has taken place over the decades to create horses that possess the athleticism and speed of the thoroughbred, with the willing temperament of the draft horse.

Some warmbloods reflect their coldblooded side, being heavier, larger animals. Others are designed for sport, and these look very similar to the hotblooded racehorse.

■ **The Hanoverian** *is the best known of the German warmbloods and is used throughout the world in competitions. Its conformation, even temperament, and athleticism make it an ideal horse for dressage work.*

Warmbloods are produced through precise crossing of specific bloodlines and breeds. They are generally named for the country or region in which they were bred, hence the Dutch warmblood, the Belgian warmblood and so on. Others include the Holsteiner from Germany and the Selle Français from France.

Crossbred horses

Believe it or not, there are horses that are "Heinz 57" – some people would call them mutts. In fact, horses with mixed bloodlines are called grade horses. Even if you know what breeds the horse's parents are, it is still a grade horse.

Grade horses usually do not appear in any breed associations since they are crosses. However, the International Grade Horse Association "registers" all grade horses so that they can be counted in an equine census.

There are new breed associations cropping up in the United States to support all types of wild and crazy crosses. The AraAppaloosa (Arabian/Appaloosa cross), the Quarab (quarter horse/Arabian), the Welara (Welsh pony/Arabian), and the Walkaloosa (Tennessee walker/Appaloosa) are some of the new organizations that have formed to give these crossbreeds a home.

America's most popular breeds

AMERICA IS KNOWN for its ingenuity and, in this respect, its horse breeds show no exception. Crafted with resourcefulness and purpose, American horse breeds are among the most popular in the world.

INTERNET

www.aqha.com

Check out the official web site of the American Quarter Horse Association.

The American quarter horse

Named for being the fastest sprinting horse to run a quarter mile, the American quarter horse is celebrated for its temperament, versatility, and speed. There are more quarter horses registered than any other breed in the world. The breed started in Colonial times when thoroughbreds were crossed with Spanish feral ponies to produce a horse that could work hard during the week and then race on the weekends. Today's quarter horses are talented western horses, and they also do 3-day eventing, jumping, and dressage.

The paint

The paint is distinguishable by its colorful coat. Native Americans treasured these horses because they believed they had magical powers. Paints excel in a wide variety of disciplines, including cutting cattle, racing, jumping, driving in harness, and rodeo.

■ **The coat of an American paint horse** *is always a combination of white with another color. These paint horses exhibit attractive, differing coat colorings.*

The Appaloosa

One Native American tribe, the Nez Percé, elevated the Appaloosa to sacred status. Named for the Palouse River that ran through the tribe's homeland, these spotted horses faced near extinction following the surrender of Chief Joseph, who fought to save the tribe's land from being taken by white settlers. Luckily, years of careful crossbreeding brought the Appaloosa back. Familiar Appaloosa patterns of a blanket, spots, snowflakes, or splashes are its trademarks. Additionally, the horse must also display the mottled skin on its face and/or genital area. It must also have striped hooves, or the whites around the eye must be visible.

Trivia...

A paint horse can be a pinto, but a pinto is not necessarily a paint. That's because paint horses derive from certain bloodlines and are registered with the American Paint Horse Association. A pinto is a horse with splashy markings, but it can be found in a variety of breeds.

The Morgan

The Morgan got its start in colonial Vermont, where a horse of unknown parentage (although it is thought that he had Canadian blood) was given to schoolteacher Justin Morgan as payment for a debt. From this single horse came a new breed of rugged yet elegant horses. This short, compact, and versatile horse is renowned for its intelligence, high head carriage, sound legs, and animated trot.

DEFINITION

*When a horse **trots,** her legs move in diagonal pairs in a two-beat gait. The **pace** is a human-made gait, where the horse's legs move in horizontal pairs with the help of guides fastened at the top of the legs. The front and back legs reach forward at the same time.*

The standardbred

In 1849, a foal named Hambletonian was born from a thoroughbred father and a mother who was reported to be a Norfolk trotter. He became America's all-time fastest trotting horse and the foundation sire of the standardbred breed. The original qualification for a horse to be registered as a standardbred was the ability to trot a mile in less than 2½ minutes. Renowned as the racehorse that **trots** or **paces** with a racing buggy behind, the standardbred also has many uses for those who prefer to get in the saddle. Former racing standardbreds can be retrained for English and western riding, as well as for trail riding.

The Tennessee walking horse

When the standardbred stallion Black Allan was bred to a Morgan mare named Maggie Marshall, the Tennessee walking horse was founded. The smooth-gaited, sweet-tempered horse was ideal for carrying farmers across fields and hillsides. Bred for its smooth movement and its docile disposition, the Tennessee walking horse excels in saddleseat classes. What makes walkers unique are their gaits, which include the flat-foot walk, the running walk, and the canter. The breed also makes a sure-footed trail mount.

■ **The American saddlebred** *can be trained for almost any task, inside and outside of the show arena.*

The American saddlebred

Initially bred to provide a smooth ride to Kentucky farmers, the American saddlebred was soon carrying generals on both sides of the Civil War into battle and making stagecoach runs through gold rush-era California. Bred from a mix of thoroughbred, Morgan, and the now-extinct Narraganset pacer, the saddlebred is known as "the peacock of the showring." With the high-stepping, graceful action that comes naturally to the breed, these graceful horses are showstoppers in saddleseat competitions, where they compete at five gaits: walk, trot, canter, rack, and slow.

DEFINITION

*A **hand** is the unit used to measure the height of a horse. It originally referred to the width of a hand placed horizontally with the thumb held flat. A horse is measured from the ground up to the withers. These days, a hand is equal to 4 inches (10 cm).*

The mustang

The modern mustang is a product of horses brought to America by Spanish explorers over 500 years ago. Most mustangs begin their life in the wild but can adapt well to domesticity, and they can develop deep bonds with their owners. They are small (usually 13–15 *hands*), very intelligent, and found in every color and pattern. Their wild history has also given them hard hooves that rarely require shoes. With proper care and understanding, mustangs have proven themselves as endurance horses. They are skilled at gymkhana, and games such as barrel racing and pole bending, and they have even found their way into the dressage ring.

The Missouri fox trotter

The Missouri fox trotter is a horse that naturally performs a unique gait in which she walks with her front legs and trots with her back legs. Westbound pioneers who developed the breed in the 19th century were attracted to the horse's ability to continue at this gait for many miles, providing a smooth, sure-footed ride. The Missouri fox trotter is an excellent endurance and trail horse. It is also shown in gaited classes at breed-specific events.

Gaited simply means paces that are different from the normal walk, trot, and canter. Gaited horses have tendencies to perform these paces naturally, but training brings gaits out to their fullest.

Exotics from the Far East and Africa

TWO OF THE WORLD'S most influential horse breeds, the Arabian and the barb, originated in Africa and the Far East. These horses are renowned for their powers of endurance, having adapted to live in some of the world's harsher climates.

INTERNET

www.arabhorse.com

This web site has all sorts of links for fans of the Arabian horse.

The Arabian

Today, almost every breed can trace its lineage to the Arabian, and images of them appear in ancient Egyptian art and in the Bible. While these horses were long renowned as war mounts because they could effortlessly race across the desert, in the seventh century AD the prophet Mohammed was instrumental in spreading the breed's influence. He mandated that the number of Arabians should be increased, because the horses would be crucial in leading his army into religious conquests. He also proclaimed that Allah had created the Arabian, and that those who treated the horse well would be rewarded in the afterlife. These incentives, coupled with the Koran's instruction that "no evil spirit will dare to enter a tent where there is a purebred horse," kept Arabian breeding going.

Because of limited resources, breeding practices were extremely selective. Such practices, which eventually helped the Arabian become a prized possession throughout the world, have led to the beautiful breed we know today. The Arabian is marked by a distinctive dished profile; wide-set eyes on a broad forehead; small, curved ears; and large, efficient nostrils. They exhibit their athletic ability in many disciplines, but it is in endurance that the breed reigns supreme.

THE SHAGYA ARABIAN

The barb

The barb is a real desert horse with tremendous stamina and hardiness borne out of harsh living conditions. It originated along the Barbary Coast of North Africa, principally in Morocco, but because of crossbreeding, there are few purebred barbs around today. The barb is a tough horse with a fiery temperament, and has played an important role in the foundation of many breeds. Only the Arabian has had a greater influence on contemporary breeds.

British and Irish breeds

BREEDS FROM BRITAIN AND IRELAND range from the small and compact Shetland pony, well adapted to life on the rugged Scottish islands, to the towering shire horse, a sturdy and willing working horse.

The thoroughbred

In the 18th century, three stallions, the Byerley Turk, the Darley Arabian, and the Godolphin barb, were taken to England for breeding. The progeny eventually became known as the thoroughbred. Its courage and competitiveness has made the thoroughbred an international favorite, and famous ones include Secretariat and Affirmed. This fast horse breed revolutionized racing around the world. It is very popular for many English riding disciplines, excelling in dressage and jumping.

The shire

Known to most horse lovers as the gentle giant, the shire is the world's largest horse. Its massive size is tempered by a very kind temperament. The shire has a long history of being one of the best, most reliable draft horses in existence.

■ **Welsh mountain ponies** *have distinctively dished faces, large eyes, and wide nostrils.*

The Welsh mountain pony

The Welsh mountain pony is one of the oldest pony breeds. When the Romans withdrew from Britain in 410 AD, the horses that they had imported to help in the conquest were set free. These animals bred with native horses and produced the sure-footed Welsh mountain pony. The talents of this rugged breed have long been appreciated by the Welsh, who used the ponies for herding sheep. The hardy ponies have a strength and stamina that defy their small stature. They are particularly good at jumping and driving.

The Shetland pony

With its small stature, clever nature, and cute demeanor, the Shetland pony has always been a hit with kids. The Shetland has lived on the islands off the northeast coast of Scotland for about 10,000 years. The harsh climate and sparse food helped create a pony that is compact, rugged, and intelligent.

The Irish draft horse

The Irish draft horse was developed by farmers to be strong enough to plow the fields, yet spirited and athletic enough to provide a good day's riding. Today, it is most valued as a breed to cross to. Irish thoroughbred crosses are known as Irish sport horses, and they excel in show jumping, hunting, and eventing.

Ponies do not usually exceed 14.2 hands at the withers, while draft horses can be nearly 18 hands tall – a difference of almost 16 inches (40 cm)!

The cream of Europe

CONTINENTAL EUROPE HAS PRODUCED a wide range of horses from the prancing Lipizzaner, the plow-pulling Friesian, the mountain-bred Haflinger, and the cavalry horse, the Trakehner. These horses are some of the world's most distinctive and enduring breeds.

The Friesian

With its black coat, noble profile, high-stepping gait, and beautiful presence, the Friesian is a showstopper. This early warmblood was protected in its homeland of Friesland in the Netherlands, so it didn't suffer much crossbreeding.

THE FRIESIAN

The horse, admired for its natural affinity with humans, worked in the fields, pulled carriages of the rich and powerful, and carried armored knights into battle. In the 17th century, Dutch settlers brought the Friesian to North America. In fitting with its heritage, the striking breed excels at driving, but it is also very popular in dressage.

The Trakehner

The king of Prussia established a stud farm in Trakehnen with the purpose of developing the perfect cavalry horse. Thoroughbreds and Arabians that exhibited the desired qualities were crossed with coldblooded draft horses in the hope of refining the horses while retaining the size, bone, and disposition of the colder breeds. The horses that slowly emerged were both elegant and capable of enduring long months of battle.

The Haflinger

The Haflinger is a native of Hafling, a European village originally in Austria but now in Italy. In the steep mountain terrain, these sturdy horses played a vital role in bringing supplies to remote communities, and farmers relied on them for agriculture and logging. Their color, which can vary from honey blond to chocolate, is complemented by a long and flowing white or flaxen mane and tail. Haflingers compete in many disciplines, although they're most renowned as driving horses.

Trivia...

During the 19th century, draft horses were used to tow barges on canals, move heavy goods and equipment in industry, and to plow the land.

The Lipizzaner

The Lipizzaner is famous for being the horse from the Spanish Riding School in Vienna, Austria, where it performs 17th-century dressage movements. The athletic white horses do so well at the leaps and prancing movements, called "high school" movements, that they perform all over the world.

The Lipizzaner, which takes its name from Lipizza (Lipica), is the oldest of the European horse breeds.

Don't count on all horses in a breed to be alike. No matter what breed of horse you find appealing, remember that horses are individuals.

■ **The Lipizzaner** *has a distinctive white coat, but these horses are actually born black or dark brown – they turn white between the ages of two and seven.*

Spirit from South America

THE SPANISH CONQUISTADORS brought horses with them to the Americas, and many horse breeds have descended from these first equine arrivals in the new colonies.

The paso fino

On Christopher Columbus's second journey to America, he brought horses of Spanish breeding, specifically barb, Andalusian, and the now-extinct Spanish jennet. Crossbreeding of these horses produced the paso fino (which means "fine gait"). Paso finos got their stamina and power from the barb, and their beauty and grace from the Andalucian. What the jennet passed on, however, was a natural broken four-beat gait. The gait, performed at three speeds, produces a constant cadence in which there is little vertical movement in the croup and shoulder, creating a comfortable journey for the rider.

INTERNET

www.ansi.okstate.edu/
breeds/HORSES/

Find out about dozens of horse breeds at this informative web site.

The Peruvian paso

The native horse of Peru, the Peruvian paso was bred for its effortless gaits and easy-going personality. Originally created to carry Peruvian landowners over vast areas in a relatively short period, Peruvian pasos are well-suited to competing in endurance events, and many owners love the horse for supersmooth trail riding. In the showring, Peruvian pasos are asked to demonstrate their paces. They must also display brio – controlled brilliance and energy – and be shown under traditional Peruvian tack.

A simple summary

✔ There are many different breeds of horses, each with distinct qualities and strengths.

✔ A hotblooded horse is a spirited breed with desert origins, while a coldblood is derived from the draft horses of northern Europe.

✔ A warmblood is not a cross between hot and cold horses, but rather a result of careful breeding to develop a sport horse with traits of both types.

✔ Grade horses are the mixed breeds of the horse world.

PART TWO

First Days with Horses

GETTING TO GRIPS WITH the horse world can be demanding, so here's all you need to know about buying and looking after your own horse.

Chapter 5

Preparing Yourself for the Horse World

Y OU'D LIKE TO GET A BIT MORE INVOLVED with horses, but it's a little overwhelming. To get started, you need to learn how to ride and get some more exposure to horses. There are plenty of ways to expand your horsey horizons, from taking lessons to spending time with horses while on vacation. Whatever way you go about it, you're bound to be off on a new and exciting adventure.

In this chapter...

✓ **Getting to grips with riding**

✓ **Arranging lessons**

✓ **Getting to know horses**

✓ **Let's ride**

✓ **Getting on and off**

✓ **Aids for gaits**

TAKING RIDING LESSONS IS A GOOD INTRODUCTION TO THE HORSE WORLD

Getting to grips with riding

THERE ARE SOME PEOPLE who are born to be in the saddle. They are natural equestrians, and they instinctively know how to ride. Not only that, horses respond to these people's imperceptible commands instantly.

Are you a natural?

Don't take it hard if it feels foreign to be astride a horse. Riding, like most sports and hobbies, takes practice before you become proficient. Not only is there the physical combination of balance, muscle co-ordination, suppleness, and concentration to master, but also there are different ways to ride, and these require different methods of communication with the horse.

Riding a horse is similar to driving a classic car: You need to discover each horse's little personality quirks to have a fulfilling ride. On one model, the brakes are touchy, while on another the steering seems a little sloppy. Some have sensitive accelerators, while others have sticky clutches. Once you know how to deal with the idiosyncrasies, you can manage a very pleasant drive. Just as it's important to learn how to properly control and guide a car, it's crucial to do the same when aboard a horse.

Lessons allow you to learn at your own pace on safe horses. You'll meet people like yourself who are just starting out, as well. Eventually, you'll understand the riding lingo better, and you'll be able to ride a variety of different horses.

■ **Riding lessons** *will give you confidence and provide a solid foundation on which to build your equestrian skills.*

Like taking any other type of lesson, such as golf or tennis, taking riding lessons allows you to find out if you have an aptitude for the sport before making a huge investment in time and equipment. In the United States, there are basically two different styles of riding: western and English. Western riding has its roots with the cowboys, while English riding stems from foxhunting. But no matter what style of riding piques your curiosity, it is wise to find a knowledgeable horseperson to usher you into that world safely.

Western riding

Western riding is becoming more popular all over the world, but has its roots in America. In the 1600s, Spaniards were exploring the New World, and they brought over Spanish horses and classical riding with them. To handle the long hours spent exploring on horseback, they developed a saddle suited for this purpose. It featured a high *cantle* and *pommel* and long stirrups, similar to today's Australian saddles.

The Spanish explorers roamed through North America, Mexico, and South America, and the *vaqueros* became skilled at roping and herding cattle. American colonists, who headed west in the 1800s, cottoned on to the new form of riding that they observed the *vaqueros* performing and they began riding in a similar way. They adapted the Spanish saddle to suit their specific needs, adding a horn at the front from which to loop a rope that could be used to hold cattle. The style of riding that we know today as western riding developed from these working cowboys.

In western riding, the rider sits deep in the saddle with an upright posture. He rides with little rein or leg contact, and the horse is taught to respond to very light cues. Roweled spurs, which have a small spiked wheel, help cue the horse without the rider having to kick him. Split reins – two reins that are not attached to each other – are held together in one hand over the saddle horn, and the horse is guided by light rein pressure on the neck. This is called neck reining.

The reins are held together in one hand because, traditionally, the cowboy steered with the left hand, so that he could hold a rope in his right hand.

Today, people ride western for different purposes. Riders often hit the trail on a western-trained horse. There are also shows that competitors can enter to show off their riding style or their horse's training.

English riding

There are several different riding disciplines that fall under the umbrella of English riding: dressage, combined training, saddleseat, hunters, and jumpers can all be considered English. These disciplines developed over the centuries as society changed.

During the Middle Ages, riding became utilitarian: Horses were seen as beasts of burden, battlefield mounts, or transportation. As times changed, however, a person's status in society could be determined by the quality of the horses he or she owned. Meanwhile, the Renaissance brought a rebirth of riding as an art, and dressage was born. Around the 19th century, with the wane of the European monarchies and aristocracies, horses became more of a source of sport and competition.

Horse jumping, both in civilian shows and in military exhibitions, had long been an attraction by the time an Italian army officer, Federico Caprilli (1868–1907) revolutionized English riding – and more specifically, jumping – with his notion of a "forward seat."

Caprilli's style of riding was quite different from that popularized on the hunt fields and in steeplechases. Rather than shooting feet forward onto the horse's shoulder and virtually leaning back on the reins for balance over a jump, Caprilli's technique was to shorten the rider's stirrups and keep the rider's upper body bent at the hip, so that he or she was centered with the forward thrust of the jumping horse. His principle was that the rider should not grab onto the reins for support while airborne, and that the horse should be able to freely use his head and neck.

Arranging lessons

ONCE YOU'VE DECIDED what type of riding you would like to do, it's time to find an instructor. But where do you look? How do you find one who is compatible with your learning style? And how do you know whether your instructor is any good if you've never ridden a horse before?

■ **Many people learn to ride** *when they are young, but it is possible to learn at any age. Lessons can be one-to-one, or in small groups of people of similar riding abilities.*

Where to look

First off, understand that riding teachers are not regulated in the United States. There are certification programs available, but you don't have to have any type of credential to be a teacher. If someone wanted to, he or she could take an advertisement out in the local newspaper, declare him- or herself a coach, and wait for the students to come – that's how easy it can be. Therefore, it's important to check out your potential instructor before signing up for lessons.

Most tack stores have a community bulletin board and free horse magazines. Check these out to find out about horses and equipment for sale, boarding opportunities, trainers, and riding schools.

It is important that you feel relaxed and at ease with an instructor. Not every teacher needs to be a former Olympic rider, but it's essential that he or she is a good communicator who can help you understand the basics and give you an excellent foundation. The first place to look is the yellow pages in your town. This will give you an idea of where your closest riding center is. Other places you could try looking include your local tack shop or feed store.

Choosing a great riding teacher

When you call a riding instructor or a riding school, be prepared to ask questions. Find out how long the instructor has been teaching and whether he or she has any certification. Ask whether the instructor specializes in a particular style of riding and whether he or she has ever competed – and, if so, to what level. Find out whether the instructor offers private or group lessons, and whether he or she provides school horses for you to learn on. Most teachers are forthcoming and will give you whatever information you need to take the next step.

Be prepared to provide the teacher with the following details about yourself:

- Your age: Some teachers specialize in coaching adults, while others provide lessons for children of various age groups.
- Any riding experience: Have you only ever ridden at pony rides? Did you used to gallop your friend's horse like Secretariat when you were 14? Or did you go to summer camp and ride for a couple of weeks? Let the teacher know.
- Your goals: Do you just want to be comfortable making the horse go and stop? Or would you like to eventually compete on horseback? Do you only have time for riding at weekends or do you want to buy your own horse ultimately?
- Your preferences: Do you prefer private lessons or group lessons? Private lessons give you one-on-one attention, but group lessons can be a fun learning experience, because you can gain insight from the others you ride with.

Observing a lesson

It is also worthwhile asking if you can go and watch a lesson in progress, so you can see how the instructor behaves toward the students. When you evaluate a potential teacher giving a lesson, you have a lot to take note of. Since you may not be familiar with what to look for, here are some pointers.

If you see a lesson horse tacked incorrectly, for instance, with his saddle pad bunched up, that's a sure sign that the instructor is not that concerned about the safety or comfort of either the horse or the rider.

INTERNET

www.riding-instructor.com

The American Riding Instructors Association promotes safe riding by certifying competent instructors, running seminars, and publishing magazines.

First off, check to see the horse is properly groomed and tacked up. While many school horses might look a little scruffy in comparison to gleaming show horses, their coats should be brushed, their manes and tails should not be tangled, they should be carrying a healthy amount of weight, and the equipment that they're wearing should be properly fitted.

Once the lesson begins, listen to the way the teacher explains things. Does he or she use a lot of buzzwords or jargon that goes totally over your head? Does he or she explain a technique a couple of different ways if the student doesn't initially understand?

A good teacher might go over to the student and demonstrate visually, or even get on the horse. He or she should have a good understanding not only of riding, but also of horse care, feeding, equipment, and horsemanship.

Remember, if you select a teacher who you discover later is not ideal for you, don't fret. Just be up front about it and say that you're going to try someone else who better suits your needs.

■ **A good riding teacher** *will always speak to his or her student positively, lead lessons from the center of the arena, and give plenty of encouraging advice.*

Getting to know horses

AS WELL AS TAKING LESSONS, it is a good idea to add to your knowledge about horses in other ways. You can gather information by attending various events and by talking to other people in the horse community.

Visit a tack store

One sure fire way to get involved with horses is to visit a tack shop. Tack stores, like most specialty stores, hire knowledgeable sales staff who are immersed in the industry. Most are very friendly if you tell them that you're new to horses and want to see what it's all about. Tack shops also contain a wealth of information. Not only do they have all the equipment you'll ever need to keep a horse happy and healthy, but they are a link to all the horsey goings-on in your community. They should be able to and supply you with listings of various horse shows and competitions.

INTERNET

www.equestrian.org

This is the web site of USA Equestrian. The site provides a calendar of competitions.

Go to a show

Horse shows are a great place to see horses presented in their most splendid form – groomed from nose to tail, decked out in their finest tack, and performing at their peak. As a spectator, you can learn what goes on in various classes. There are all levels of competition, from local shows where entry level riders compete, to major international competitions held at big equestrian centers.

Most shows do not charge an admission fee. Seating can be limited or nonexistent, so be prepared to stand by the rail or sit on the grass. The top competitions, however, do have a small ticket price for spectators, but they usually have good viewing areas.

■ **Shows start early** *and usually go on until late afternoon, so remember to bring sunscreen and wear a hat.*

Let's ride

NO MATTER HOW YOU first approach your life with a horse, the biggest pleasure is being able to swing into that saddle and ride. A horse is unlike a bicycle or a motorbike, since he can do one thing that these can't: think for himself. He can be taught to go at different speeds, and to steer around or jump over obstacles – you just have to know how to ask him.

The three gaits

The most basic paces, or gaits, that a horse performs under saddle are walk, trot, and canter. Some horses are also asked by their riders to gallop. The walk is the slowest pace and is known as a four-beat gait because you can hear all four feet separately. The trot is slightly faster, with two beats to its rhythm, and has a bouncy feeling to it when you're in the saddle. The legs move in diagonal pairs – the front right with the back left, and the front left with the back right.

■ **One of the greatest** *pleasures of riding is the freedom of being out with your horse in the country.*

The canter (also known as the lope) is a three-beat gait that looks like the horse is skipping in one direction – this direction depends on which leg the horse "leads" with. He can change his skipping to the other direction by changing his lead. Although the canter is faster than a trot, it is more comfortable to sit because it has more of a rocking-horse feel to it. The gallop is like a very fast canter, except there are four footfalls to its beat. It is the horse's fastest gait.

Racehorses can gallop at speeds up to 45 miles an hour, so only an experienced rider should attempt galloping. Until you reach a higher level of skill, stick to trotting and cantering.

One of the most frightening experiences when riding is to be on a runaway horse. Horses can get very exuberant when being ridden as part of a group, and if one takes off, the others will most likely follow. Once a horse becomes a runaway, it takes skill – not strength – to bring him back under control.

Tacking up

Putting the saddle and bridle on is called tacking up. The bridle looks confusing, but you will appreciate having it securely on your horse's head, since this is part of how you communicate with him. There are a couple of ways to bridle a horse, but this is the most basic. Unbuckle the halter and remove it from your horse's head, but rebuckle it around his neck so that he cannot wander away. Put the reins over his head. Hold the top of the bridle in your right hand and the bit in your left. Bring your right hand over to rest in between your horse's ears and place the bit in front of his mouth. Gently help the bit into his mouth by inserting your thumb in the corner of his mouth.

Nosebands fit snugly to keep the horse's mouth closed so he'll pay attention to how you communicate to him with the bit.

Your horse will open his mouth to accept the bit. Then, loop the crownpiece over his ears so that the bit cannot fall out. Fasten the throatlatch loosely, allowing for one hand's space in between the strap and his cheek. English bridles also have nosebands, which fit just below the horse's jaw.

SADDLING UP

It is important to learn how to tack up properly. If you put the saddle on correctly, you will be able to ride in safety and comfort. If you put it on incorrectly, not only might you make your horse sore, but you might have a fall due to the tack sliding off. It is important to make sure all buckles are secure (but you should tighten them gradually so that you don't hurt or startle your horse).

1 Fitting a saddle pad

Approaching from the left, place the saddle pad high on the horse's withers. Slide it down so that his hair lies flat.

2 Placing the saddle

Place the saddle on top of the pad, and pull the pad up into the saddle arch in the front (called the gullet).

3 Fastening the girth

Buckle the girth on the right side, then go over to the left, reach under the horse's belly, and buckle the girth there.

Getting on and off

*NOW IT'S TIME TO GET ON –
or mount – your horse. First, check
your girth, or cinch, to see if it is tight
enough to prevent the saddle from
slipping. Move to a flat area and check
that your horse has his weight on all four
legs. Then, you're ready to mount safely.*

Mounting your horse

Stand on your horse's left side, and gather up your
reins so that he cannot walk off while you get on.
Take your stirrup and turn the back of it toward
you. Place your left foot in the stirrup, place your
left hand firmly on his neck, and your right hand on
the back of the saddle. You will need to spring up and
over, so with a few hops, push off with your right leg,
and stand in the stirrup. Then swing your right leg
over the horse's back and gently sink into the saddle.
Find your other stirrup with your right foot.

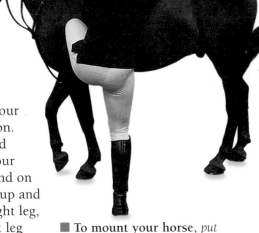

■ **To mount your horse,** *put
your weight in the left stirrup and
push off with your right leg.*

Sitting on the horse

Your basic riding position allows you to use your body so that you can communicate with
your horse effectively. Sit tall in the saddle without leaning to the left or to the right.
Keep your head up and your eyes ahead. Let your arms hang naturally bent so there is a
straight line from your elbow to your hand, all the way down the reins to the bit. Try
to relax your weight down to your bottom, through your legs, and into your feet.

*To help you get your sitting position right, imagine a vertical line that runs
from your ear, down your shoulder, through your hip, and down to your heel.*

Holding the reins

To ride with English reins, pass the leather through your hands from bottom to top as
though you were holding two ice cream cones in front of you. Slip your pinky fingers
underneath each rein so that it is looped in between your ring and little fingers, and out
between the thumb and index finger. Keep your thumb on top. Western riders thread
their reins from bottom to top, too, but in one hand. The reins are separated by the
pinky finger, with one rein placed above the pinky, and one below.

DEFINITION

*Your **natural** aids are your legs, your hands, your balance, and your voice. **Artificial** aids are devices that are supposed to help reinforce your natural aids. These include spurs, whips, and martingales (a series of leather straps that attach to the horse's bridle). Artificial aids should never replace your natural aids, or be used to punish a horse.*

What are aids?

Horses don't understand English. It's important to be able to communicate with them in a way that they can interpret, and you can do this through nonverbal cues, or aids, which can be *natural* or *artificial*. You can tell your horse to go faster or slower, to stop, to turn, and to do all kinds of things through your aids.

Ideally, your first lessons should be longeing on a longeline. Your riding instructor will have you in the saddle, but you will be making a circle around your teacher on a very long line of about 30 ft (9 m). The lead is attached to the horse's bridle and halter. This allows you to have your teacher control the horse while you relax and focus on your position. It's important for you to feel secure in the saddle, and once you do, you can have that line unclipped and be free to roam the arena.

Aids for gaits

MOST HORSES ARE TRAINED to understand similar cues. I will describe the most basic aids that you would use to get your horse going the speed you want him to go. However, it is possible that your teacher's basic aids vary slightly from the ones I describe here.

Walk on

Squeezing with both calves inward, you should be able to make your horse walk. Maintain the basic position described above, keeping your lower back moving with the motion of the horse. Allow your horse's head to bob in rhythm with the stride by not restricting his reins.

Trot steps

A trot can be ridden sitting, but it may shake your fillings loose unless you really know how to ride it properly. Novice riders may prefer to have a neckstrap to grab onto – this helps to steady you if you feel insecure.

Ask for the trot by nudging with your heels just behind the girth. You might need to give your horse a stronger nudge if he doesn't respond. Look where you're going and give your body a slight incline forward.

Trivia...

Posting, or rising, trot derives from the time when postmen used to ride to deliver mail. They developed this technique so that they could spend those hours in the saddle in more comfort.

The posting trot, or rising trot, is ridden when you sit and rise in time to the movement of your horse. This is called riding your diagonal. You're riding on the left diagonal when you're sitting in the saddle and the horse's left foreleg and right hind leg are on the ground. Then you rise when these feet are off the ground. The right diagonal is the reverse. There's a right beat and a wrong beat to rise to. To correct the wrong diagonal, sit an extra beat. Keep your hands steady and try not to pull yourself up out of the saddle with the reins.

To check whether you are on the right diagonal, use the phrase "rise and fall with the leg on the wall" and look at the position of the horse's shoulder blade. When the shoulder blade nearest the arena fence is at its most forward position, you should be sitting in the saddle. When the shoulder swings back, you should be out of the saddle.

When rising to the trot while out trail riding, you should change the diagonal occasionally to alternate the shoulder you are sitting on.

Go for a jog

In western riding, a jog is a slow trot. It was developed because western riders sit every beat, so if the gait is slow, it's a lot more comfortable than a bone-jarring, long-strided English trot. You can get to a jog from a walk by nudging both heels evenly into the horse's sides. Absorb the movement by sinking your weight down into your western saddle. It may feel really bouncy at first, so relax your hips and try to make them move forward with the motion.

Canter and lope

These gaits are pretty much the same thing, except lope is a term used in western riding, while canter is used in English – perhaps a lope is a more laid-back version of canter. Either way, these gaits are the most fun to ride because of their speed and rocking-horse motion.

It's easier to ask for the canter on a circle or around a corner. This allows you to strike off

■ **Cantering and loping** *are three-time gaits, which means that three hoofbeats are heard at every stride.*

on the correct leading leg. Let's say you're going around the arena clockwise. To get the correct lead (in this direction, it's the right lead) you would shorten your right rein so that you could see the horse's right eye. This gets him to bend in the right direction. Keep your right leg at the girth, and slide your left leg behind the girth farther back. Squeeze with your left calf muscle, and nudge with that heel. It may seem like an out-of-control gallop, but just relax and go with the motion. Once you do that, it is a very comfortable pace. Do not try to balance yourself using the reins. That's your direct line to your horse's mouth, and if you yank on his face he might oblige you with a close-up view of the arena dirt.

Going at a gallop

We're off! Only when you're really confident in your ability should you try to gallop. It is the most exhilarating gait, but can easily get to be a wild ride if you don't have a secure seat. Your stirrups should be shortened so that you can get out of the saddle and keep your weight forward. If at any time you feel your horse is getting too fast, use a give and take pull, instead of just a steady haul. And above all, don't scream. You'd be surprised how horses don't like that and will actually run faster.

■ **When you're galloping,** *keep your heels down and your lower legs steady around your horse.*

A simple summary

✔ Lessons can teach you how to be a proficient rider.

✔ English riding includes jumping, while western riding is similar to what is done on ranches.

✔ Riding instructors vary in ability and skill, so choose carefully.

✔ Tack stores are worth a visit to gather information and insight into horse equipment and events.

✔ Horse shows give a good overview of the different types of riding.

✔ Riding involves knowing how to communicate with your horse.

Chapter 6

How to Find Your Horse

As I've mentioned, owning a horse is not like owning a typical pet. In fact, in the United States horses are not officially thought of as companion animals. They are regulated by the Department of Agriculture and are considered livestock, right there beside cows and pigs. Horses may act more like pets than other barnyard animals do, but you still have to treat them differently from most domestic animals, and you'll need to go about acquiring one differently, too.

In this chapter...

✓ **Before you buy**

✓ **A space for your horse**

✓ **The equine for you**

✓ **Match your skill level**

✓ **Taking the plunge**

✓ **The vet exam**

BREEDING FARMS ARE A GOOD PLACE TO START LOOKING FOR A HORSE

Before you buy

IF ONLY IT WERE AS EASY to acquire a horse as it is to get a dog or cat! You'd be hard-pressed to find a horse in a pet store – you'll most likely purchase a horse from a breeder, a dealer, or a private party. And although people generally buy kittens or puppies (as opposed to cats or dogs), it would be disastrous for a first-time buyer to purchase a foal and try to raise and train her.

Buying a horse is a lot like buying a historic house. A house-hunter researches a certain type of house or particular architecture and works with a professional – a real estate agent – to help find the one that is ideal. Then there's all the qualification and paperwork, and the final inspection that shows the new owner the pros and cons of the structure.

It's important to figure out ahead of time how you're going to handle the responsibilities of ownership. It's also good to know yourself and what you want out of this new relationship. And because horses take a lot of time, you need to know if you've got that time to spare.

Similarly, savvy horse shoppers determine well in advance what kind of horse is right for them, and then they enlist a professional horse person to help them select the best match. A test ride, trial period, and prepurchase exam reveal the unique attributes of that animal. Finally the bill of sale, a check, and registration papers are exchanged. Hopefully, neither the house nor the horse will have termites.

Contemplate time

What type of schedule do you have? Are you already so booked up that you can barely muster the enthusiasm to turn on the television when you come home from work or school? If you're involved with other activities, whether they be sports, groups, friends, or family commitments, you may not have much extra time to devote to a horse. Also, if there are a lot of people who depend on you already, you might not be able to take on one more "dependent." But let's say you have a manageable work or school week, and your free time is ample. You're over the first hurdle.

Evaluate your experience

Sometimes, people think in grandiose terms when it comes to horses. If Elizabeth Taylor in *National Velvet* can hop on a horse that she trained herself (well, with a little help from Mickey Rooney) and go belting across the English countryside to win the Grand National steeplechase race, then you can certainly tackle more humble riding goals, right? Right – as long as those relate to you and your personal ability, not your

■ **Looking after a horse** *takes up a lot more time than simply riding her. You need to evaluate the amount of free time you have available before you opt for horse ownership.*

neighbor who's been in the saddle since diapers, and not your fellow riding classmate, who for some reason turned out to be a riding natural and is now the regional champion in her show division.

Think about what you'd like to do with your horse, whether it's leisurely riding in the park or competing in a show. If you've been taking lessons and you are getting more secure about being on a horse, so much the better. Talk to your instructor to get an honest opinion about where your riding is headed.

Consider overall expenses

If you're going to take the plunge, your first order of business is to see how much horses cost in your area. You'll also need to find out how much other services and products cost where you live. For instance, in some parts of the country, a bale of hay can cost $15, while in other places, that same bale might be $5. There will be both initial expenses and ongoing ones.

In addition to the amount the seller will charge you, your horse-buying budget has to include veterinary evaluations (as you might look at several different horses before settling on one), fees or commissions to trainers for their advice, and transportation costs to bring your new horse home.

EXPENSES

As well as the initial cost of buying your horse and equipment, you will need to budget for all the ongoing expenses involved in horse ownership. Use this checklist to find out what the costs of services, feed, and equipment are in your area:

Initial expenses

- Horse
- Professional's fees
- Transportation to horse's home
- Vet check
- Barn equipment
- Barn or stable (if you own horse property)
- Boarding fees monthly (if you don't own horse property)
- Feed

Essential gear

- Grooming supplies
- Horse blanket
- Horse equipment (lead rope, halter, etc)
- Tack (saddle and bridle)

Services and ongoing expenses

- Deworming
- Equine mortality insurance
- Farriery
- First aid
- Veterinary costs, including routine vaccinations

Additional costs

- Rider equipment, including boots, apparel, and helmet
- Riding lessons
- Training fees

These costs just skim the surface. There are certainly ways to cut costs, but it's good to know from the outset what you're getting into.

■ **Investment in good tack** *and other essential equipment is a long term, but worthwhile, expenditure that you won't regret.*

A space for your horse

THE LITTLE GIRL NEXT DOOR told me once how she'd plotted out her backyard so that she could keep her dream pony back there. There would be a fence all around the lawn (a perfect pasture, in her eyes), and right by the patio there would be a tiny barn – like those aluminum storage sheds – featuring one stall. When I asked where her feed would go and where her tack room would be, she just stared at me blankly. Her dreams hadn't included practicalities such as these, let alone whether her yard was even zoned for livestock.

A horse at home

Horses need space. And if you are indeed zoned for horses, you need to provide ample shelter for them. This means sturdy fencing, a barn, stable, or **run-in shed**.

You also need to have room to exercise your horse. Many people build arenas on their property so that they can practice riding at home. But if you don't have that much acreage, you need to have access to a place to ride, such as a large field, some nearby trails, or even a community riding ring.

> **DEFINITION**
>
> A **run-in shed** is a three-sided shelter with a roof on the top. It gets its name because a lot of horse owners build them in large pastures, so that the horse can shelter during inclement weather.

Don't overestimate your horse management skills. They have to be pretty sharp to keep a horse at home. You should be in tune to equine behavior, and know when a horse isn't feeling well. If you overlook the subtle signs of an ill horse, you may end up risking her life.

Keeping horses is not a life of glamour. It's wonderful to look out of your window and see your equine charges grazing. The reality is that you are responsible for everything: shoveling manure daily (and arranging its disposal), feeding twice a day, and arranging veterinary visits and shoeing.

■ **Your stable will** *need regular maintenance. You also need to keep fencing and arenas in good repair.*

Your horse away from home

Boarding your horse is the other option. You can go to a public boarding facility, known as a boarding barn or equestrian center, or you can find someone with horse property and pay him or her to feed and clean after your horse. An equestrian center is a good option for someone new to horses. Farriers and vets visit boarding barns regularly. Your horse is fed with all the others on a regular schedule. Her stall is cleaned daily. There are usually riding instructors connected with the facility for you to take lessons with. If your horse has any training issues, there's usually a horse trainer there. You can often ride in shows held on the premises, too. If you're ready to take the horse-ownership plunge, keep your eyes open and be realistic.

If you're boarding your horse but you make the decision to bring your horse home, you'll already have watched the professionals care for your horse, and you can devise your own horse management program based on theirs.

The equine for you

EVER SEE THE MOVIE The Black Stallion? *What a gorgeous horse – a coal-black Arabian stallion, as fleet as the desert wind, and as loyal as a Rottweiler to his master. Wouldn't we all love to own a horse like that?*

The truth of the matter is that a horse like that should never be put in the hands of a novice. In real life, a stallion should be handled only by experienced equestrians.

Moreover, an Arabian is a highly intelligent, spirited breed of horse, and only one that is trained properly (not on a desert island, as in the film) would be suitable for a beginner. Remember that there's no such thing as a perfect horse.

■ **By getting to know** *all kinds of horses, you'll soon find out which type is the best match for you.*

Each horse comes with its own characteristics, including age, breed, height, color, sex, and level of training. These combine to be one-half of the horse-and-rider equation. A horse is as individual as you, and the horse your friend buys might be the perfect mount for her, but might not be so suitable for you. It's important to stay flexible and open minded. If you say, "I only want a young horse," you might pass up the horse that could make you very happy, only because she's had a few more birthdays than your prerequisite. Don't limit yourself to strict requirements, such as only wanting a white horse, or a Morgan, or a gelding.

Ponies versus horses

"Look at that cute little pony!" I heard a woman say at a local show. "He must be a very young horse." The owner replied that the pony was 35 years old – not a baby in any sense. You need to understand the difference between a horse and a pony.

A pony is not a baby horse. Ponies are, in basic terms, small breeds of horses. They are not just stunted horses but a different class of equine. They are hardy, sturdy, and intelligent, and they often outlive their taller horse relatives. And yes, some can live into their 40s, even.

If you have decided that a pony is what you need, keep in mind that an adult pony will not grow any larger, and so if you do purchase one that is a little on the small side, a child can outgrow her in a short period of time.

Breed specific

Of the dozens and dozens of horse breeds in the world, you might wonder which breed is right for you. Speaking in basic terms again, some breeds excel more than others in certain riding styles. Although a horse can be trained to do a variety of things, you should aim to purchase a horse that excels at the activity you enjoy the most.

HORSE BREEDS AND THEIR COMMON USES

- **Western breeds:** Appaloosa, Paint, Quarter Horse
- **Saddleseat breeds:** Arabian, Morgan, Saddlebred, Tennessee Walker
- **Hunt seat breeds:** Thoroughbred, Quarter Horse, Warmbloods
- **Gaited breeds:** Tennessee Walker, Missouri Fox Trotter, Peruvian Paso, Paso Fino
- **Dressage breeds:** Thoroughbred, Warmbloods, Standardbred, Freisian

THE BASIC TYPES OF RIDING HORSE

English riding

Horses trained in the English style have a classical and elegant way of riding. This style is popular throughout the world.

(a) **Jumper:** Her job is to clear a course of jumps as quickly as possible without knocking any down.

(b) **Hunter:** This horse also jumps, but her job is to do it in style. A hunter is supposed to mimic the well-mannered horses that do foxhunting. She jumps in an elegant, sedate style.

(c) **Dressage horse:** Trained in the classical art of riding, a dressage horse performs unique movements and patterns in a manner similar to compulsory figure skating. A highly trained dressage horse can pirouette, change leads with every stride, and trot in place. Dressage is graded into different levels.

■ **When you train** *your horse to jump, start off with low fences. You can work up to higher fences once you and the horse have more confidence.*

(d) **Eventer:** These horses perform three different styles of riding in one event. They first perform in dressage, then gallop over a set of challenging fences out in the open (the cross-country phase), then jump a set of fences in an arena (the stadium-jumping phase).

If your main interest is to learn the English style of riding, make sure that you research an equestrian center that specializes in teaching the various English skills. You also need to be sure that the horse breed you choose is well-suited to this style of riding.

Western riding

The western style of riding has its origins in the cattle ranch work of the United States and South America. A special saddle is used and the reins are usually held in one hand. The stirrups are longer than those used for the English style of riding.

e **Western pleasure horse:** This horse walks, jogs, and lopes in both directions.

f **Horsemanship horse:** This horse is judged on how obedient and trained she is while performing a pattern in the middle of the arena.

g **Gymkhana, or games, horse:** This horse is speedy and agile, and competes in fast events such as barrel racing (dashing around three barrels in a cloverleaf pattern) or pole bending (snaking through a series of poles in the arena).

h **Reiner:** In a way, the reining horse is similar to the English dressage horse. This horse also performs different movements during a compulsory pattern.

i **Cutter:** A cutting horse works like a Border collie or Australian cattle dog: She separates a cow from a herd and then holds it off for a certain amount of time.

j **Trail horse:** There are two kinds of trail horses: one that performs at a show over simulated trail obstacles, and one that can take you for a ride in the country. The horse and rider must deal with each challenge in a relaxed manner. A trail horse must be level headed and sure-footed.

k **Endurance horse:** Besides having a good head on her shoulders and solid feet under her body, the endurance horse has to have stamina – lots of it. An endurance horse might trot and canter 25, 50, or even 100 miles (40, 80, or 160 km) a day.

■ **A reining horse** *performs circles, roll-backs, spins, and even slides.*

Levels of experience

Since people don't buy horses so that they can grow up together, there are usually two types of horses available: "green" horses and "made" horses. Green horses have received their basic training but still have a long way to go. They may not understand all the riding cues or be able to respond to them correctly. And because they haven't been ridden all that much, they may spook at unfamiliar things. Over time, however, a green horse becomes more seasoned.

Green horses are generally young horses (3 to 8 years old). They are usually less expensive than made horses.

A made horse is well trained and well mannered. She's been around the block a time or two. She has been to shows or is an experienced trail horse. There isn't much that ruffles her feathers. She knows how to do her job and can probably teach you a thing or two as well. A made horse is uncomplicated to ride and is usually at the top of her game. Made horses are usually older (9 to 13 years old). Since horses can live to be around 25 or 30 years of age, 9 years certainly is not old for a horse. A made horse is more expensive than a green horse because you're paying for all the training that went into making her safe and responsive.

Learning from a wise horse

Then there is the older horse – 14 years and older. Physically, she has a bit of wear and tear on her (perhaps some arthritis or other ailment), but this is normal for any sort of athlete at her age. She's settled down and is fairly tolerant. Older riding horses are worth their weight in gold, although many people will pass over them, thinking that these horses are past their prime. They aren't really – although their serviceable years will be fewer than a younger horse's, obviously. As a first horse, they can often be the perfect mount.

■ **An older horse** *is likely to be calmer and more accustomed to distractions, such as traffic, than a young horse. She may be more susceptible to illness and injury, however, so you will need to look out for changes in her normal pattern of behavior.*

Match your skill level

ABOVE ALL, SELECT A HORSE that complements your riding ability. There is nothing scarier than being on a horse that is too much for you to handle. Too much doesn't mean too expensive, it means that the horse is either too challenging for a beginner, or that she might have some behavioral issues.

Still, people fall for a pretty face. They see a gorgeous creature and think they can grow into her. Well, a horse is not a pair of sneakers. Riders like this often get a horse that is a handful for them, and they end up getting bucked off, riding a runaway horse, or having some other catastrophe. If you opt for a horse that may be too much to handle, you risk losing the confidence to ride her. Be honest with yourself. An older, wiser horse can still give you plenty of wonderful rides if you just want to have fun.

INTERNET

www.horseforsale.com

This web site features classified listings and ads for hundreds of horses for sale.

■ **Learning how to jump obstacles** *that you might encounter while you're out on a trail ride will take time and experience. You must feel comfortable with your horse before attempting new skills.*

Taking the plunge

YOU HAVE YOUR PLAN, you know the type of horse you're looking for, and you know what you'd ultimately like to do as a rider. Now it's time to start shopping and to wade through all your various options.

Buying from a breeder

Many people purchase horses directly from a horse breeder. Breeders normally have one or more stallions that they *stand* on the premises for the purpose of selling the offspring. Breeders have young colts and fillies, certainly, but they also have mature horses that are already trained and ready to go. Horse breeders usually don't have large farm operations; they're normally on a small plot of land with very humble facilities.

DEFINITION

*When breeders **stand** a stallion, they are offering stud services to mare owners. This is how stallion owners earn their living. A "stud fee" can be several thousand dollars.*

Advertisement lingo

Whether you begin your search at a breeding farm or with a private party, you will undoubtedly read a lot of classified advertisements. They can be found in the back of local and national magazines, on the Internet, and at your local tack store. The ads can be very confusing, since they have lingo and abbreviations that you might not understand at first. After seeing a bunch of them, you can figure out what is true about the horse, and what is stretching the truth.

■ **Visit local breeders** *specializing in the breeds of horses that interest you. Breeders have horses available at various ages and levels of training, so you should be able to find the one that suits you best.*

Horse auctions

Some people have discovered nice horses at auctions, and there are deals out there. But this is rare because you as the buyer don't have much information on the horses – sometimes you are not allowed to even ride them. Their histories, as well as their breeding, may be unknown. Sadly, most horses that end up at auction are there for a reason, due to health or behavioral problems. So buyers beware!

Horse sales

A horse sale is different. These sales are usually breed specific and are held during large breed shows, such as the Quarter Horse World Show or the Appaloosa World Show. You can see the horses before they go on sale (often the trainer or agent will be exhibiting the horse during the show). This is a good opportunity to gather information on the animal, and you would be purchasing a horse with known parentage, history, and show record.

Word of mouth can lead you to the right horse. Keep in touch with people around equestrian centers and tack and feed stores. They might find a perfect candidate for you.

The Internet is also a good place to look up potential horses to buy (type in "horse+sale" in your favorite search engine), but you still need to exercise caution. Horses that are located across country can be risky to pursue, so ask for a video of any horse that tickles your fancy online before you take any further steps. You should follow the same procedure as if the horse was located down the street – organize a physical exam by a vet and a test ride.

INTERNET

www.therighthorse.com

This site is a database that matches buyers' wants with available horses.

COMMON PHRASES IN ADVERTISEMENTS

- **Bombproof**: unfazed by traffic and unusual noises; calm and steady
- **Seasoned**: knows the ropes
- **Needs experienced rider**: may have behavioral issues
- **Green-broke**: has only the minimum amount of training
- **Ready to start**: has never had a rider on her back
- **Prospect**: having the potential for a certain type of riding, but no formal training. A jumper prospect might be a horse who leaps out of her corral daily
- **Flashy**: a horse that stands out, whether it be her color (such as a Pinto), or the way she carries herself

Finding out the details

Once you think you've found a horse to look at, don't just call the owner for directions to his location and show up. Do some legwork on the phone. You can find out whether or not to take the next step by asking about the horse's background. Some good questions to ask include:

- What is the horse's breed, age, sex, and height?
- What has the horse done during the time the owner has had her (for example, what riding disciplines, showing, or special events)?
- What is her personality like (is she spirited, gentle, quirky, temperamental)?
- Does she have any health problems?
- Does she handle trailering, clipping, and being tied to a hitching post?
- Does she need any special equipment to be ridden or handled?
- Does she have any *vices* or behavioral problems?

> **DEFINITION**
>
> A **vice** is a bad habit that a horse can develop – often through boredom or by copying other horses. Common vices include chewing up fences, pacing, or kicking in her stall. These habits can be very difficult to change.

If you get some promising details from a seller about your potential mount, bring in your experienced horse person for the next step. Your expert can be your riding instructor, a local trainer, or even a knowledgeable friend. This equestrian can lend an expert eye while still remaining objective about the horse. He or she will know what to look for and can ride the horse for you, as well as evaluate any potential problems. He or she can also judge the animal's conformation and suitability.

Steer clear of any seller who won't willingly provide you with any information you have requested. If a seller seems upset or angry about your questions, then you would be wise to pass on that horse.

Watch your potential horse as the owner grooms her and tacks her up. See how the horse behaves. Look for obvious warning signs such as laid-back ears and an angry swishing tail. See if it is easy to groom her coat and pick up her feet for cleaning. Observe how the saddling up goes: How does the horse react when the girth is tightened? Can she be bridled easily? Ask your expert to look at the type of tack the horse wears. The owner should explain the use of a severe bit or a device such as a tie-down for the horse's head.

On your first visit to a horse, it is a good idea to arrive a little ahead of schedule. This allows you to see the horse before she is taken out for you, and can even prevent an unscrupulous owner from having the opportunity to wear out a feisty horse or drug a mean one.

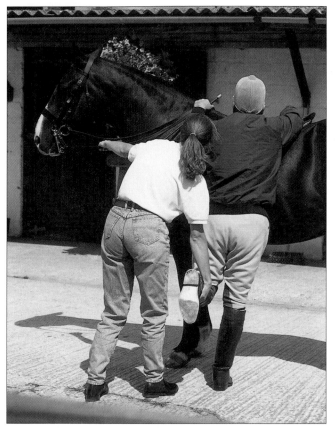

Assessing the horse

The owner should ride the horse first, so you and your expert can observe the horse together. The horse should be ridden at a walk, trot, and canter both clockwise and counter-clockwise around the corral or arena. See how the horse behaves with the owner – this is the person who knows the animal the best. If the horse misbehaves or doesn't do as she is told, you might stop the session there and move on.

When you're taking a horse for a test ride, do only what you feel comfortable doing.

If the horse is okay being ridden by the owner, your expert should ride her next. If you're buying the horse for a particular purpose such as jumping, ask your expert to take her over a fence.

■ **Once your horse expert** *says that the horse is okay for you to try, it's time for you to hop aboard.*

Taking your test ride

Take your time getting used to the way the horse steers and walks before you move into a trot or canter. If you feel confident and secure, then begin your ride in earnest. Besides seeing what her trot and canter are like, see how well she responds to your cues for stopping and turning. Make circles and change direction often. If you are buying a trail horse, you have to be able to try her out on a trail – this way, you can see if the horse can do the job.

If this doesn't seem like the horse for you, tell the owner up front. But if you are interested, you might want to see if you can take the horse on a trial basis while you have a prepurchase exam performed. If the owner is reluctant to let her off the property, ask if you can come back another day to ride. That way you can find out a little bit more about the horse.

INTERNET

www.AAEP.org

This is the official site of the American Association of Equine Practitioners, and it can help you find a veterinarian in your area.

The vet exam

SINCE A HORSE IS AN EXPENSIVE VENTURE, you want to know exactly what her overall health is like as well as uncover any potential problems. A horse that goes lame two weeks after you buy her is one of the biggest liabilities you could saddle yourself with, so get as much medical information as you can before you write your check.

The physical evaluation

Your vet will make a physical examination and will form an evaluation based on what you intend to use the horse for. There is no "pass" or "fail" on a vet check – it's more like creating a picture of a horse at that particular time in her life. Then you will discuss the results together, and your vet can give you his or her opinion on whether or not the horse can do what you would like her to do.

Many behavioral problems are an indication that the horse is in pain. A vet will pick this up.

Finally, if this horse (or the one that finally makes it to this stage) is the one you are comfortable with, it's time to get it all on paper. Draw up a bill of sale that discusses the terms of sale, if any, as well as a detailed description of the horse.

Make sure that any registration papers you receive on a purebred horse match the horse standing in front of you (yes, sometimes you can get bogus papers). Now you can hand over your check. You've just bought yourself a horse!

■ **The vet's exam** *will also include a lameness check. If your vet has serious reservations about the health of the horse, you should not proceed with a purchase.*

The bill of sale

Having the purchase in writing can prove invaluable in the event of any future disputes. You can draw up a contract in just a few minutes that can protect both you and the seller. Make sure you include the following details:

- The names and addresses of both the buyer and seller
- The identification of the horse such as distinguishing marks, age, breed, color, any tattoos (some breeds tattoo a number inside the horse's upper lip), brands, or microchips
- The price that has been agreed upon and how it will be paid (some owners only want cash or a cashier's check, while others will agree to personal checks or even to paying on installment)
- Any warranties or disclosures. If the horse is being sold for a particular purpose and you want it in writing, have the owner put that down. By the same token, if there is something that came up in the vet check, such as the horse is slightly arthritic in one ankle, the owner might want to have that put in the bill of sale, so it doesn't come back to haunt him or her later
- Signatures and dates from both buyer and seller

A simple summary

✔ Develop a purchase plan based on how much time you have to spend with a horse, your riding ability, and your budget.

✔ Determine whether you can keep a horse at home, or whether you need to board her at an equestrian center.

✔ There are many types of horses that can perform all types of different activities. Find out which one is most likely to suit you best.

✔ A young horse is relatively inexpensive to purchase, but a well-trained horse is more suitable for a novice rider.

✔ Horses can be found through breeders, at horse sales, on the web, and through local advertisements.

✔ Bring a professional along to help you view horses.

✔ Have your horse checked by the veterinarian of your choice.

Chapter 7

Bringing Your New Horse Home

THE FIRST FEW DAYS WITH YOUR NEW HORSE can be a little nerve-racking, especially if the only time you've ever spent with equines has been during riding lessons. If you want to make that special connection with your horse, be prepared to spend time with him. During the "newlywed phase," you'll get to know his quirks, and you'll start to familiarize him with a regular routine. Horse ownership is not just about saddling up and riding into the sunset – the fun part comes the day you find out that your horse has great affection for the person in his life: you.

In this chapter...

✓ **Room and board**

✓ **Home on the range**

✓ **The ride home**

✓ **Home preparations**

✓ **Dinner is served**

✓ **The daily routine**

ONCE YOU'VE FOUND THE HORSE FOR YOU, YOU CAN START PREPARING TO TAKE HIM HOME

Room and board

MOST HORSE OWNERS DON'T have the luxury of owning horse property. But that doesn't mean that they are stuck with keeping the horse next to the lawnmower in the garage. A good option is to rent a place at a boarding stable, where your horse can be kept in the company of other horses.

■ **When you arrive** *at a potential stable, take note of your first impression. A good boarding barn is tidy and uncluttered.*

There are a lot of different ways to board your horse, from a humble pasture board situation, where he'll be in a large field with other horses and little else, to palatial furnishings at top boarding barns, also known as equestrian centers. You can keep him at a full-care facility, where you pay one monthly fee for all stable and health care responsibilities, or there are shared-care options, where you might just pay for your stall space, but you have to perform all feeding and cleaning duties.

Selecting the perfect boarding facility

Keep your horse's safety in mind when choosing a boarding stable, and look at more than one for comparison. A good boarding stable does not have a lot of extraneous farm equipment lying around. The fencing and barns are in good repair, the hay and bedding storage areas are organized, and the arena footing is not packed down like cement. A conscientious boarding barn should have its own safety rules and health requirements for new horses coming in. There should be a contract or boarding agreement for you to sign.

You might be looking for extra amenities at a boarding barn, such as lighted arenas for night riding, and wash racks with warm water. You might want a hot-walking machine to allow your horse to cool down after exercise, or a locker to store your extra feed and tack.

■ **Good hygiene** *is a serious business in the best stables.*

Life at the boarding barn

Each boarding facility will have its own atmosphere. Some of them are community oriented, encouraging active involvement with other boarders. Riding clinics (private riding lessons with special instructors) are often scheduled so that riders can advance their education. Some facilities hold special play-days – mounted games on horseback – for the kids. Some plan regular get-togethers, such as potluck barbecues or pizza parties.

Other barns like to stress training and competition. They might hold a regular show series on the premises. The instructors and trainers located at these facilities often have show schedules where they take their students on the show circuit annually (good if you're going to get serious). A training barn will have good equipment for its clients to use (such as fences to jump, western trail class equipment to practice on, and round-pens for working with young horses). Some barns are laid back, some are super serious. Some have an enjoyable atmosphere, while others can be a little cliquish. Spend time walking around the facility you're considering and check out the ambience. See what types of facilities would suit you best.

RED FLAGS FOR A BAD BOARDING BARN

You might rethink keeping your horse at a potential boarding facility if you inspect it and run across any of the following warning signs:

- Protruding metal or wood in stalls
- Old farm equipment all over the place
- Hay that looks like it's seen better days
- Multiple sightings of large rodents
- Combustible clutter in barn aisles
- Children jumping horses without safety gear on
- Riding arenas that have not been harrowed (dragged) in several days/weeks
- Cars parking in areas that are for horses
- Inoperable hot walkers or other broken equipment
- Turn-out rings or pens that have poor gates, latches, or fences
- No security lights or gates around the property
- Boarders that are the cattiest bunch you've seen since the tabbies were born

■ **If you see horses** *that look ill-cared for, you should avoid that boarding facility.*

Be a great boarder

Being a great boarder is easy: You just need to follow the "do unto others" rule. Of course, you'll run into people from time to time who seem to have forgotten their boarding manners. Set a good example by being at your best while visiting the stable, and you'll find that people are generally friendly and helpful in return.

First off, clean up after your horse. If he relieves himself in the aisle or in the grooming stalls, get a pitchfork and clear it up. Do whatever tasks you have to do in the stable's common areas promptly – for example, don't just let your horse stand in the wash rack for an hour when other people might be waiting for it. Don't borrow things such as someone's stable rake or washing hose without asking first. If you do borrow any tools or tack from someone, make sure you return them in the same condition.

If you have children and you want to bring them with you to the barn, it is crucial that you watch over them at all times. Not only is it annoying for other boarders to have to deal with your children if they get bored of the horse thing and get into mischief, but it is also dangerous for the kids.

When using the arena, keep your eyes up and learn how to ride in arena traffic. When you are passing a horse in the ring, pass left shoulder to left shoulder, just like driving a car. If someone is in a lesson, stay out of his or her path. You wouldn't want someone interrupting your schooling session.

Good personal relations

Try not to gossip about other boarders or trainers. Yes, all barns do have their share of dirt – and not just the type on the floor. Steer clear of catty conversations. If you do have a problem with another boarder, don't just go running to the facility manager. Try to work it out with that person in the most pleasant way possible. If this step doesn't work, then you can involve the manager.

A good boarder pays all fees on time. Don't wait until the barn manager has to call you up to see where your check is – or worse, puts a lock on your stall door until you've paid up.

If you have a problem with the service at the barn, make sure that you let the management know as soon as possible and in a tactful way. Don't fly off the handle and make demands just because you found your horse was getting the wrong hay, for instance. A simple conversation with a follow-up note will suffice. However, if you have hard-core problems with the facility that cannot easily be resolved, you might need to move your horse to a more appropriate stable.

Home on the range

MANY HORSE OWNERS DREAM of having enough land and money to design and build a place to keep their horses at home. Rural living definitely has its appeal, and small farms can be a quiet solace from the everyday rat race.

Owning horse property

If you are in the market to move yourself to horse country, you have two options. You can purchase acreage with rural zoning and start to design your facility from the ground up, or you can buy a house that already has a barn and fencing setup. If you want to develop your own horse property, there are several issues to consider.

Check with your local planning department to see what type of permits are required for building and what sort of structures are allowed in your area. See if you can change the lay of the land (for instance, can you dig into a hill?).

You'll need to determine where to put your barn in relation to your own house. Keep in mind how the wind blows, and take advantage of morning sun and afternoon shade. Figure out where the property drains, because you don't want to situate your horses on a floodplain.

■ **Look at the lay of your land** *and think about how it could best be devoted to equestrian use. What sort of boundaries can you erect around the property and what buildings will be required?*

Considering options

Figure out what kind of barn you'd like. There are various styles – some are large structures like the traditional red barns, while others are motel-style stables (the stalls are lined up next to each other, with all doors facing out to the yard). Barns can be custom made or bought prefabricated and ready to assemble. Consult a manufacturing company for ideas – it will be valuable information when you finally decide to break ground.

Never, ever use barbed wire fence around horses. Barbed wire was developed for use with cattle, not horses. Cattle have tough hides and are shorter and more compactly built. A horse can rip himself to shreds if he's caught in a barbed wire fence. He can cripple himself for life if he rips a tendon or leg ligament.

Other things to consider building include corrals, sometimes called paddocks, to let your horse play and snooze during the day (it will save you stall bedding costs and give your horse extra freedom). You'll need a place to store your tack, a room or shelter to put your hay and feed, and a bin or area away from the barn and house to keep your manure and old bedding.

The good side

Keeping a horse on your own farm or ranch can be more affordable than boarding in the long run. Besides your mortgage on the property and initial startup costs, you will have reduced feed, maintenance, and bedding expenses. You can keep your horse as you would like to, not as the stable manager dictates. If you develop your land properly, you can provide your horse with optimum exercise in his pasture during the day, instead of cooping him up in his barn stall.

The bad side

Managing horses does take time and money. If you're considering moving to a rural property so that you can keep a horse, think about how long it will take you to commute to work. Are you a handy person? You will have to do the maintenance on your property, or hire someone to handle this role. You'll have to be responsible for getting your feed delivered, your farrier appointments set up, and your veterinarian calls scheduled. If you ever decide to take a vacation, even for one day, you'll need to find a trusted person to take charge of the feeding and cleaning chores.

Trivia...

There are many options on offer as far as boundary fencing is concerned. The fencing that encloses your horses must be extremely sturdy. Wood fencing is attractive, but horses have a tendency to chew it. Metal pipe fencing is strong, but can injure horses if they run into it. Wire mesh fence is an affordable alternative. High tensile polymer rail fence has supportive wires running in flexible "fence boards." The rails slide through brackets on the posts to absorb any impact a running horse might make.

INTERNET

www.yourhorseshealth.com

This site can help you locate recommended equine practitioners in your area if you haven't selected a vet for your horse.

Whatever way you decide to keep your horse, make sure it suits your lifestyle and remember that there is no perfect facility. Horse-keeping should reflect how you like to deal with your horse and your ultimate goals with him. You'll have to decide what suits you before you bring your horse to his new home.

The ride home

ARRANGE FOR YOUR HORSE'S RIDE HOME well in advance of the day you decide to pick him up from his previous owner. You probably shouldn't go out and buy a ¾-ton pickup and matching horse trailer for the event. Instead, rely on your network of horse friends or professionals for help.

You can find a professional horse hauler, called a commercial transporter, through equestrian directories, classified ads, or local equestrian centers. A company will pick your horse up and deliver him to your address.

If you're transporting locally, your horse will be on board the trailer for only a short time. A long-distance ride, however, requires more consideration. Not all companies offer the same level of service or care, so find out what specifics the transporter provides. If you are unsure about picking a commercial transporter at random, look for one who is based locally first.

Your veterinarian, county extension agent, friends at other stables, and other equine contacts that you trust may be able to recommend transporters. Personal references of satisfied customers give the best information to go on.

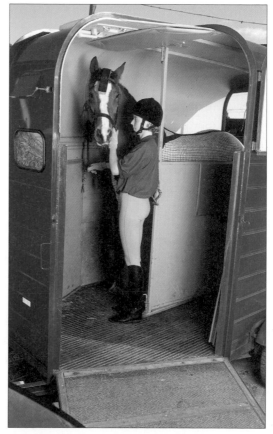

■ **Make sure you are happy** *with the transport you have organized to bring your horse home.*

Help for the long haul

On a long-distance trip, your horse will be traveling with other horses. A journey can become lengthy if the driver picks up other charges along the way – traveling several hundred miles out of the way can mean an extra day aboard a trailer. Make sure your shipping contract outlines important details about the time frame for picking up and dropping off the horse, resting and layover procedures, and when payment is expected. Don't pay everything in advance. Make sure your horse arrives healthy and happy before you hand over all your money.

You don't have to go with a commercial hauler, however. Many times your local equestrian facility can give you the name of a trainer who will pick up your horse for a fee. You can also check with a local horse friend – there are always people willing to join in on the excitement of bringing home a new horse.

INTERNET

www.overnightstabling.
com

_This web site provides
information on purchasing
the Nationwide Overnight
Stabling Directory and
Equestrian Vacation Guide._

A safe trip

Once you've sussed out your horse's ride, it's time to get him. But don't just run out the door and hop in the cab of the driver's truck empty handed. You'll need to have a few items with you to make for a smooth transfer.

First off, call the seller and ask what type of feed your horse is currently getting. You want to have a supply of feed ready for your horse when he steps into the trailer, as well as when he steps off.

Gather some supplies to ensure that he gets home safely: A halter to place on his head, a lead rope to lead him with, a trailer tie that features two special snaps that can be released in an emergency, and protective leg wear. Now, obviously, horses travel every day by just being shoved in a trailer and off they go. But it's better to get your horse home safely and without a blemish.

When you arrive at the horse's old home, it's a good idea to ask the seller any last-minute questions. Find out if the horse goes off his feed when put in an unfamiliar situation. See if there are any ways that you can make him feel more at home initially.

Before loading your horse onto the trailer, let the seller spend a couple of moments with him. Some people are very attached to their horses, even if they are selling them. Have the seller help you load the horse into the trailer. He or she knows the horse better than you do, and sometimes horses can be touchy about getting into an unfamiliar trailer. This is not the time to retrain a truculent horse. Have your experienced friend and the seller get the horse aboard, secure him, and latch all doors and ramps tightly.

Home preparations

IT'S THE MOMENT YOU'VE BEEN waiting for. The truck is in the driveway, and it's carrying your precious cargo. You've prepared for him ahead of time, so all you need to do is take him off the trailer and settle him in.

Savvy stall setup

Your horse will spend a major portion of his life in his stall. If he's at a boarding barn, his **turn-out** time will be limited to when you visit. You should, therefore, ensure his stall is safe and comfortable.

The way modern equestrians keep horses is very strange. We take a free-roaming animal and confine him to a small space for 23 out of 24 hours a day. No matter how cozy a stall seems to humans, it's an unnatural existence for a horse. Horses are quite adaptable, however, and soon get used to a regular barn routine.

> **DEFINITION**
>
> **Turn-out** *is the time that a horse gets to spend in a small pasture, paddock, or arena by himself. Be sure to turn out your horse regularly for the benefit of his physical and his mental health.*

Your stall should also be in good shape. If the barn is wood, look for areas that might give way if the horse leans against them or kicks. You should always have a halter and lead rope at the stall door in case of an emergency.

Many stalls are prefabricated structures, made of aluminum or other metal. Look to make sure that any bolts and screws are seated completely so that they won't catch on your horse's skin.

Ensure that the feeding tub or hay rack is mounted securely, with no broken edges. Also, clean out the automatic waterer, if appropriate. This has a float or lever system that allows it to keep a constant flow of fresh water, but algae and dirt can accumulate, especially if the waterer is located in the sun.

■ **Your horse's stall** *should be well-maintained. Make sure that there is a good supply of bedding on the floor.*

Stall comfort

Your horse's stall floor is important, since it can often determine his level of comfort. If you've ever been to an amusement park or trade show, you know how tired you get standing all day on concrete. Imagine having to do that day in and day out! Stall floors can be cement, dirt, or sometimes a complex commercial drainage system. You can make the stall floor more comfortable by using stall mats – these are large sheets of rubber placed under the bedding that provide a cushion to delicate legs as well as improve the condition of the floor. Ventilation is important for your horse's health. Respiratory problems can develop in horses that are kept in stalls with little air flow. Therefore, make sure that any windows or grilles can open up to allow fresh air to breeze through – this not only allows ammonia from urine to dissipate, it also keeps your horse from living in cell-like conditions.

Safety considerations

His surroundings should be given a safety check, too. The feed room should be locked so that he cannot break into it and gorge himself, leading to devastating health consequences. Feed should also be stored in containers with strong lids to prevent a rodent invasion. Clear the barn aisles of any bags of shavings, wheelbarrows, pitchforks, or items that could be knocked over or injure someone. Some things you might not even think of as dangerous could harm your horse. There are dozens of plants that are toxic to horses. Unfortunately, many of them are ornamental shrubs and flower bushes found in everyday gardens.

INTERNET

www.ansci.cornell.edu

To see a list of plant species that are of particular concern to horse owners, log onto this Cornell University web site.

He's arrived!

Many horses are panicked when they come off a trailer. If your horse is too distracted, you might need to place a small linked chain, called a stud chain, over his nose. This is not to be used as punishment, but just to reinforce that the horse needs to pay attention to you.

Usually, the panic doesn't last long. Most horses will look around and maybe prance a little when first coming off a trailer. Have your friend remove the horse's protective leg wear while you hold on to him. Gently walk the horse around so that he can stretch his legs and survey his new surroundings. Some people recommend turning the horse out in a corral to give him the opportunity to shake off the confines of his trip. Finally, once you're ready to put him up for the evening, lead him into his stall, take his halter off, and get his dinner ration together.

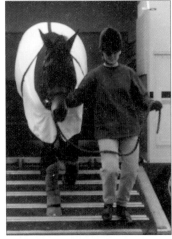

■ **Take care** *when you take your horse off the trailer – he may feel disorientated.*

Dinner is served

SINCE YOU DISCUSSED YOUR HORSE'S feed with his previous owner, you already know what he has been eating. But you might want to make changes in his diet to reflect his life with you. (And just because his previous owner fed him a certain type of hay doesn't mean that it's the ideal diet.)

A nutrition plan

First off, consult the veterinarian who performed your prepurchase exam to help you devise a complete diet plan for your new horse. Many vets will tell you that most horses do just fine eating only high-quality hays such as Bermuda grass, timothy, or alfalfa hays.

Don't make sudden changes to your horse's diet as he could become ill. Any changes in a horse's feed must be done gradually.

However, there are times when you'll need to supplement your horse's regular diet with a different type of feed, such as a grain. (For a complete guide to feeds, see Chapter 12).

Feeding schedules

Ever been around a large stable at feeding time? You'd think there were equine piranhas being housed there with the stamping feet, banging pails, and heads looking at the feed tractor going by. Horses get used to a routine, and if there is variation, they'll let you know.

■ **Horses enjoy** *a regular feeding schedule. They thrive on being fed the same food in the same quantity at regular intervals.*

Horses have delicate digestive systems, so if a new forage or grain is thrown in the mix, if their meal is late, or if too much is given to them, they can become very ill. Stick to the same meal plan daily, and you can minimize the number of tummy aches your horse gets. Baled hay, however, can provide a natural stimulation for a stall-kept horse. It allows him to chew longer, which in turn helps his digestive system. Even horses that are fed nutritionally complete feeds should often be given hay for this reason.

The daily routine

IT'S YOUR FIRST DAY AS A HORSE OWNER! How exciting and how frightening at the same time. All of a sudden, you have this huge animal depending on you for everything – what do you do first?

Set up a daily schedule for your horse. It doesn't need to be as regimented as your feeding system, but your horse shouldn't stand in his stall all day waiting for you to come and "spring him." He could become bored and develop behavioral problems. Also, lack of regular work will make a horse unfit in just a few weeks. Regular attention and exercise will enhance his health and well-being.

Getting used to each other

During the first few weeks, no doubt you'll be on cloud nine. You'll want to spend most of your free time with your new partner. It's a good idea to give your horse a day or so to settle in. Your time will be spent walking around the property, getting exercise in turn-out, and just handling your new horse, in general, through grooming. You can get a good idea of what his personality and **ground manners** are like from spending time with him in this way.

Working around horses

Your new horse doesn't know you from Adam at this point, so use common sense around him. Move in a smooth, not jerky, fashion. People who are nervous around big animals often make quick, darting motions, which can startle a horse. Put your hand on his hindquarters and walk closely around his rump to the other side, speaking to him so he knows you're back there. Some horses enjoy being patted and stroked, while others might not care for it. The only way you're going to find out is by doing it. The more confident you are around your new horse, the easier he'll settle in. Horses will often react badly to a timid or uncertain individual.

Tack and equipment care

No doubt you'll soon be in the saddle. Make sure that you take care of it when you've finished a ride. Your bridle and girth, which lie next to the horse's skin, get sweaty and will also need to be cleaned and conditioned. Purchase a saddle rack and bridle pegs so that you can put your tack up correctly after each ride. Rinse your horse's bit after every ride – you wouldn't want to put a disgustingly crusty metal thing in your mouth, either, would you? Saddle blankets, pads, and leg wraps all need regular washing, too. Dirty blankets can cause your horse to develop skin problems. A blanket that gets washed only once a year is impossible to get back to its original color or shape.

Your tack needs to be cleaned otherwise it can become brittle, dry, and develop cracks. Cracks lead to weakened leather, and a broken bridle, or a buckle that comes loose from a girth, spells disaster.

■ **Take care of your saddle** *by cleaning it regularly to keep the leather supple and flexible.*

A simple summary

✓ Whether you keep your horse at a boarding barn or on your own property, there are pros and cons.

✓ You can arrange for your horse's first trip home through a commercial hauler or private party.

✓ Your horse's living quarters should be set up and checked for safety before he arrives at his new home.

✓ Consult your vet to develop the optimum feeding plan.

✓ Horses like order and routine, so set up a daily schedule.

✓ Work around horses in a confident manner so they are calm and trusting with you.

✓ Clean your tack and equipment regularly, both for your safety and for your horse's health.

Chapter 8

Gear Guide

IF YOU LIKE SHOPPING, you're going to love horse ownership. Not only is there a slew of tack and equipment for your horse, there is riding apparel in every style and color to completely drain your bank account! Luckily, when it comes to purchasing gear for you and your horse, there are only a few important items that you'll need right away. The rest of the equipment you can accumulate later. Also, there are several ways in which to cut corners on your spending. But be forewarned: As the saying goes, "Anyone who said they made a small fortune in horses probably started out with a large one."

In this chapter...

✓ **Horse essentials**

✓ **Your riding clothes**

✓ **The saddle**

✓ **The right bit and bridle**

✓ **Leg protection**

SPEND TIME GETTING TO KNOW WHAT EACH PIECE OF TACK IS FOR

Horse essentials

GET READY TO SAY GOODBYE to your disposable income. You thought the cost of a horse was pretty steep? That was just the beginning. Now you'll need to invest in a fair amount of tack and equipment for your new addition. The good news is that you won't need it all at once.

Your main source for horse products will probably be the local tack store. If you have more than one in your area, select the one that offers the best prices for its service. You might have to drive a little farther, but in the long run you will feel as though you have spent your money well.

Used equipment is a solid option if you're just getting started. Plus, it makes you look like you've been involved with horses a long time.

For instance, there's a tack shop within walking distance from my office. It's a beautiful Spanish building, filled with gorgeous displays, the top-of-the-line tack, and plenty of new products to entice the impulse buyer. Yet I'll travel 20 extra miles (32 km) to the small, aging storefront in an industrial center. Why? Its prices are really good, and its people are even nicer. They'll special order for me or beat someone else's price. The elegant Spanish building with the fountain? I'd probably pay a third of its rent with the prices it charges! But you can also shop in horse catalogs, over the Internet, and at consignment shops.

Halter and lead rope

A halter is called a headcollar in England because that's exactly what it is. It fits over the horse's face and fastens behind her ears to allow you to lead and control her as you would when you'd take your dog for a walk. Halters are made of nylon or leather (or some are nylon with a strap at the top – the crownpiece – made of leather for safety.)

■ **Halters come in several different sizes,** *but the most common ones are "cob" (for Arabians or dainty-headed horses); "horse" (for average-sized heads); and "warmblood" (for the big guys).*

The horse's leash, the lead rope, should be a sturdy length of nylon, cotton, or leather. You can select a rope that complements the halter color. It's also a good idea to have a spare lead around for emergencies – while the lead rope itself rarely breaks, horses have been known to break some of the flimsier snaps that attach the rope to the halter.

Do not turn your horse out or leave her alone in her stall with a nylon halter on. Should she get hung up on a fence post, she could break her neck struggling to get free. Leather halters are much safer because they will break if the horse pulls hard enough.

Basic grooming tools

Here are the brushes and tools that you'll need right off the bat:

- Body brush: this is an all-purpose brush that allows you to vigorously groom your horse's coat to remove the daily dirt and scurf. This is usually a large oval brush with a flat back, a hand strap, and short, medium-soft bristles.

BODY BRUSH

- Curry comb: not really a comb at all, but a round rubber or plastic brush that has little nubs on it to massage the horse's skin and remove heavy dirt, mud, and hair. There are curries that have pointy teeth, while others have soft, flexible fingers. Use one that matches your horse's sensitivity. If she's thick-skinned, you'll be fine using the pointy curry. A delicate horse will prefer the softer variety.

CURRY COMB

- Hoof pick: this simple device is one of your most important tools. The metal pick is used to remove rocks and debris from the bottom of your horse's foot. It is designed to scrape round the *frog*. Remember to clean out your horse's feet daily so that they will stay healthy.

DEFINITION

*The **frog** is the V-shaped pad at the back of the horse's hoof, which acts like a shock absorber for her foot.*

■ **Use the hoof pick** *to clean out stones and dirt from the hoof. Work from the back to the front of the hoof, and be careful not to damage the soft parts of the foot.*

Your riding clothes

IF YOU'VE EVER TRIED TO CLIMB aboard a horse in a pair of jeans that just came out of the dryer, you'll appreciate why riding clothes were created. Most riding apparel is designed to reflect the sport's origin, whether it is the classic style of English, or the relaxed lifestyle apparel of western.

Riding clothes are made to move with you in the saddle. They make it easy and comfortable to mount up, to spend hours trail riding, to jump over fences, and to do barn chores. Riding clothes should not hinder movement or impede contact with the horse.

Safety gear

I'm going to go out on a limb here: Anyone who gets on a horse without a safety helmet is a fool. You want some statistics? According to the American Medical Equestrian Association, the most common reason that riders are admitted to hospitals is for head injuries. Sixty percent of deaths associated with equestrian sports are the direct result of a head trauma.

Once upon a time, helmets were hot, heavy, bulky, unattractive, and expensive. But now, manufacturers have developed lightweight, ventilated, durable helmets that are actually stylish. There are schooling helmets that are affordable as well, so the excuse of expense is not realistic. The visor helps to protect your eyes in the sunlight. The harness keeps the helmet firmly attached to your head. Show helmets are designed for style with a low profile silhouette and have the look of the traditional black velvet hunt cap.

■ **Dress for comfort** *and safety when you go riding: A padded body protector will minimize injury during a fall, especially if you're out on the trail; a helmet is essential for all types of riding; boots and clothes should fit you properly.*

Helmets basically cushion your brain if it were to experience an impact with the ground, a jump, a tree, or the like. With its protective polystyrene shell, the inner materials actually compress to absorb the shock that your head would normally take on by itself. While no safety equipment can protect you 100 percent, helmets certainly reduce the likelihood of severe injury or death.

Helmets work. Most deaths from head injury could have been prevented by wearing a well-fitting, secured safety helmet approved by the American Society for Testing Materials and the Safety Equipment Institute. A bike helmet is tested and approved for a totally different sport – therefore it is not recommended for wear while riding horses.

However, it's a free country, as they say. Wearing a helmet is a personal choice. Many riders and trainers never put a helmet on top of their heads, and they have made it through life without a mishap. Are you willing to gamble on yours?

The correct footwear

All riders should wear a boot with a heel. The heel acts like a stop, preventing the foot from getting caught in the stirrup. If a rider gets thrown, but the foot is still stuck in the stirrup, the rider could be dragged to death.

Boots don't have to be any particular style or color. You can wear a western- or English-style boot. Manufacturers have even developed "riding sneakers," which look like high-top athletic shoes and are an affordable alternative.

■ **Leather English-style** *boots can be expensive. Alternatives include tall or ankle boots in rubber and synthetic materials.*

Boots also protect you when you're on the ground. Horses can sometimes forget where your feet are and place a hoof on them. If you're just wearing sandals or a thin little tennis shoe, your toes could be crushed. Boots can offer your feet some protection.

If you did want to select a particular style, stay away from those pointy-toed cowboy boots. Those are good for line dancing, but not for western riding. The western boot of choice is a lace-up ankle boot called a roper. English riders have a lace-up ankle boot, as well, called a paddock boot. They also have a choice of tall boots that come in two different styles: field boots (lacing at the top of the foot) and dress boots (without laces).

INTERNET

www.devonaire.com

Check out the clothing manufacturer Devon-Aire's site to get some ideas about the variety of boots, shirts, jackets, and more available.

Clothes made for comfort

Western riders wear riding jeans in the saddle. Wranglers seem synonymous with cowboys, but there are plenty of other brands found at both western wear stores and tack shops for you to try on. Today's riding jean is more of a relaxed fit, which allows the rider to swing a leg up without having to hop around or struggle, with seams that are sympathetic to the rider's position in the saddle. English riders wear breeches (which in some circles are pronounced *britches*.) Breeches fit underneath tall boots, and their close-fitting fabric moves with the rider – especially helpful when jumping fences. Lightweight fabrics that stretch and breathe are most desirable.

Minimize sun damage by applying a sunscreen or wearing a long-sleeved shirt. Even when it's warm, many trainers wear light-colored cotton or CoolMax® long-sleeved shirts to protect them from harmful rays.

Riding shirts can be anything from your favorite T-shirts or tank tops, to specially designed athletic wear. New materials that wick away moisture keep you cool during a strenuous ride. Women should don a sports top or bra for support while in the saddle.

The saddle

UNLESS YOU WANT TO BE AYLA, Empress of Horses, and ride bareback, you're going to need tack. You might have been able to strike a deal with your horse's former owner to purchase her old saddle and bridle. But many owners like to hold onto their tack for their next horse, and, also, their saddle might not be something that you wish to take home with you.

Even if you're just trail riding, tack can get expensive. But it is a solid investment. If a saddle doesn't fit properly, it can make your horse sore, and a horse with a sore back often develops behavior problems such as bucking to show you her discomfort. A horse in pain will often try to compensate in other ways, and may end up going lame. If you invest in good quality tack, it has a good resale value. Do some research and get as much advice as you can before purchasing. Choose your saddle carefully and consider your horse as well as what type of riding you will be doing. A well-made saddle can last many years, if you take proper care of it, and if you do decide to sell it (let's say you buy a different horse down the road which needs a different saddle size, or you change from English riding to western), you can often get a good price.

Quality cues

How can you tell if a saddle is well made? First off, smell it. Good leather has a warm, inviting aroma. Poor quality leather smells harsh or like fish. Even new, good leather is firm but flexible. You can also tell by the standard of workmanship. The edges of the saddle should be smooth and the stitches should be even, tight, and small. Any tooling should be carefully done, and rivets or silver should be secure. Buckles and rings should be of stainless steel or brass, not cheap plated metal.

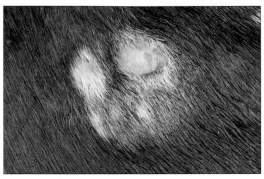

■ **An ill-fitting saddle** *can cause swellings on the horse's back known as saddle sores. A horse with saddle sores should not be ridden until all of the affected skin has healed completely.*

Avoid false economy

You'll see saddle and bridle packages in catalogs that are unbelievably inexpensive. They'll feature a saddle, girth, stirrups, and bridle for one low price. And in the picture, they look pretty much like the more expensive items on the following pages. Please, for the sake of you and your horse, stay away from these. You don't want to run the risk of ending up with leather that is smelly and stiff, and a saddle that is haphazardly sewn together. By spending only a couple hundred dollars more, you can get tack that is durable, comfortable, and attractive.

To get an idea of what types of saddles are available in different price ranges, first check out some Internet pages by typing "English riding tack" or "western riding tack" in your favorite search engine. Then visit your local tack store and ask for some help in seeing some of the subtle differences between all the different types of western and English gear.

BUYING SECOND-HAND EQUIPMENT

Second-hand equipment can be found in classified ads, at regular tack stores, and at consignment shops. There are deals to be had. Look at the used saddle the same way you'd look at a new one, but be a little more critical about extra wear and tear. Check for rotting or weakened leather, loose stitching, or missing hardware. Buy with the stipulation that if it doesn't fit, you can return it for your money back.

Your saddle will be the most expensive piece of tack you own. It also has to fit two: you and your horse. There are many variations on English and western saddles, so check with your riding instructor, trainer, or experienced horse person to help you select the one that is right for your type of riding.

English saddles

English saddles are generally made for either jumping or dressage. The jumping saddle is flat and the flaps on the side are designed to follow the position of your leg (kind of hiked up) when you are jumping over a fence. The dressage saddle has a deep (concave) seat and long side flaps because your legs hang down straighter and need to have greater contact with the horse than when you're jumping.

Western saddles

Western saddles have a deep cantle and a horn in front, which sometimes acts like a handle. Its side flaps, called fenders, are long and made of stiff leather. English saddles, being smaller, weigh about 20 pounds (9 kg), but western saddles often weigh in at 45 pounds (20 kg).

How to choose the right fit

You could spend thousands of dollars on the nicest saddle in the store, but if it doesn't fit your horse, it's worthless. Think of searching for your saddle as being like searching for a new pair of athletic shoes. In the sporting goods store, you'll find running shoes, sprinting "spikes," cross trainers, walking shoes, basketball shoes, hiking boots, and a host of others. Each pair, depending upon style and manufacturer, is going to fit differently. That fit will mean the difference between agony and a winning performance.

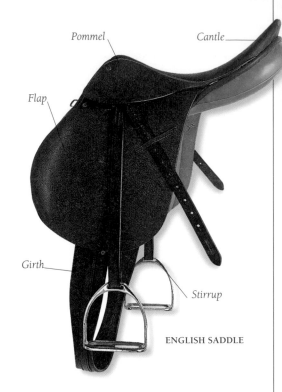

Pommel   *Cantle*

Flap

Girth

Stirrup

ENGLISH SADDLE

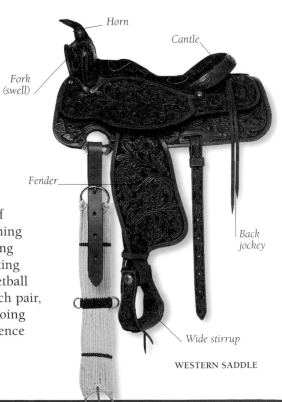

Horn

Cantle

Fork (swell)

Fender

Back jockey

Wide stirrup

WESTERN SADDLE

You're going to have to try a saddle out to see how it fits. At the tack shop, you'll see saddles on special stands, so you can actually swing your leg over and sit on them. The part you sit on, the seat, is measured in inches, and most "sizes" are in the upper teens: 16", 17", etc. But they can vary among manufacturers, so use sizes only as a guide.

Sit in a half dozen saddles until you find one that is comfortable for you. The sales associate can help you determine the best fit. Some have "deep" seats, meaning that they are concave, allowing you to slide into the right spot for a more secure feeling. The flatter seat allows you to move around more, which is good for people who jump, for instance. Saddles can also feel wide or narrow.

If the saddle is too small for you, you can end up with some painful bruises down below from hitting the front or the back of it. If the saddle is too big, you'll be floundering around trying to sit in the proper position.

Once you have a model that you're comfortable in, you need to take it home and try it out on your horse. Every horse's back is different, so be prepared to "test drive" more than one. Have a horse friend with you to help you examine the fit (it's a good idea to have your vet look at how it fits as well, since medical problems result from a bad fit).

SADDLE-FITTING NOTES

- Too wide a saddle "tree" (skeleton of the saddle that is covered in padding and leather) will press down directly on the horse's withers and backbone, causing pain, while a too narrow tree will dig painfully into the horse's shoulders
- The panels (underside that lies against the horse's back) should follow the horse's contours smoothly
- The girth should fit about 4 inches (10 cm) behind the horse's elbow. If it slides ahead or behind this position, the saddle does not fit the horse

■ **While the seat** *does have its own slope, it should not look like it is tipping forward or back when viewed from the side.*

The right bit and bridle

YOUR BIT AND BRIDLE are important equipment, too, since you will be communicating to your horse through them. These vital pieces of tack help you to control the horse's movements.

The bit

The bit rests in the toothless gap of the horse's mouth, over his tongue. He responds to how you put pressure on his mouth through the reins that you hold in your hands. Imagine placing a pen in your mouth sideways. You'd want that pen to not hurt your tongue or corners of your mouth, right? Choose one that is mild (easy on the horse's mouth), not severe. A snaffle bit, which is a thick bit that generally is jointed in the middle to allow flexibility, is considered a gentle bit. Bits with long sides that hang down from the mouthpiece, the shanks, can be severe. A bit that has a port in the middle, a U-shaped hump in the mouthpiece, can be harsh or gentle, depending upon how tall the port is.

Any bit can hurt a horse if it is put in the wrong hands. A mild bit can be jerked on as easily as a severe one. Learn the proper use of all equipment so you won't unwittingly hurt your horse.

For help with selecting the right size, take a pencil and tie a string to it. Place the string inside the horse's mouth and pull it until the pencil rests on one side of his face. Mark the string on the other side of his face and remove. Measure this in inches and take your measurement to the shop. Most horses' mouths are about 5 inches (13 cm) wide.

The bridle

There are all types of bridles on the market – some basic and some pricey. Like saddle leather, your bridle leather should also be of good quality. Bad leather stretches or is very stiff (something that you won't like when your reins are hard to hold). It won't clean up well, and will begin to look shabby quickly. A good leather bridle has even stitching, rust-free buckles, and supple leather. If you are going to be riding western, you will need a western bridle, which is designed to work with western-style bits.

Mouthpiece fits horse's mouth

■ **Choose a bridle** *to match your horse's head size and your riding style.*

Leather-cleaning equipment

Good leather can last for many years if you treat it properly. To clean your tack, you'll need leather soap (liquid or bar), cleaning sponges, clean rags, and leather oil or conditioner. Apply the soap to your dampened cleaning sponge and work into the leather. Circular motions will help dislodge ground-in dirt. Then, remove all soap with a second clean wet sponge. With the leather still damp, apply your conditioner with another sponge or with a soft brush. Apply a thin film of conditioner to the outside and the rough underside as well. Let the conditioned tack sit for a half-hour. Wipe off any excess oil residue.

Some products have both cleaners and conditioners in them. These products are good to use when time is tight, but they cannot really do the job of separate products.

LEATHER SOAP

Leg protection

LEG WRAPS AND SUPPORT BOOTS are designed to help your equine athlete stay sound. Wraps protect your horse's lower legs from getting cut or banged up if the horse "interferes" (knocks one leg against the other).

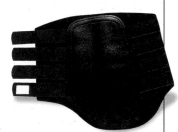

Support boots bolster the tendons and ligaments, which can often be strained under heavy work. Not all horses need these boots, but some, such as jumpers and reiners, can benefit from the extra protection.

PROTECTIVE BOOT

A simple summary

✔ You have several options for your horse equipment purchases – stores, catalogs, and the Internet.

✔ Your tack will last a lifetime only if you select quality workmanship and materials.

✔ Riding apparel not only makes you look the part, it is designed with safety and comfort in mind.

✔ Once you have chosen your tack, you need to look after it properly using the correct products.

Chapter 9

More at the Store: Extra Equipment

NOW THAT YOU KNOW THE BASICS, you'll need to start collecting a few more items that will make your horse-keeping life much easier. Special grooming supplies help keep your horse clean and healthy, while barn tools allow you to keep your stable area tidy. Some of the biggest ticket items – such as a horse trailer – are a personal choice. However, don't rush to your bank manager just yet. No one says that you have to turn into the urban cowboy overnight.

In this chapter...

✔ **Grooming kit**

✔ **Seasonal equipment**

✔ **Around the barn**

✔ **Travel gear**

YOU WILL NEED DIFFERENT EQUIPMENT FOR YOUR HORSE DEPENDING ON THE SEASON

Grooming kit

THERE'S A JOKE ABOUT how grooming is the process by which you transfer dirt, debris, and shedding hair from your horse's coat to your own clothes and face. But actually, this daily task helps maintain your horse's health.

Not only does proper grooming before and after your ride remove dirt that can create soreness under a saddle or bridle, it also allows you to spend time checking out your horse's overall condition. You will be able to spot any unusual lumps or bumps or swelling early on, and possibly prevent a small situation from becoming a large health ordeal.

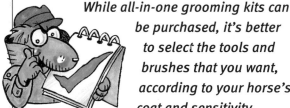

While all-in-one grooming kits can be purchased, it's better to select the tools and brushes that you want, according to your horse's coat and sensitivity.

Hoof oil

Curry combs

Hoof pick

Cloth

Sponge

Sweat scraper

Mane and tail combs

■ **You can put together** *your own grooming kit to suit the particular needs of your horse.*

You can put make up your own grooming kit in a variety of ways. Some people use wooden containers, while others just put together a makeshift one in a box or a bucket. The best way to keep your tools together is to put them in a compartment tote, which allows you to find what you need quickly and easily.

Brushes and curries

Besides a body brush, you should have a stiff brush to use on sweat-dried coats or to break up dirt. Stiff brushes, which are slender, natural, and stiff-bristled, are good for tough hides or winter coats. You should also have a finishing brush, which has soft bristles to remove fine dust particles and for use on your horse's face. The finishing brush brings the oils of the horse's coat up to the surface to finish him with an extra shine.

Trivia...
Hoof oils don't exactly restore moisture to the foot, they simply block moisture from getting out.

You'll also need a shedding blade – a metal-toothed tool which looks like a hacksaw blade bent into a teardrop shape. When used in long, stroking motions, it catches any loose hair and removes it from the coat. It should not be used in a circular motion because the sturdy metal might hurt if used too aggressively. Another tool is called a slick block. The slick block is a little square brick, reminiscent of lava stone, and it performs the same duties as the shedding blade – to **slick out** a horse.

DEFINITION

A horse is **slicked out** *when his winter coat is finally gone, and what is left is the short, shiny new hair underneath. He's slicked out because his coat is shiny and sleek looking.*

Massaging curries are more like mitts that work to loosen up dead hair, old skin, and dirt. Horses love to have these mitts used in a circular fashion on their coat. Because the "teeth" on these are either small nubs or a swirly plastic mesh, they do not irritate sensitive skins.

INTERNET

http://gprix.com

Grand Prix Equestrian Products is an on-line catalog – it will give you lots of ideas about types of grooming equipment available.

Mane and tail

Tail hairs take a long time to grow. That's why a lot of show grooms never use any combs or brushes on tails at all, but instead just condition the tail, then painstakingly pick apart the strands. If you don't have the time to keep your horse's tail like that, there are still plenty of mane and tail brushes that will keep the tail pretty. Large brushes with flexible, rounded plastic teeth seem to work best. A horse's mane grows faster, however, so it's less of a problem if some of the hairs break off.

Using a sweat scraper

A sweat scraper is another grooming tool you should have on hand. Ironically enough, very few of these are used to scrape the sweat off of a horse, since most horses don't come home wringing wet after a ride. They do get wet after a bath, however, so that's when the scraper comes into play.

Working like a squeegee, the scraper pulls water off the horse's coat, one stroke at a time.

■ **Sponges are useful** *for cleaning out eyes and ears, wiping off stains, and applying medications and shampoos.*

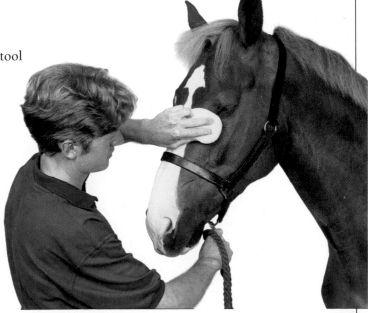

The extras

During the winter, a horse can have a hard time cooling down under his shaggy winter coat. Clipping the long hair means that you have to blanket him from the elements, but if you ride daily, this will make your horse easier to care for. Clippers come in various sizes: small for clipping the long muzzle hairs or trimming the ears; regular for detail work on the legs, face, and mane; and heavy-duty for shearing the horse's whole body.

Hiring a professional groom to clip your horse is good perhaps for the first time, but that would be so you can observe and learn – after all, your horse will need to be clipped more than once, and that expense can add up.

Sheen sprays put the finishing touch on a clean horse. Most people use these when they are competing in a show to catch the judge's eye. Hoof oils are used for this purpose too, but they are also used daily to keep the horse's hoof moisturized.

Seasonal equipment

WHETHER IT'S A BLISTERING SUMMER or a chilly winter, you need to be prepared for what comes with that time of the year. Your horse will thank you if you've done your homework well before the weather changes.

Blankets

Horse clothing for the winter months, blankets are designed to be worn when the horse is not being ridden. Some horses wear blankets all day during the winter, while other horses living in milder climates might only wear them overnight.

Blankets are available in a range of fabrics to suit different purposes: There are blankets designed for horses that live indoors, and there

■ **Lightweight blankets** *may be used in summer to help keep the horse's coat clean before a competition.*

are "turn-out" blankets that are tough and durable, for horses that spend most of their time outdoors. Some blankets are quilted with a waterproof outer shell, just like a ski jacket. Others are very light and are nothing more than heavy cotton or nylon.

Fly protection

You can provide your horse relief from flies by putting him in his own protective suit of armor. Fly sheets, fly masks, and fly leg wraps provide a physical barrier against a horse's winged enemies.

Made of the same material as the screens on your windows, fly sheets allow air to circulate underneath them, so they can be worn in the hot months when pests are the most prevalent. Some horses need protection on their legs, since flies bite this area, drawing blood easily. Flies are extremely bothersome around a horse's face, so a fly mask can provide relief from flies crawling around the eyes.

HORSE WITH
FLY MASK

INTERNET

www.bmbtack.com

This web site features BMB blankets, sheets, and other tack and supplies, made in America.

MEASURING AND FITTING A BLANKET

Finding a blanket for your horse is easy. Take a cloth measuring tape and have a friend place the beginning of the tape right in the middle of the horse's chest (below his neck). Then, pull the tape along the side of the horse, around to the back of the horse's tail. You're going from front to back, keeping the tape horizontal. Your measurement will be the size of the blanket. Blankets are sold in even number increments, so if you come up with a measurement of 79 inches (200 cm), you would purchase an 80-inch (210-cm) blanket.

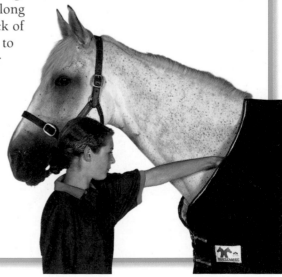

■ **The blanket should fit** *well and have straps or ties to hold it in place. If there is too much slippage, this will irritate the horse.*

Around the barn

TOOLS OF THE TRADE will help keep your horse, as well as his surroundings, spick-and-span. Some items don't have to be from the tack store, while others are made expressly for the job at hand.

Clean-up and maintenance equipment

Buckets serve many purposes around the barn, including bathing and feeding. Keep a couple so that your horse doesn't receive a soapy meal.

A muck bucket is a large tub used for manure. It can be used in place of a wheelbarrow if you're just cleaning out one stall. A muck bucket is also a handy place to deposit manure that your horse leaves in barn aisles or in the grooming and washing areas. An empty one can be turned over and used as a step stool or a **mounting block**.

Tools of the trade

You may want to invest in a future fork, which differs from a pitchfork because it is specially designed to pick up manure, leaving behind the clean straw or wood shavings. Why it's called a future fork is a mystery. Your rake can help you distribute your stall bedding evenly, as well as clean up loose hay in barn aisles and a host of other maintenance duties. You'll also need a flat-ended shovel to help you pick up messes and move dirt around – this is ideal for maintaining corrals and cleaning small pens that get a lot of hoof traffic.

■ **Assemble a kit** *of all the cleaning tools you need. Larger items, such as a wheelbarrow, rakes, and future forks make barn maintenance much easier.*

Another invaluable piece of cleaning equipment is the industrial type broom your school janitor swept the sidewalk with. This is a top choice because the large rectangular heads with stiff bristles help keep aisles and wash areas tidy.

Feed stores, farm equipment stores, and tack shops all carry barn equipment. However, you can find many items at your local home improvement stores and usually at lower prices. Shop around for the best deals.

You'll probably want a garden hose with a sprayer, not for hosing clean the walkways (conserve that water), but for giving your horse a bath. A sprayer with adjustable streams will give your horse a perfect rinse.

Stable savvy

Horses are big animals, and they can inadvertently hurt you just as easily as they can hurt themselves. Prevent accidents by keeping your stable as safe as possible. Keeping the stable clean is the first step to safety.

Do not leave clutter in your barn aisle. You don't want to be tripping over wheelbarrows and watering hoses. Keeping the stable clean also means keeping it clear of all the cleaning equipment!

Remove cobwebs and old bedding to reduce the possibility of fire. Make sure that your fencing is safe, and keep only horses in your pastures (remove old equipment or dangerous items). Lock up your horse's feed so he cannot break into it and overeat, which can make him seriously ill. Close all gates and stall doors to prevent your horse from running loose. Keep a fire extinguisher handy for emergencies, and make sure that there are "No Smoking" signs prominently displayed.

■ **Clear away your tools** *once you've finished the job and store them safely.*

123

Travel gear

YOUR HORSE SHOULD HAVE his own travel wardrobe, and not just because you want him to look like a million-dollar racehorse when he steps off his trailer. Horses need gear that allows them to travel in safety.

Shipping boots are protective boots that fit from above the horse's knee (and his pointy hocks on his back legs) all the way down to cover his feet. In a small space, a horse can get jostled around and accidentally step on himself, which can lead to cuts and bruises. Padded shipping boots reduce the likelihood of injuries on a horse's delicate legs. The poll cap is a little hat for your horse to wear to protect his head. Horses are tall, and trailers only have so much headroom. There's always a risk of a horse banging the top of his skull, his poll, on the trailer roof. A poll cap works as padded protection.

It's a good idea to have your horse wear a leather halter instead of a nylon one. A leather halter can break free in a bad situation (such as a trailer accident). A horse who is trapped in an overturned trailer can kill himself in a struggle.

A trailer tie is a short adjustable nylon strap that features two safety buckles that have a quick release in case of an emergency. Anyone who has watched a horse panic to get out of a trailer will appreciate being able to give their trailer tie a quick yank at the snap to free the horse.

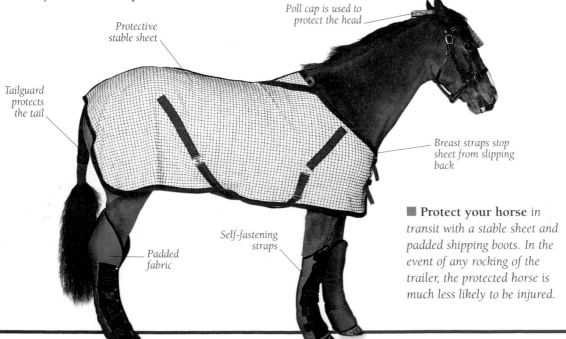

Poll cap is used to protect the head

Protective stable sheet

Tailguard protects the tail

Breast straps stop sheet from slipping back

Padded fabric

Self-fastening straps

■ **Protect your horse** in transit with a stable sheet and padded shipping boots. In the event of any rocking of the trailer, the protected horse is much less likely to be injured.

Another essential travel item for your horse is a stable sheet – a lightweight blanket that protects his coat from little nicks and dings that might occur during transport. Make sure the sheet is in the right position before fastening the straps.

Truck and trailer specifications

If you're looking to really get into some shopping, your truck and trailer, known as your rig, is the Holy Grail. The right sized truck with the right amount of horsepower, coupled with the trailer that meets your horse's needs, will make you more flexible and can lead you to endless riding opportunities.

Buying a huge truck may be a case of road overkill if all you need to do is bring your horse out to the trails every month or so. Figure out what your basic needs are and go from there. Start with the truck's towing ability. For example, a two-horse trailer that weighs 2,500 pounds (1,133 kg) with two 1,200-pound (545-kg) horses requires a truck that has a towing capacity of at least 4,900 pounds (2,200 kg). Since most ½-ton trucks come with a standard V6 engine and a towing capacity of only 3,000 pounds (1360 kg), you will need a V8.

You'll want to buy the "towing package" with your new truck. This includes a larger radiator and fan, a heavier-duty transmission cooler, electrical plugs for your trailer, a heavy-duty alternator and battery, and a heavier suspension system.

The ¾-ton and 1-ton trucks offer even bigger engines (this is where you will hear the term "power plant" being used for the truck's motor – it truly is a mean machine).

Think buying a truck is confusing? Step onto the lot of a horse-trailer dealer. Trailers come in different sizes to accommodate small or large horses, and there are many different styles and materials, as well as price ranges, to get any shopper thoroughly confused. For first-time horse owners who just have one or two horses, I'd recommend looking only at a two-horse trailer.

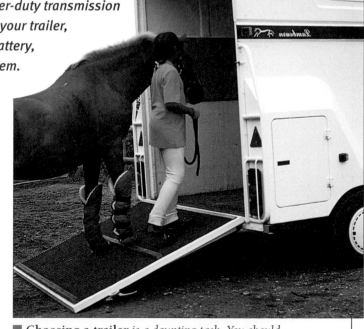

■ **Choosing a trailer** *is a daunting task. You should have an understanding of your horse's size before you commit to buying a trailer.*

Two-horse trailers are generally bumper-pull style, where the trailer attaches to the tow vehicle with a hitch installed on the bumper (as with a boat). There are straight-load styles, where the horses stand side by side inside, or slant-load styles, where the horses travel at a diagonal angle. There are stock trailers, which have an open design inside, as well as those that have a divider to keep the horses separated.

Choosing your trailer

Trailers are made of different materials. Steel and aluminum are the most common. Galvanized steel is strong and durable, and today's steel trailers are much lighter than those of the past. Steel, however, can rust if not maintained properly. Aluminum is lighter in weight (crucial when figuring out how much weight your vehicle can tow) and doesn't rust. But aluminum trailers can be more expensive than steel ones.

Trailers have feed, tack, and sometimes dressing compartments. Some have mangers placed in front for the horses to be able to eat on the go. Most have padding along the walls and on the back door to increase the horse's safety. Decide what equipment is going to be particularly useful to you and your horse.

TOWING TERMINOLOGY

You'll need to figure out some numbers first: Add up the approximate combined weight of the trailer you best like, your horse's weight, any additional cargo (like hay, tack), and passengers. This is your payload.

Here is a list of terms that you'll need to know:

- Base curb weight: the weight of the empty vehicle with a full tank of gas
- Cargo weight: any additional weight being added to your empty vehicle
- Gross vehicle weight rating (GVWR): the maximum allowable weight of the fully loaded vehicle, including passengers and cargo
- Gross combination weight rating (GCWR): the maximum allowable weight of the towing vehicle and the loaded trailer – including your cargo and passengers – that the truck can take on before it experiences damage
- Maximum loaded trailer weight: the maximum amount of weight that a fully loaded trailer can tow
- Tongue weight: the amount of trailer weight that pushes down on the trailer hitch
- Tow rating: the manufacturer's rating for how much the truck can pull, which includes the loaded trailer, maximum tongue load, and GCWR

Another style consideration is how your horse will get into the trailer. A step-up trailer is exactly that: The horse must step up into his compartment, and the doors close behind him. If the trailer is built fairly low to the ground, it is easy for most horses to figure out that they need to climb in. A ramp-style trailer allows the horse to walk up the ramp, and the ramp acts as the closing door. Some horse people think that this is the safer option of the two.

Always consider the following safety equipment for your trailer: anti-sway bars, a safety release mechanism for your electric brakes, and escape doors for you to make a quick exit out of the trailer when loading your horse.

Safe trailering

Now that you have your rig, just brush up on some towing tips before you start singing *On the Road Again*. Make sure your trailer is securely hitched to your truck and that the lighting system is properly working. After your horse is loaded, make sure all doors are latched tight. Allow ample time to get to your destination – you'll need plenty to get him there safely and with a good attitude.

When driving, make sure your braking is planned well in advance. Accelerate slowly and smoothly, and make your turns gradually. Always signal, and don't weave in and out of traffic. This is for your horse's comfort. When haulers give their horses a bad ride (banging them around like freight), the horses become reluctant travelers and can be a problem to load the next trip.

INTERNET

www.horsetrailer
classifieds.com

This site features advertisements placed by people selling trailers as well as those who are looking to buy a used trailer.

A simple summary

✓ The right grooming items will keep your horse looking good and feeling healthy.

✓ You need extras for the winter as well as for the summer.

✓ The right equipment will make your horse's environment safe.

✓ Trucks and trailers come in many styles and price ranges. Buy one that's suited for your purposes.

✓ Remember to do all your safety checks before setting off.

✓ Consider your horse when driving your trailer.

PART THREE

Care and Health

MAINTAINING THE HEALTH of your horse is vital if you want to carry on riding her. Remember that prevention is always better than cure.

Chapter 10

Other People in Your Horse's Life

HORSES DON'T, AND SHOULDN'T, live in a vacuum. They should have visitors on a regular basis – important ones. Besides friends who come and feed carrots and dole out pats, horses have other visitors who are even more valuable to their well-being, such as the veterinarian and the horseshoer. These individuals not only work to make horses happy and healthy, they can prevent difficulties that might crop up in the future. Find out all about the people who will take care of your horse's various needs, and how you can get the most out of these special relationships.

In this chapter...
✓ **Your veterinarian**

✓ **Your horseshoer**

YOUR HORSE WILL NEED TO BE ACCUSTOMED TO BEING HANDLED BY DIFFERENT PEOPLE

Your veterinarian

SINCE HORSES ARE SO LARGE, they give the air of being infallible, but nothing could be further from the truth. A horse is a delicate animal, and it takes only one little mishap to set her back for a long while.

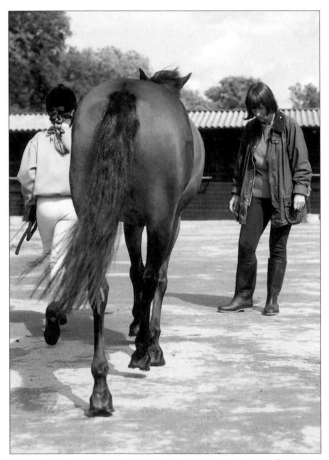

■ **You can learn a lot** *about the health and treatment of horses just by spending time with an equine practitioner.*

That's where your veterinarian comes in. A horse vet can open up worlds of understanding to you in the areas of health care, preventative treatments, and what to do in an emergency. It's fascinating to watch a vet at work because you can find out about all kinds of ailments and witness treatments being given at firsthand.

Equine vets

Large animal vets are somewhat different from equine vets, because they are like general practitioners for the many different types of livestock. Equine vets not only know about the physiology and maladies that affect horses, but they also have a special knowledge of subjects such as horse lameness. A cow or sheep doesn't depend on its soundness to get by, but a horse needs to be able to trot and canter to do her job. The vet needs to be observant in these areas and know how to treat any related issues that come up.

A veterinarian has to have a good "stall-side" manner. Horses get anxious when they are around an intimidating person, and if a vet is brusque, aggressive, or downright forceful, horses will remember that experience and will often be reluctant patients the next time.

Does the vet make house calls?

An equine vet does make barn calls, which is a good thing. It is quite an ordeal trying to haul a horse to the doctor's for her vaccines, but it's another thing to attempt to put her in a trailer when she's very ill or perhaps gravely injured.

Your vet can see your horse for her regular scheduled checkups, as well as to administer vaccines, to perform dentistry, and to come to her aid in an emergency. Vets often work out of their mobile offices, which are usually large trucks with special drawers, cabinets, and compartments in the truck-bed. They have access to all sorts of medications, surgical equipment for outpatient operations, X-ray and ultrasound gear, running water, and sometimes even computer services. If your problem can't be solved by your mobile vet, such as when your horse needs extensive surgery or specialized equipment, your horse will have to travel to a hospital.

Keep the numbers of your vet and the hospital in your tack room, your wallet, and by the phone. Some hospitals are affiliated with universities or veterinary colleges, while others are near racetracks.

Ask your vet where the nearest horse hospital is so that you know in advance and don't have to spend time finding out during an emergency situation.

What motivates a vet?

Vets work long hours – sometimes putting in 70 or more hours a week. They are often on call on their days off and receive emergency calls at odd hours. A thriving practice usually means little time off. Yet these people keep these grueling schedules, day in and day out. Why? They certainly don't make the money that human doctors do. Most say that they do it because they truly love being involved with horses. They enjoy the work because they are able to help an animal that cannot tell them what is wrong. Unlike a house pet, a horse has to return to her job, and most vets enjoy the challenge of getting their equine athletes back to work.

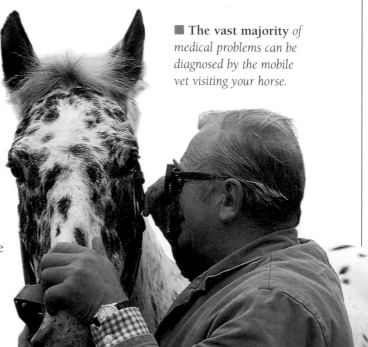

■ **The vast majority** *of medical problems can be diagnosed by the mobile vet visiting your horse.*

The good patient

Make sure that your horse is well mannered when she sees her doctor. Generally, you'll be on the premises when the vet arrives so that you can describe your horse's symptoms and what action you've taken. Lead your horse out of her stall when the vet tells you to.

Your horse should be trained to stand quietly through an exam. She should not pull back on her lead rope if tied. If she's fussy because she's frightened, that's one thing, but a horse that fidgets and is naughty just because she's allowed to get away with bad behavior is a problem. She should have no problem lifting her feet and allowing people to touch tender spots such as her belly or ears.

Don't let your vet be kicked backward just because your horse is touchy about getting her temperature taken. If your horse has a training problem that you haven't yet conquered, let the vet know about it.

The key to having your horse behave with a vet is to establish good ground manners before the first visit. You can achieve this through consistent handling and training. Make sure that you can easily control your horse on her healthy days, so that when your vet arrives, your horse is accustomed to being touched everywhere.

A vet's daily schedule

No two days are the same in a vet's life. They begin early in the day with a full schedule of appointments, but invariably someone throws them a curve ball: an emergency. Vets generally carry pagers and mobile phones for this purpose, and they usually have answering services if they don't have an actual office taking messages.

WHAT IT TAKES TO BE A VET

Most people think that they'd like to be a vet because they want to help horses, but they also have to deal with the reality of not being able to save every patient. Veterinary school is difficult work, and to be accepted by a veterinary college, you have to have excellent grades with at least a 3.0 grade-point average. You have to be good in subjects such as math and science. In addition to your preveterinary studies, you also have to spend 4 years attending vet school.

A vet's day will include routine examinations such as lameness evaluations, vaccinations, "well-baby" exams for newborn foals, and diagnosis of ailments. Then there are the urgent calls – the ones from owners who are panicking and need the vet to come out right away. These might involve a horse who has gotten *cast*, or one who has a health-threatening laceration, or colic. Vets will squeeze in the emergency calls, or if they cannot make it, they will refer the client to a different doctor.

Your horseshoer

THE WORDS "HOOVES" AND "FEET" are used interchangeably in the horse world. It is actually the horn of the hoof that grows. The foot encompasses the bone and tissue and outer covering.

Horses' hooves are constantly growing. Wild horses walk many miles each day over rough and varied terrain, and this action causes their hooves to wear down naturally. In the wild, weaker animals are at an immediate disadvantage, and it's the horses with tough, durable feet that get to pass on their genes. Because they don't generally walk on hard road surfaces, wild horses don't need shoes.

A domestic horse leads a somewhat different life to her wild counterparts – her hooves have to be filed down by a horseshoer to keep them healthy. She also has to have shoes fitted.

FARRIERS' TOOLS

■ **Your farrier** *will trim away the excess growth from the sole of the foot before sizing and shaping a shoe. He then selects a shoe of the right size and molds it to fit the horse's foot exactly.*

Why do domestic horses need shoes?

It might seem strange that a domestic horse needs to wear shoes and have her hooves trimmed, when equines get by very well in the wild without this attention. However, although we breed horses for various purposes, survival traits are not usually one of the things we factor in, and so our domestic horses may not have the toughest of feet. Also, our horses don't have the natural lifestyle of trotting along the plains in search of food and water, which helps to keep hooves trimmed. Finally, domestic horses have to do one thing that wild horses never do – they must carry a rider, and that major difference changes their weight and their balance as they travel.

Don't ride your horse if she has a problem with her feet. When it comes to equine feet, no matter what book or magazine article you read, you'll see the quote, "no hoof, no horse."

Shoes are necessary to protect the wall of your horse's hooves and to prevent wear, especially if you ride on hard road surfaces regularly. But regardless of whether you slide into the saddle five times a week or once a month, your horse must have her feet trimmed and/or **shod** at regular intervals. This is essential to keep your horse's feet in good working order – if you neglect them, you risk not being able to ride your horse.

The role of the farrier

When a farrier pays a visit, he or she will start by taking off your horse's old shoes. He or she will do this by straightening the nails that hold each shoe on – this is called unclinching – and then taking a pair of tongs to work the nails out and the shoes off (the nails come out with the shoe). The old shoes are usually discarded.

The farrier then checks the alignment of each hoof to see how the foot grows out in relation to the way the horse is built. Like our fingernails, which might curve or bend when they get long, a horse's foot will do the same. Some hooves flare out when they

■ **The farrier uses** *hoof nippers to clip off parts of the hoof that may have grown too long – this helps make the hoof neat and even.*

grow too long, or some might grow really long at the front part – the toe. Your farrier will clip the hooves to the right length. He or she will then "balance" the foot with a giant nail file, rasping the bottom so that it aligns underneath the horse properly. This is so that your horse can put her weight down on a level bearing surface. The foot is not changed to suit any particular cosmetic shape; it is always trimmed to reflect its own natural shape and size. The horse is then ready for her new shoes to be fitted.

It takes from 9 to 15 months for a hoof to grow from the top of the coronary band – the hairline that divides the end of the horse's leg with the hoof – down to the tip of the toe. If a foot never gets trimmed, it can curl up to the point where the horse will be unable to walk.

How a shoe is nailed on

Nail placement is extremely important. The nails are driven into the outside wall (the edge) of the hoof from the bottom, and out through the side at approximately ⅝ inch (1.5 cm) high. If they are driven in too deep, they can put pressure on the inside tissues within the horse's feet. They can also quick the horse – just as if you were to have your fingernail pulled off too close to the skin. If nails are placed too far out toward the outside of the wall, they won't be able to hold the shoe on for long and will end up breaking off the wall.

■ **Nails come in different sizes,** *and your farrier will avoid using ones that are too big for your horse's feet.*

There are usually eight places on a horse shoe in which to nail it on. But that doesn't mean that the farrier will use eight nails. Generally, he will tack the shoe on with six nails if it will hold well, and he will choose the shoe's nail holes that are best suited for that horse's foot. For instance, he might use the top two holes then skip the second two, then nail in the last four.

Horseshoe nails

The nails are tapped in, then the extra nail length that protrudes out of the side is snipped off and then bent – clinched – to anchor the shoe on.

Special shoes for special problems

Have you ever noticed the wear and tear on a pair of running shoes? You'll often find that one side wears down faster than the other does, or perhaps the heel is lopsided. This is because of the way you run. It's the same with horses. Some horses travel over the ground more evenly than others do.

Horses often strike their front legs together when they trot, or they may hit the back of a front foot with the toe of a hind hoof. They might also have diseases, such as arthritis, that make them travel stiffly. These horses can often get a little help by having their feet trimmed differently and having their shoes set to allow them an easier way to travel.

When a horse doesn't travel well, there are ways to help her compensate. The technique used to be called corrective shoeing but now it is more often referred to as therapeutic shoeing. A farrier can't correct the way your grown horse is built, nor can he fix a horse that travels oddly. He can, however, devise a shoeing program that can alleviate extra strain placed on limbs that aren't quite perfect.

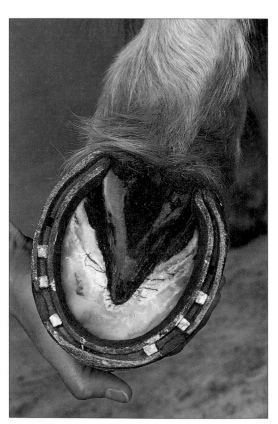

Types of shoes

Horseshoes are basically made of two materials: aluminum and steel. Aluminum is softer and lighter than steel, and it is more easily shaped, but it does wear out faster. The lightness allows the farrier to tack on a wider width shoe (a thicker U-shape), which covers more of the horse's foot and this gives added support and protection.

Steel shoes last longer and are heavier than those made of aluminum. Most horseshoes are not beaten into their perfect shape out of a bar of steel, as in the olden days. They are actually sold premade and according to different sizes. A farrier uses a premade shoe and changes the shape slightly so that it fits each particular hoof.

■ **A good shoe** *will be a perfect fit. In this case, only six nails were needed and the shoe itself has been altered to fit the hoof of this horse exactly. The final result provides an even walking surface.*

Choosing the right shoe

The shoe you choose will depend on the sort of riding skills you perform. Lighter shoes allow the horse to have a long sweeping stride, while heavier, or even weighted shoes, tend to make the horse travel with more of a high-stepping pace.

There are shoes that are made entirely from scratch. These are custom jobs and are pricey to get. Many top competition horses have custom shoes made every time they go for shoeing.

You also need to consider how hard your horse will be working, and on what types of terrain. There are many materials and styles of shoe available for different types of riding. For example, racehorses wear aluminum racing shoes, called plates. However, since aluminum is a lightweight, soft metal, these shoes should never be used on an endurance horse, which has to traverse rocky terrain over long distances. Be realistic about the shoes you choose.

■ **Round eggbar shoes** *are used to provide heel support for horses that may be prone to foot problems.*

To give the shoe a better hold on the foot so it is not easily pulled off, a farrier might secure it with toe clips or side clips – these are small sections of metal that clamp close to the hoof, like old-style roller skates.

Bear in mind that your horse's shoes may not last as long as you plan because horses sometimes pull their shoes off. They're not doing it deliberately. It's just that occasionally, a horse might be trotting along and step on the back of her shoe and yank it off.

Scheduled maintenance

Ensure your horse receives her trimming and shoeing on a regular basis. If you go too long without making that call to your farrier, you could cause your horse's feet to change their form, such as when a horse's heels grow too close together, or contract. You might also cause her to strain her lower legs, such as when unbalanced feet cause strains in leg tendons. If this happens, remedial action will be necessary.

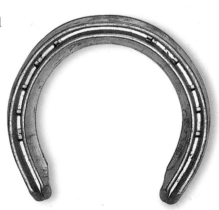

■ **Light, aluminum** *shoes are used in races and shows. They are suitable for soft surfaces only.*

As a generalization, most horses need to have their feet trimmed every 6 to 8 weeks. There are some horses, however, that need their feet tended to as often as every 4 weeks, and others that can wait 10 weeks. Some horses can go a little longer between trimmings during the winter, when their hoof growth slows slightly. But always work with your farrier to determine the best schedule for hoof care.

Making a farrier's day

Shoeing is physically demanding work. To be hunched over all day, pulling off shoes and bending new ones into place is hard on the back. Farriers start their days early – sometimes as early as 7:00 a.m. They have to go over their list of clients for the day and make sure that they have everything they need in their mobile trucks (yes, there are electric forges these days – instead of the old-fashioned furnace where iron is shaped and molded). They'll typically do around seven horses a day, spending about 90 minutes with each client. Traveling from equestrian center to private barn, they've got to plan what area they will be in ahead of time, or else they'll be on the road unnecessarily. They have to deal with juggling phone calls, a few clients who don't pay on time, misbehaving horses, and loads of billing and paperwork.

INTERNET

www.horseshoes.
net/school and
www.horseshoes.
com/okstate

The Oklahoma Horseshoeing School and the Oklahoma State Horseshoeing School both offer vocational programs for prospective blacksmiths.

HORSE SHOEING AS A CAREER

Being a farrier is a tough but rewarding career. Farriers are self-employed, which means success depends on their talent, yes, but also their attitude and ability to market themselves. They need to be able to promote themselves and let people know the benefits of their services. While farriers don't need to be licensed, not many people have the inborn ability to form metal and stick nails in a horse's foot, so farriers need the right training.

There are vocational schools that offer 2- to 15-week courses in horse shoeing. Some schools use volunteer horses from the public to practice on, while others must learn the craft on dead horses' legs taken from the rendering plant. Farriers study anatomy, lameness,.different techniques (general and specialized), and business management. Once they've completed the program, they have to understand the fundamentals of setting up their own business and working with animals for a living.

A good working relationship

To be a good client, make sure that you treat your shoer fairly. He or she knows what he is doing better than you do, so try not to be overbearing. This doesn't mean that you can't discuss things, however. You should let your shoer know how the horse is traveling when she walks and trots; if any problems have cropped up (such as, "she keeps pulling her shoes off" or, "her feet are growing really fast"); or if you have any general concerns about the health of your horse's feet. Set up your appointment in advance – don't just wait until the day before the big trail ride for your farrier to drop everything to come out and work on your horse.

Prepare for the farrier's visit in advance. Make sure there is a suitable area available for your farrier to work in. A grooming stall is nice, but even a flat, clean, dry area works well. There should be a safe place for your horse to stand tied. Farriers don't really enjoy shoeing horses in the rain, so if you have an area where you can shelter from a sudden storm or from the midday sun, so much the better. It is also good for you to have your horse in her stall so that the shoer can just walk over and halter her – the farrier won't have time to chase your horse around a large field.

As a good client, you should pay your farrier's bills on time. If you were the one doing backbreaking labor, you'd want to see your check at the end of the day, wouldn't you?

A simple summary

✔ An equine vet is different from a livestock vet because horses have athletic issues that livestock don't.

✔ An equine vet works long hours dealing with emergencies and routine calls.

✔ Consistent training and handling of your horse will make her a good patient when your vet comes to examine her.

✔ Your horse needs regular attention paid to her feet whether you ride her very often or very little. Don't be tempted to put off having her shod.

✔ Farriers have tough schedules, so make sure that you are a good client by communicating with your farrier, sticking to a regular schedule, booking appointments in advance, and paying on time.

Chapter 11

An Ounce of Prevention

WHOEVER CAME UP WITH THE MAXIM "healthy as a horse" was probably not an equestrian. While horses are really strong and powerful animals, it takes careful handling of their health to make sure they stay well. Horses can be susceptible to several diseases, so like you, they need routine checkups and regular health maintenance to stay in the pink. Additionally, a few horses can be accident-prone, so you'll need to make sure your horse's safety is looked after, too.

In this chapter...

✓ Signs of a healthy horse

✓ Deworming for well-being

✓ Essential vaccinations

✓ Safety around horses

✓ Poisonous plants

✓ Lost and found

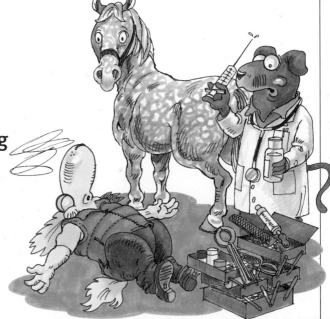

A HAZARD-FREE ENVIRONMENT IS ESSENTIAL TO KEEP YOUR HORSE SAFE AND HEALTHY

Signs of a healthy horse

IT'S EASY TO TELL IF A HORSE is feeling well or not. The more time you spend with your horse, the more you'll be able to see if he's feeling perky or peaked. If a horse isn't feeling up to snuff, you'll know in both subtle and obvious ways. You just have to get used to reading the signs.

From nose to tail, here are the hallmarks of a horse that is feeling great:

- Eyes are bright, with no discharge in the corners. He has an alert expression
- Nose is relatively dry and clean. When a horse exercises, he might have a little nose trickle, but it should be clear. It's time to worry when a horse has a serious runny nose or thick grayish mucus
- Ears are clean and free of bug bites, bleeding, warts, or other growths
- Gums are pink, not gray or whitish
- Legs are not swollen, and feet are cool to the touch
- His manure is firm and ball-shaped, not runny
- Mane and skin should be clean, without too much *scurf*. Skin should be smooth, and the coat should be relatively shiny, not dull or lifeless
- Hooves should be dry and without cracks. They should be trimmed properly. The underside of the foot should be without odor (a foot that smells foul often has disease)

> **DEFINITION**
>
> **Scurf** *is the equivalent of horsey dandruff. It is the combination of dirt and skin particles.*

■ **If your horse has been mixing** *with other horses, the risk of infection will be greater, and it is especially important to check him daily for any signs of disease.*

A horse's overall body should be carrying enough muscle and body fat so that the horse is lean, but not skinny. A horse that is too thin will be more susceptible to diseases, and a horse that is too fat will have a host of obesity related problems.

Taking vital signs

To know if your horse is sick, you first have to know what the signs are when he's well. Some riders, such as endurance riders, must know their horse's vital signs as part of their routine for competing. They closely monitor their horse's pulse, respiration, heart rate (commonly known as his P & Rs), and temperature. Your horse's vitals should be taken when he's at rest (before he exerts himself) and over a couple of days.

To measure a horse's respiration, you need a watch with a second hand. Turn toward the horse's hind end and watch as his flanks bellow in and out. Then look at your watch, find your starting point, and count how many times the horse's flank rises and falls within one minute (each in/out breath counts as one). To count a horse's pulse, find one of your horse's pulse points. They can be found in three spots: the inside of the jawbone just below the large cheek muscles; at the back of the knee; and just below the fetlock on the inside of the leg. Count how many beats you feel per minute.

To take a horse's temperature, you have to use a rectal thermometer. Shake the thermometer down below 97° F (36° C), and coat it in petroleum jelly. Insert it gently into the horse's rectum. Hold it firmly and do not push too far. Leave the thermometer in for about 2 minutes. Remove and examine the reading.

You can find the perfect thermometer for taking your horse's temperature at your local tack store. It will feature an alligator clip attached to a long string, which runs through the eye at the thermometer's end. The clip attaches to the end of the tail so you can be assured the thermometer won't get lost.

NORMAL VITAL SIGNS

- On the average, a horse breathes about 10 to 15 times a minute
- His temperature is normally 99–101° F (38° C)
- His pulse is 30 to 40 beats per minute
- Don't be alarmed if your horse is slightly different (for instance, has respirations of 16, or a temperature of 101.5° F.) If your horse is healthy but has vital signs that are slightly different from the norm, take these as your baseline

When to call the vet

Your horse's vital signs might be slightly different from one day to the next, but you can get an idea of what the average normal signs are for him. If they are very different, it is likely there is something wrong.

Another sign horse owners pick up on when a horse is feeling ill is listlessness. Whether he's standing in his corral with a droopy head, or he's performing dully in the arena, take care to notice this lackluster attitude. Take it easy on your horse and watch him for a day. If he seems worse, then you should phone the vet for advice.

■ **Taking a horse's pulse** *is a good way of checking how healthy he is.*

Deworming for well-being

THIS IS NOT A PLEASANT SUBJECT, but since horses are outdoor animals, they get involved with all sorts of creepy crawlies. Of course you've noticed the large numbers of insects that buzz around the stable yard. Unfortunately, there is a whole community of pests that actually live inside horses, too. These internal parasites are worms.

Body invaders

Worms are ingested as larvae, usually in a pasture or from the floor of your horse's stall. Once swallowed, the larvae migrate to the horse's stomach or intestines and attach themselves to the gut lining. When they mature, the worms lay eggs, which are eventually shed with the horse's manure. In the environment they develop into larvae and the life cycle begins again. But while they are inside your horse, they wreak havoc on his intestines, lungs, heart, and even blood vessels.

If your horse is carrying worms, he'll have a dull coat, and he'll not be able to put on weight. He might rub his tail to ease the itchiness.

So what's a horse owner to do? There are special medications called anthelmintics that are designed to kill internal parasites. Your veterinarian can administer these dewormers, either through a special metal syringe inserted in the horse's mouth to squirt the worming medicine far down the throat, or through a stomach tube.

This old-time method is where the vet takes a flexible plastic tube and inserts it into the horse's nose, down the esophagus, and into the horse's stomach. The good thing about this method is that it ensures that the horse gets the complete dose. The bad thing is that the horse may get his esophagus damaged by an improperly inserted tube. It can also go down the wrong pipe – the trachea – which can cause the horse to develop pneumonia.

While you're deworming your horse, keep an eye on him so that he can't spit out the medicine. Avoid feeding him for at least a 1/2-hour to prevent him from dropping the dewormer with his feed.

The larvae grow and develop into adult worms inside the horse

The larvae are eaten by the horse

Adult worms release eggs in the droppings

Eggs hatch and new larvae emerge into the grass

■ **The life cycle** *of a worm can be difficult to break. Unless you can remove your horse from the affected pasture, the life cycle will continue. It can take several years to eliminate a worm problem.*

The good news is that there are over-the-counter dewormers that you can give to your horse yourself. They are just as effective as the vet's dewormers, because your vet uses the same medication. You can buy dewormers that can be added to your horse's feed, or you can squirt it down his throat with a plastic syringe. Stick the tube in the corner of your horse's mouth, hold his head still, and depress the plunger smoothly.

Controlling worms

Make sure you give the right dosage. Each dewormer is administered according to the horse's weight. Your horse should be dewormed quarterly as a rule. However, there are new dewormers on the market that are formulated to be administered at different intervals. Keep the worm population down by cleaning your horse's stall, paddock, and pasture areas regularly. Feed him in a manure-free area. Don't crowd a pasture with too many horses. If you have two pastures, let one rest for 60 days. The worms burden may then have a chance to be reduced in the "used" pasture.

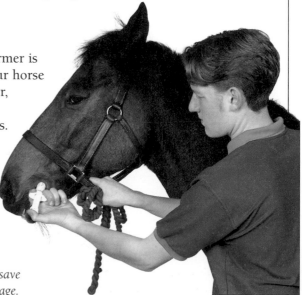

■ **Deworming your horse** *is a simple procedure and can save your horse from a great deal of discomfort and internal damage.*

Types of worms

There are several types of worms that can cause problems for horses. Some of the most common parasites include small strongyles and large strongyles, which damage a horse's blood vessels, digestive system, and other internal organs. Large strongyles are known as bloodworms because of the bloodsucking nature of the adults. Small strongyles mature in the liver, then migrate into the intestine and colon. Ascarids, also known as roundworms, begin in the horse's small intestine, but move into the horse's circulatory system, liver, and lungs – possibly causing respiratory problems. Pinworm eggs can be found in the horse's rectum, and you'll see an afflicted horse rubbing out his tail.

There are more than 150 species of internal parasites that affect horses. When worms are not brought under control, it's possible for all species to be present at the same time, often at different life-cycle stages.

Botflies lay their tiny yellow eggs on the horse's legs or lips, where the horse swallows them. The ones that hatch attach themselves to the horse's stomach lining, where they mature, often causing ulcers. These larvae are eventually shed with the manure to develop into adult botflies – big ugly bumblebee-looking menaces.

Essential vaccinations

YOU CAN PROTECT YOUR HORSE from the big bugs, but you also need to keep the small bugs – viral diseases and the like – at bay. Horses' unique immune systems can be hit by equine-only viruses as well as the more common ones that affect all mammals.

First off is influenza, which is very much like our common flu. While it's not particularly life threatening, it is easy for your horse to catch, so make sure that he (like you) receives his annual flu shot (show horses may need to be vaccinated quarterly). A horse with the flu will exhibit symptoms similar to ours: runny nose, cough, sore muscles, poor appetite, and even a fever. It will take a horse more than a month of resting up to recover fully.

Rhinopneumonitis is a highly contagious disease that often occurs after a bad flu bout. Symptoms may be similar to the flu, including a high fever, runny nose, poor appetite, and general listlessness. It can also cause pregnant mares to abort their unborn foals. A horse will need to have stall rest for 14 days to recover without any relapse. Try to vaccinate your horse at least once a year (again, show horses may need to be vaccinated quarterly). This vaccine will often be combined with the flu shot.

Rabies and tetanus

Rabies is the same in horses as it is in all other animals, including humans. Since there is no treatment for a horse that contracts rabies, prevention is key. Horses can catch rabies through contact with wild animals. A horse with rabies will be uncoordinated, depressed, and aggressive. Because rabies always kills its victim, the horse will have to be destroyed. To help prevent rabies, try to keep the varmint population down at your barn (this not only includes rats, but opossums and raccoons, too), and get your horse an annual shot.

While you'll see vet supply catalogs that list vaccines for sale through the mail, it is better to get your veterinarian to administer them. The vet will know the proper way to give a shot, and will also know the proper conditions for storing vaccines before use.

Tetanus is a big concern since horses are one of the few creatures that actually wear metal. Tetanus is caused by the bacterium *Clostridium tetani*, and a horse can get it through a bad shoeing job, a deep wound, or by stepping on a rusty nail. Tetanus causes the muscles to become extremely stiff and rigid, and is fatal if untreated.

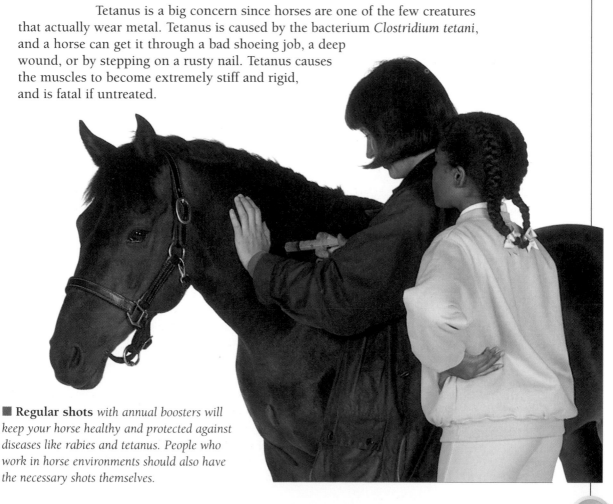

■ **Regular shots** *with annual boosters will keep your horse healthy and protected against diseases like rabies and tetanus. People who work in horse environments should also have the necessary shots themselves.*

147

Strangles and encephalitis

Strangles is passed from horse to horse by eating or drinking from the same source, or by direct contact with an infected horse. A horse with strangles runs a fever, develops a runny nose, and stops drinking water. The disease affects the lymph glands under the horse's throat, which swell to large proportions, making it difficult to swallow and even to breathe – hence the name. The swollen glands turn into abscesses, which eventually drain in a very unpleasant manner. Some horses have bad reactions to the strangles vaccine, so you want to make sure that your horse is healthy and strong before you have him vaccinated.

■ **A sick horse** *may show signs of depression and weight loss. Always contact your vet if you notice any of these symptoms.*

Encephalitis (western, eastern, and Venezuelan strains) – sometimes called sleeping sickness – is one of the more devastating equine diseases. Some strains are more deadly than others. The virus infects the horse's brain and spine, causing abnormal behaviour (for example, they may walk into walls or in circles). Infected horses are severely depressed, weak, uncoordinated, feverish, and have difficulty eating. Even if a horse survives, he may be permanently brain damaged.

Spread by mosquitoes, encephalitis is less of a problem for horses living in very dry climates. No matter what your local environment is like, vaccines should be given annually to protect your horse from this deadly disease.

Swamp fever

Equine infectious anemia (EIA) is also known as swamp fever because, at one time, it was thought that mosquitoes were the vector that carried the disease. A horse with EIA has a high fever and swollen limbs, and is listless, depressed, weak, and anemic. There is no vaccine or cure for the virus, which is normally fatal. Even if a horse recovers from this disease he will then be a carrier and may have to be put down.

Remember to keep vaccination records. These should detail what vaccines were given to your horse and when. It can be difficult for your vet to treat your horse if his vaccination history isn't known.

Safety around horses

EVEN THE MOST LOVING HORSE can accidentally hurt his owner. And even the most conscientious horse person can occasionally get careless and make a mistake. The trick is to reduce the instances of problems by taking precautionary measures. The old adage "It's better to be safe than sorry" is particularly true when around half-ton animals.

You should always be dressed appropriately around horses. If you go to visit your horse in shorts and sandals, don't be surprised if your toes get crushed or even severed underneath a horse's steel-shod hoof.

Proper horse management

Many safety measures can be taken to reduce the likelihood of an accident should your horse get frightened and run away. Make sure to lead your horse by a lead rope – not just by his halter. A horse led only by the side of his halter can break away from you more easily or could drag you by your trapped hand. Your lead rope should be looped and grasped like a bunch of flowers, not wrapped around your hand, otherwise if the horse were to pull away suddenly, you could get a serious rope burn or even lose your fingers. Tie your horse with a safety knot, which is a version of a slipknot, so that if he were to panic and pull back, you could release him before the situation escalated.

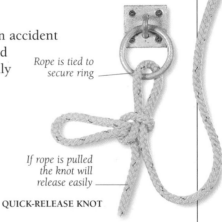

Rope is tied to secure ring

If rope is pulled the knot will release easily

QUICK-RELEASE KNOT

■ **Always wear a helmet** *and sturdy boots around horses, not just when you are riding. Walk level with the horse's shoulder or neck, and don't let him get ahead or drag behind – you could get trampled.*

Learn how to lead your horse properly – under any circumstances. Don't let him get bossy and barge over you. Keep him so that his shoulder and yours are even when you walk, and give him a tug on his lead rope if he tries to go too fast. Like your dog, you want him to behave when he's "on-leash." A misbehaving horse at the end of a thin rope is a hazard. If he does become really fractious, it is better to let go than get trampled.

If a horse pulls back so quickly that you can't undo your safety knot, you'll have to cut the rope, and quickly. Have an emergency knife around and keep away from flailing hooves as you set your horse free. A struggling horse can injure or break his neck in a panic.

A well-trained horse will not give you problems when you turn him out. However, some horses bolt away before you have a gate latched or halter off. Have an experienced horse person work with you so that your horse waits until you are finished before trotting away.

Good barn management

Keep clutter to a minimum. Apart from causing injuries, leaving clutter lying around creates a fire hazard. Old feed bags and bedding should be stored away from the barn. Post "No Smoking" signs prominently and make sure everyone adheres to the rule.

Keep your barn-cleaning tools in a certain area. You're not going to find it amusing if you do an impression of your favorite cartoon character by stepping on a rake and getting whacked in the head.

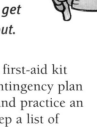

Don't lock your horse in with a combination or key lock – you might need to get him out quickly in an emergency. However, make sure that your horse's stall and corral gates latch properly. Clever horses can get out of any gate, so get gate fasteners that won't let him out.

■ **Fires can start** *at any time. Make sure that every stable has easy access to a fire extinguisher.*

Be ready for any emergency with a first-aid kit for you and your horse. Have a contingency plan for a flood, fire, or other disaster, and practice an emergency drill for evacuation. Keep a list of emergency numbers posted prominently at the stable, including one for your doctor and vet.

Poisonous plants

HORSES EAT GREEN THINGS, but many plants are toxic to them. Many ornamental shrubs and flowers that are used in backyards, or to pretty up show arenas, can be deadly. Horses don't usually eat toxic plants in their pastures unless they are very hungry and there is nothing else to eat.

INTERNET

www.erc.on.ca/
poison.htm

The Horse Council of British Columbia, Canada, offers advice about poisonous plants.

Fortunately, most poisonous plants don't taste good to horses, but you should find out which poisonous plants grow in your area and remove them as best as possible. You should also make sure that any hay you feed to your horse does not contain traces of these plants. Some toxic plants can just make your horse ill, but others have more devastating consequences and can kill.

POISONOUS PLANTS

There are dozens of plants around the world that can be toxic to your horse. Find out from your vet which ones grow in your area. You can show your vet the following list and have him or her check off or add those poisonous plants that are native to your region.

■ **Ragwort causes** *liver failure and lung congestion, leading to death. There is no cure.*

- Azalea
- Black walnut
- Bracken fern
- Buckwheat
- Castor bean
- Cockleburs
- Crown vetch
- Dogwood
- English yew
- Fiddleneck
- Foxglove
- Groundsel
- Heliotrope
- Horse nettle
- Hound's tongue
- Japanese yew
- Jimsonweed
- Johnson grass
- Kleingrass
- Locoweeds
- Milkweed
- Mountain laurel
- Nightshade
- Oaks
- Oleander
- Poison hemlock
- Poison oak
- Ragwort
- Rattlebox
- Red Maple
- Rhododendron
- Rhubarb
- St-John's-wort
- Sensitive fern
- Sorghum
- Sweet clover
- Tall fescue
- Tarweed
- Water hemlock
- Wild cherries
- Yellow star thistle

Lost and found

YOU LOVE YOUR HORSE. But someone might want to take him from you. Horse rustlers are still prevalent in America, but for different reasons than you might expect. While some beautiful show animals might be stolen and resold to an unsuspecting buyer, the sad truth is that many stolen horses end up with dozens of others on a truck to the slaughterhouse. The price of horsemeat, sold as a delicacy to some European countries, is steadily increasing, and because of that, our American horses may end up on someone's dinner plate overseas.

Beating rustlers

The best thing to do is protect your horse from thieves. Keep stable areas well lit at night (make sure you don't have a light shining directly on your horse, though – he needs his beauty rest). If you can secure him behind a locked gate, that's even better. Keep a lock on your horse trailer to make it more difficult for a thief to make a quick getaway. Don't lock your horse in his stall, though. If there were ever a disaster such as a barn fire or tornado, you would want someone to be able to free him from being trapped inside.

Keep photographs of your horse so you can identify him. Take pictures of him in the summertime, when he's sleek and shiny, as well as in the winter, when he's furry or clipped. Take shots of each side of his body, and note any distinguishing marks. You can also create a ***signalment*** by drawing his markings on a line drawing of a horse. If he has a white star on his forehead or one white sock on his leg, you would note that on paper.

> ### DEFINITION
>
> **Signalment** *is the term for using the horse's color and markings for identification. Usually, a standard series of numbers and letters correspond to each mark, giving the horse a code which can be recorded on his papers. This is the oldest method of ID and by far the most common. Every breed registry utilizes signalment, recording a physical description of the animals registered with them.*

Hi tech branding

Microchipping, a new technology that is used on other pets, is now crossing over to horses. A microchip is a small, rice-sized capsule that is injected via syringe into a crook in the horse's neck. When scanned, the microchip reader comes up with an ID number, and your horse's records will come up in the microchip database, so he can be returned to you safely. (Don't forget to register your horse, or the chip is useless.)

Many microchip manufacturers are providing slaughterhouses with scanners, so that any microchipped horse will come up as a "wanted" horse. It's still a little murky whether or not the scanners are being used 100 percent of the time, since slaughterhouses may not always comply.

Identification

Horses can be identified through various different methods. The Old West way was to brand the skin with a hot iron. Freeze branding, a newer branding method, uses an ultra cold iron on the horse's skin.

■ **Brand marks** *are permanent, obvious, and easily readable, allowing identification from some distance away.*

A freeze brand is a symbol that is usually applied to a number of animals, such as a warmblood registry brand. A freeze mark, however, is a series of symbols that is placed on the neck of a horse and serves as a unique ID.

In freeze branding, the hair grows back in white, showing the mark, whereas a hot brand leaves a scar on the body, and the area is bald.

Keeping it in perspective

While a lot of this chapter focuses on all the bad things that can happen to horses, remember that the likelihood of these things happening are slim, especially now that you're such a well-informed, prepared horse person!

A simple summary

✓ Learn to read the signs of a healthy horse.

✓ Internal parasites can compromise your horse's health.

✓ Vaccinate your horse and get him annual booster shots.

✓ Horses can unwittingly hurt their owners, so safety around the barn is essential.

✓ Poisonous plants are prevalent, with some causing sickness and even death.

✓ Prevent your horse from being stolen by ensuring all gates are properly and securely latched. Install outside lighting.

✓ You can protect your horse from being stolen by placing an ID on him using various methods.

Chapter 12

A Nutritious Beginning

THE MOST DEVOUT HORSE PEOPLE actually love the smell of fresh cut alfalfa hay, have probably dipped into the grain bin to test it out personally, and probably concoct a wonderfully nutritious diet for their equine charges – even though they themselves exist on burgers and fries. (It's a good thing, too, since there's not really the equivalent of a "McHay Bale" yet.) But that doesn't mean that all horse food is created equal. Learn what role nutrition and feeding play in your horse's life.

In this chapter...

✓ **Dinner is served**

✓ **All grasses are not alike**

✓ **Daily requirements**

✓ **Special needs feeds**

✓ **Other dietary needs**

FRESH GRASS FORMS THE BULK OF THE HORSE'S NATURAL DIET

Dinner is served

WHEN YOU LOOK AT THE FORAGE available to wild horses, it's hard to believe that they are getting any nutrition out of those weeds at all. But would it be wise to take a wild horse and let her eat like the racehorse Cigar?

Wild and hardy

As I've mentioned before, the prehistoric horse Eohippus was a browser, eating leaves and shrubs to survive, later developing into a grazing animal. As an animal that once fed upon lush grasses across the plains, the horse had to adapt many years ago to exist on the scant scrub that even cattle won't eat. As a result, the wild horse's constitution became hardy and tough, able to pull what little nutrition there was out of those slim pickin's. So, if you were to put a wild horse in a pasture full of tall, succulent grass, she would become ill because she isn't used to such rich food.

Even though horses are grazers, they are not above chewing on bushes, weeds, trees, and bark. They graze constantly throughout the day, and their digestive systems constantly process and eliminate small amounts of food. Moving from one area to the next in search of a full meal stimulates the horse's *gut*, which allows her to move the fibrous roughage through, while still getting the vital nutrients out of it. The food is broken down by microbes living in the gut.

Domestic diet

Horses eat a variety of greens because they need to pull the right nutrients out to complete their diet. Grasses give the horse fiber, while leaves and shrubs provide a mineral and vitamin balance. To keep the digestive system working properly, it is essential that a horse has adequate roughage in her diet.

■ **Grass is the natural food** *for horses. It contains cellulose, which provides the fibrous bulk needed to move the food through the body.*

In domestic life, hay is the main staple of the horse's diet. Domestic horses don't have the iron constitutions of their wild brethren, so good quality hay must be available for them. Hay is made from grasses or legumes, or from a combination of the two. The grasses most commonly used for horse hay are timothy, Bermuda grass, orchard grass, and fescue (some names that you might recognize from your lawn). Legumes, which have the ability to fix nitrogen in the roots and leaves, include alfalfa and clover (and for us humans, peas and beans). Some hay growers mix a combination of these plants in one field to produce mixed bales, providing a more varied diet.

All grasses are not alike

WHEN YOU GO TO THE FRUIT and vegetable section of your grocery store, you undoubtedly select the nicest produce for your salads and meals, leaving the bruised, unripe, or rotten stuff behind. You should do the same for your horse's greens. Some hay is cut at the height of its nutrition, while other hay is only a little more nourishing than sawdust.

Is your hay okay?

Three ways to spot quality hay are:

1. Bales are tightly bound together and neat

2. The color should be green – not yellow or brown, which are signs that it dried for too long or that it might have been rained on

3. It should smell sweet – bad hay might smell dusty or moldy

When you take a bale apart and it seems to have large puffs of dust, it may have mold. Do not feed it to your horse. A horse can get very ill from moldy or bad hay.

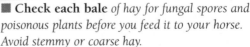

■ **Check each bale** *of hay for fungal spores and poisonous plants before you feed it to your horse. Avoid stemmy or coarse hay.*

The hay's texture is another sign of whether it's good or bad. If it's stemmy (without leaves or flowers), it was probably harvested late, and it won't have as much nutrition as if it were cut at peak time.

Ask your feed dealer to point out different types of hays to you so you can begin to tell them apart by sight, touch, and smell.

One surefire way to see if you are feeding high-quality hay is to go straight to the horse's mouth. Horses will devour tasty hay, and will seek out each wisp to make sure there are no leftovers. If a horse doesn't finish her hay rations, or if she tramples it, she's telling you one of two things: You're feeding her too much or her hay is not exactly okay.

INTERNET

www.foragetesting.org

Got some hay that you want to know more about? The National Forage Testing Association can provide names of test labs in your area, and can tell you if a lab you want to use is certified.

Grass-kept horses

A horse "at pasture" is kept in a field and can eat all the grass she wants. This doesn't mean, though, that you can just stick her on the lawn and expect her to get all the nutrients she needs. The nourishment that's available will depend on the time of year.

■ **If a horse looks fat** *then it may be a sign that she is eating too much. Obesity can cause respiratory and heart problems.*

In the winter, a horse at pasture will need to be supplemented with other food, since the field might actually be covered with snow for most of the cold season. Compare this to early spring and summer, when you might have to restrict your horse from eating too much grass, as some horses develop a "grass belly," not unlike a beer belly. These horses have a bloated paunch as a sign of overindulgence. They can also get ill from too much spring grass.

Some horses are prone to laminitis, a sometimes-deadly condition that can occur when a horse eats too much food or food that is too rich. Laminitis can result in permanent or chronic lameness.

Daily requirements

YOUR HORSE'S SIX MAIN dietary requirements, in order of importance, are water, roughage (bulk), energy, protein, minerals, and vitamins. Good quality hay or pasture used to be able to deliver sufficient amounts of these components (except for water, of course) to the working horse. These days, however, with hay harvested from depleted soil, and grass pastures being the exception rather than the rule, you will probably need to look elsewhere to make sure that your horse receives a balanced diet.

First, talk with your veterinarian. He or she will be able to evaluate the quality of hay in your area and determine if your horse needs anything extra to round out her diet. Also, discuss the performance you expect from your horse and what behaviors, if any, you'd like to curtail. Many horses get labeled as lazy, spooky, or crabby, when a thorough analysis of their diet and appropriate adjustments could solve the problem. Based on your horse's age, general health, and her workload, your vet will be able to make suggestions concerning supplemental feed and vitamins. If you are happy with the way your horse looks, if she has a shiny coat, bright eyes, and good solid hooves, you may not need to supply anything other than good-quality hay, constant access to fresh clean water and a *mineral block*.

DEFINITION

Mineral blocks *contain salts and trace minerals that are otherwise missing from the diet. The horse licks the block to ingest the minerals.*

When we feel sluggish, we grab a cup of coffee or an energy bar to perk us up. Too perky? We'll have some turkey – it not only rhymes, but it also contains tryptophane to make us sleepy. There's substantial scientific and anecdotal evidence of how certain foods affect the human body. There is no reason to think that things would be different for our horses.

Feed in a bag

When you go to a feed store, you'll notice all types of feed bags that could confuse even the most knowledgeable equestrian. Some are alfalfa cubes, pellets, grains, "sweet feeds" (they have molasses added), and even beet pulp. Some look like the equivalent of big dog kibble bags. Since most of us don't eat anything remotely close to some of the ingredients listed on these bags, we could be in deep trouble trying to guess what is best.

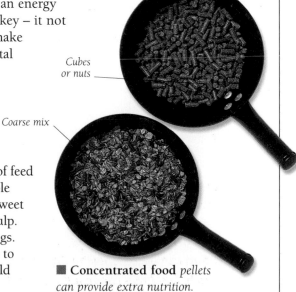

Cubes or nuts

Coarse mix

■ **Concentrated food** *pellets can provide extra nutrition.*

Choosing the best products from the vast amount of feed out there can be a challenge, even if you've owned horses for a long time. Once you acquire a basic understanding of your horse's feed requirements, you will have the know-how to build a complete equine diet.

Is horse kibble enough?

There are generally two kinds of bagged feeds: complete feeds and supplemental feeds. A complete feed is just that – it's a cube or pellet that has hays and grains compressed with ingredients such as vitamins and minerals. Complete feeds are specially formulated to address various levels of performance and are an excellent way to make sure your horse receives the proper amounts of energy, protein, and vitamins.

Using a complete feed doesn't necessarily mean that you should skip giving your horse hay, however. Complete feeds supply some roughage, as most are alfalfa or beet-pulp based, but your horse's main source of roughage will be grass or legume hays. Plus, a horse's digestive system is supposed to be working throughout the day. If you only feed your horse a ration of complete feed, she'll probably finish her bucket quite quickly. A bored horse might start chewing on other things such as the fence, her stall, or buckets. She might also begin bolting her food down when she does get her concentrates. Hay fills the need to chew, and even if your horse needs to be put on a diet, there are hays that won't put the pounds on.

Added extras

A supplemental feed is designed to work in tandem with hay to target a horse's specific dietary needs. For example, some horses are naturally very thin, no matter how much hay they ingest. There are special supplemental feeds that can help these skinny minis put on weight in the right areas.

■ **Leaving your horse** *with hay in her stall will keep her occupied until you visit again.*

Special needs feeds

FEED MANUFACTURERS constantly update their formulas to consider environmental pollution and cutting edge nutritional research. There are also types of supplemental feeds that can help give horses more energy (good for those in serious training) or improve their outward appearance, such as enhancing their coat's shine. There are feeds that are designed for working athletes, very young horses, pregnant mares, and very old horses.

INTERNET

www.cybersteed.com/

Cybersteed is a web site from Kentucky Equine Research, Inc., which conducts equine nutrition studies and works with nutritionists to provide information on the latest feed advances.

Select a feed that matches your horse's activity level and age. Obviously, you wouldn't feed something like SuperColtVitaGrow® to a 20-year-old gelding that is hitting the trail only three times a week, right? Like humans, older horses have slower metabolisms, and may find it harder to chew. Similarly, pregnant or nursing mares may need extra protein and mineral supplements.

FEED MIXES

Feed mixes are generally separated into these categories: Maintenance, Performance, Junior, Senior, Special Needs.

- **Maintenance feed** is good for horses that do light work and have easy schedules. It's balanced so that it doesn't overload a horse with proteins and carbohydrates
- **Performance feed** is for horses that are in training for competition or otherwise have heavier schedules. It has higher fat, carbohydrates, and protein content to aid working muscles
- **Junior formulas** are for growing youngsters, providing the essential nutrients growing foals require, especially with their smaller digestive systems
- **Senior feed** is made to help the older horse whose health might be compromised or who can't digest as well as he used to
- **Special Needs feeds** include formulas for breeding stallions, for pregnant mares, for lactating mares, and for horses with certain medical conditions. Each is packed with ingredients that can keep the horse in optimum health

Your optimum feeding plan

Ideally, a horse should be given hay often but in small portions. Many good equestrian centers feed their boarded horses three times a day. Select the type of additional feed (maintenance, performance, senior) and read the specific amounts recommended by the manufacturer. If you have any questions, contact your feed store, or better yet, your vet.

For new owners, sometimes it is better to aim for a diet that includes lower energy feed, such as maintenance feed. Too much protein and fat can make a horse too energetic – even spooky sometimes. Once you settle into your routine with your horse, you can gradually introduce a higher energy feed into your horse's diet.

How much is too much?

A healthy horse is neither too fat nor thin, and her coat should be soft and shiny, not rough and dull. Horses by nature are supposed to be on the more slender side. If a horse is obese, her body has to work harder to get blood and nutrients to fat cells just to maintain them, and if her organs are surrounded by fat, they have to work harder. Joints also take on more wear and tear when they have to carry more weight.

A weight tape is like a measuring tape for your horse, specifically designed to show you roughly how much your horse weighs. Place the tape behind the horse's elbow, around her belly, just where the withers join the horse's back. Read the number where the tape's starting point meets the numbered tape below.

If your horse looks as though she's got a crease forming along her back and over her loins, and has fat deposits at the top of her neck and to her withers, she's probably carrying too much weight. Careful, gradual diet management needs to take place so that you don't cause a nutritional imbalance or give your horse a tummy ache.

To get that fat horse on a diet, you will need to treat her like a human: decrease her energy intake and increase her work. Reduce her calorie intake by reducing the volume you're currently feeding or by changing to a lower calorie dense food. If she's on pasture during the day, decrease her grazing time.

■ **Measure feed rations** *carefully. You should weigh feed each time, since its bulk can vary from day to day according to how much moisture it absorbs from the air.*

Other dietary needs

YOU MIGHT WANT TO SUPPLEMENT your horse's hay diet with specific vitamins and minerals. Or you might believe that you are feeding a complete feed that doesn't completely address your needs. In these cases, there are literally hundreds of products that offer, either alone or in combinations, vitamins, minerals, herbs, enzymes, and other ingredients to promise better equine health.

Keep in mind that nutrition is one area where more is not necessarily better. Before you scoop and pour assorted powders or liquids into your horse's feed, consider this: When experts discuss a balanced equine diet, they're not talking about broccoli versus potato chips. The balance is one between vitamins and minerals. You might choose a certain nutrient to address a specific issue but, for it to work, the nutrient may need to be supported by other vitamins, minerals, or amino acids. Remember, though, that if you use several products, you can easily overdose your horse.

Water-soluble vitamins (B complex and C) are not a problem, as excess is eliminated through urine. Fat-soluble vitamins (A, D, E, and K), however, are stored in muscle, fat, or the liver, where they can reach toxic levels.

To avoid potential problems of excessive intake, add the totals of the different ingredients and make sure you are feeding nutrients at safe levels. Take advantage of manufacturers' toll-free numbers – they're there to help you.

Special supplements

There are other dietary supplements that are designed to do more than just balance the diet. They are made to increase stamina, eliminate "free-radicals," make joints move better, or calm a nervous personality. Supplements are simply feed ingredients fed at a higher level than normal.

A nutraceutical is a combination of nutritional ingredients that have a pharmaceutical action. It is not a drug.

Additives, on the other hand, are chemicals that are designed to replace some of the vital compounds in your horse's body.

■ **Vitamin supplements** *in the form of a powder can be mixed easily into your horse's feed.*

The most common supplements

Use your head when choosing a supplement. Some vets swear by them, others swear at them. They can be fattening or even dangerously toxic in large quantities.

- Antioxidants (vitamin E and selenium): get rid of free radicals that cause cell damage
- Biotin: improves the quality and growth rate of hooves, mane, tail, and coat
- Herbs: these are natural sources of painkillers, immune system boosters, etc.
- Joint supplements: chondroitin sulfates, glucosamine, and methylsulfonylmethane (MSM) all are supposed to reduce cartilage breakdown and improve the joint fluid for horses that suffer from arthritis
- Probiotics: digestive aids that help the horse's "good" gut bacteria digest fiber better
- Psyllium: helps eliminate sand in the horse's digestive tract

Water – a horse's best friend

Horses drink a lot of water. Drinking 10 or more gallons (38 liters) a day is not an uncommon consumption rate for a horse. Make sure that your horse has a clean, fresh, endless supply of water every day. Horses will stay away from a water source that is muddy, polluted, hot, or frozen.

Water hydrates the horse and also keeps him cool after exercise. In the summertime or during peak performance, horses can sweat out large amounts of water. As an example, a racehorse running 1 mile (1.6 km) in 2 minutes can lose up to 2½ gallons (9 liters) of sweat in order to cool her body.

Sometimes, horses do not like the taste of new water. This can be troublesome, especially if you've traveled to do an overnight riding trip or a horse show. Finicky horses who refuse to drink "foreign water" can be retrained. Simply spike the water at home a few weeks in advance with a small amount of flavored powdered drink mix or molasses. Then when you arrive at the new destination, do the same to mask the taste of the strange water source. (You can reduce the amount of flavoring daily until you no longer need it).

■ **Refill your horse's water supply** *once a day. Clean buckets and troughs regularly to prevent bacteria growing.*

Ways to feed

Wall feeders and hayracks are found in nearly every barn stall around the country. But the best way to deliver a horse's feed is at ground level. This mimics their grazing posture and reduces the risk of a horse ingesting too much dust from hay. You should be careful when feeding a horse directly on the ground, though. A horse that eats from the dirt may ingest sand and other debris, which can cause digestive upsets. Get a floor feeder or pan, or feed on a large stall mat. Treats should be fed in small quantities that are easy for the horse to chew and break down. While a horse may swipe an entire carrot, it may choke her when she swallows the whole thing.

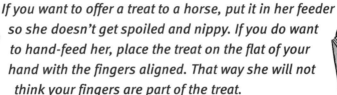

If you want to offer a treat to a horse, put it in her feeder so she doesn't get spoiled and nippy. If you do want to hand-feed her, place the treat on the flat of your hand with the fingers aligned. That way she will not think your fingers are part of the treat.

While you do have many options for feeding and treating your horse, the one option you don't have is to skimp on her nutrition. Your horse depends on you to give her the healthiest food so she can look, feel, and perform at her best.

■ **Treats should** *be cut into small, easy-to-digest pieces.*

A simple summary

✓ Wild horses have adapted to scant feed rations, but domestic horses must have good-quality feed at all times.

✓ Your horse's six main dietary requirements are water, roughage (bulk), energy, protein, minerals, and vitamins.

✓ You can learn to spot quality hay by the way it looks, smells, and feels.

✓ Supplemental and complete commercial feeds have been developed for horses in all stages of life and career.

✓ Overweight horses should be trimmed down through reduced energy intake and increased exercise.

✓ A constant supply of clean water is the most crucial element to a horse's well-being.

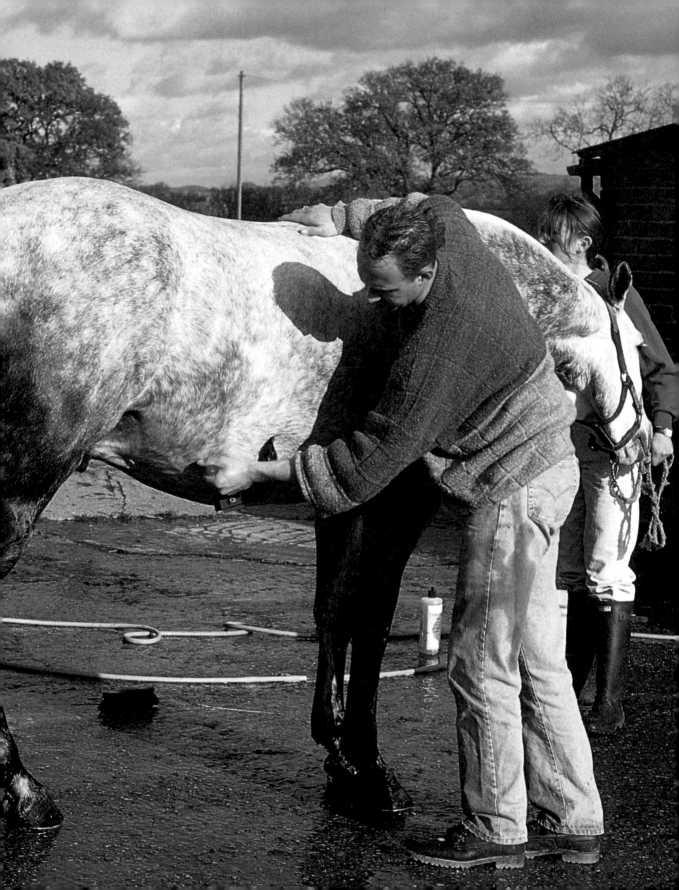

Chapter 13

The Nuts and Bolts of Grooming

Horses like stability and structure. That's why a daily regimen is so important. It's spending time with your horse in a different way – by bonding with him while you care for him. A daily routine doesn't have to be mundane. The little things you do around the stable eventually lead to better times in the saddle. Looking after your horse with regular care leads to a happy, enthusiastic equine.

In this chapter...

✓ **Good grooming habits**

✓ **Bath time**

✓ **Once-over for good health**

GET YOUR HORSE ACCUSTOMED TO REGULAR BATHING

Good grooming habits

GROOMING IS THE ONLY ACTIVITY associated with horses that is guaranteed to show you instant and rewarding results. But, as anyone who has ever put an immaculately bathed and groomed horse back in his stall and then turned his or her back for just a minute knows, these moments of achievement can be short-lived. But even though your horse has the tendency to undo in seconds what you've labored long and hard to accomplish, a daily grooming routine is essential for a few reasons.

■ **Horses groom each other** *as part of their natural social instinct. This keeps their coats clean and free from irritation.*

First, it lets you spend time bonding with your horse on the ground, and he will know that there is affection for him. Second, grooming allows you to take stock of your horse's overall condition.

In the wild, horses are "groomed" by their herd friends. You will see horses in the pasture scratching themselves and each other with their mouths, as well as rolling to get rid of mud, dirt, sweat, and loose hair.

How to brush your horse

Your horse should be brushed daily, whether you are planning to ride him or not. It's good for his coat, his circulation, and it is a relaxing time for the two of you to spend together, deepening the bond between you. Pick an area for grooming that is outside your horse's stall – preferably well lit – with good ventilation. If you groom your horse in his stall, you're just going to be putting the dirt back where he found it!

Do not tie your horse to a wood fence when you are grooming him – it may not be strong enough. There are plenty of instances of horses pulling back and galloping away merrily with fence rails banging along behind them and this could cause a serious injury.

Secure your horse using a quick-release knot, and keep the length of rope to a limit of about 2½ feet (75 cm). This will keep him from moving around too much or turning to nip you while you're brushing him.

Many good grooms don't tie their horses directly to a tie ring or rail. Instead, they tie to a loop of baling twine or string that is then attached to the tie ring. This way, if the horse pulls back, the twine will eventually break, which minimizes the chance of horse or handler getting hurt.

Assess what type of job you're in for, then arm yourself with the necessary tools. Start at the top of his neck with the body brush, behind the ears, and work your way down. Brush with the lay of the hair in light, brisk strokes. After a few strokes, take your body brush and run it against the nubs of the rubber curry. This will knock the dirt out of the brush. Tap your curry comb occasionally to remove the dust. Don't forget the hard to reach places, such as under the horse's belly and mane, and between his legs.

Massaging and finishing

If your horse is shedding, or has mud or caked manure in his hair, you can break it up with your curry. The currycomb should be used with a circular motion to bring up dead skin and dirt, too. The massaging action also stimulates a horse's circulation. Don't use it on the delicate areas such as the face and legs. Use your finishing brush to whisk away the finer dust particles and put a fine shine on your horse's coat. Then, use it to clean the horse's face. Be gentle on this area, especially around his eyes and forehead.

Work with smooth, light strokes. If you are too harsh with your brushing, or if you bang your horse in the head with the brush, he could become headshy.

Dampen a small sponge with water and wring it out. Wipe out the corners of your horse's eyes, mouth, and nose. Finally, take a soft terry towel or sheepskin and smooth out the coat to remove any final dust. Voilà! The biggest part of the job is done.

■ **Do not stand** *directly behind your horse when grooming him, in case he kicks.*

Mane and tail maintenance

To brush the tail, select a brush that is flexible (like a flat-backed human styling brush), and grasp the tail 6 inches (15 cm) from the bottom. Hold it and carefully brush out the tangles as well as any bedding stuck in that bottom part. Then move up another 6 inches (15 cm), and so on. Take your time when you come to a tangled section. Finally, brush the top of the tail and you're tangle free.

Sometimes manes don't want to behave. We like them to lie on the correct side, but somehow your horse looks like he has dreadlocks on both sides by the morning. Wet the mane down (make sure it's clean first), then add hair gel and comb it out. Separate the mane in 1-inch (2.5-cm) sections, take a rubber band, called a braid-binder, and wrap it around the base of each section. Tighten so that it lies flat. Leave these in for a couple of days, then remove and comb out.

GROOMING DO'S AND DON'TS

- Do make sure you clean your brushes regularly in lukewarm water mixed with mild soap, and then rinse them completely
- Don't let your brushes get filthy so that they add more grime to your horse
- Do brush according to your horse's sensitivity level
- Don't use harsh brushes or vigorous strokes on a thin-skinned horse
- Do begin pulling the mane after your ride, while the pores of the skin are open
- Don't use scissors on the mane
- Do curry a muddy coat vigorously using a plastic or rubber curry to remove dirt and hair
- Don't wear lip-protector during grooming sessions, or you will be wearing the removed dirt!

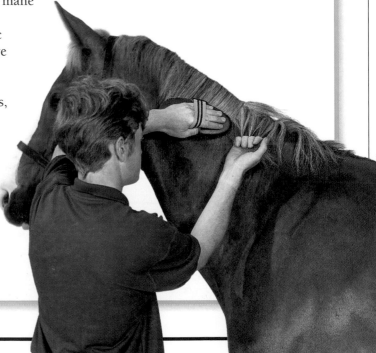

■ **Gently untangle** *the hairs of the mane with your fingers before carefully brushing through to smooth it down.*

Styles of manes

Manes for trail horses and for some western or gaited breeds are often left long and flowing. But English riders and many western show riders keep the mane even at about 4 inches (10 cm) all the way down the neck. It's kept this way so it will lie flat and neat against one side of the horse's neck, and also so it is the right length for braiding. The length is maintained by pulling the mane.

Pulling a mane basically means plucking out the longest hairs until the mane is all one length and thickness. Most horses don't mind this process, as they are less sensitive along the crest of their necks. You want to make your horse as comfortable as possible during this process, so you should pull the mane over the course of several days instead of during one session. It is also easier if the horse is warmed up and his pores are open.

Using a mane-pulling comb – a sturdy metal comb with short teeth – start at the top of the horse's neck. Take a firm hold of a small section of mane at the end of the strands, maybe a ½-inch's (1.2 cm) worth. With your other hand and comb, back comb that small section upward, as though you were ratting a hairdo from the 1950s. The longest hairs will still be in the first hand. Wind the longer hairs around the comb and, with a quick jerk, pull them out. Work down the mane to create an even length.

Pay attention to feet

The feet are the most important part of your grooming session. If you leave for a trail ride with a stone wedged between your horse's shoe or stuck in his frog, you can cause a painful bruise to his foot. Cleaning the manure out will prohibit bacteria from taking hold of his sole, too.

When you're picking out your horse's feet, remove any manure or mud and any stones. Check that his shoes are on securely and that they are not missing any nails.

With the hand closest to his leg, squeeze the tendon at the back to get your horse to lift his foot. A nifty trick for stubborn horses is to pinch the chestnut, the hard callous on the inside of the upper leg, which for some reason causes most horses to lift that leg right away. The more you groom your horse, the easier this will be. Use the sharp hoof pick to remove any bedding, mud, or manure, working from the heel to the toe. The cleft of the frog, that little indentation, is more sensitive than the rest of the foot, so refrain from completely gouging in this area.

Horses like their grooming routine to be performed in a particular order. For instance, if you usually pick out the feet, then brush the body, they appreciate it when you don't come back and do it in reverse.

Bath time

GROOMING YOUR HORSE is excellent for daily maintenance, but there will be times when you need to get your horse completely clean. So that's where bathing comes in. Bathing removes the deep dirt, sweat, and scurf that brushes just can't get at. Using the right type of medicated shampoo can help a horse with a skin condition.

The best time to wash your horse is after your ride. You'll get him sparkling after his workout, and you'll also get a deeper clean, since the pores of his skin will be open. He'll probably be feeling more relaxed, too.

Select your bathing area. The ideal place for the job is a horse wash-rack. Wash-racks vary in their design. Some are just concrete slabs that have a place to crosstie your horse, while others are like a chute to walk your horse in and out of. Rubber mats allow your horse traction on the concrete.

You can wash your horse anywhere, but remember that if you've selected a dirt surface, it will soon turn into a muddy, gooey mess. Large rubber mats can minimize the mud you and your horse stand in, and so can a slight slope that allows for drainage. Always tie your horse to something solid. Gather your gear for the job: garden hose; adjustable multispray nozzle; large bucket; large sponge; horse bath mitt or curry; sweat scraper; shampoo and conditioning agents; *cooler*.

> **DEFINITION**
>
> *A **cooler** is a large absorbent blanket that drapes from the horse's ears down to his knees and over his tail. It is used to help cool down a horse gradually after he's had a sweaty workout. The warmer wool and synthetic versions can trap body heat and are used to keep the horse warm.*

Let's get wet

Most outdoor facilities don't have warm water, and most horses are bathed in only cold water. Turn on the water to a medium flow and slowly introduce the spray to your horse. Most people start at the shoulder, which is a less sensitive area than the belly or face. Work your way down the front legs, then across the back and down to the haunches. Then head backward and wet the neck (save the face wetting for later).

If you want to give your horse a warm-water bath, you can do it bucket style, heating the water with a heating coil, which is a copper coil that runs on electricity. It might take twice as long as a cold-water bath, but it may be a good solution for sensitive horses.

Next, fill your bucket with shampoo. Most manufacturers recommend that you don't put the shampoo directly on the coat (as it can be hard to rinse out in its concentrated form), but dilute it in the water bucket instead. Take your sudsy solution and soap up your horse's coat with your large sponge. Work from front to back. Some people take the sudsy water and pour it over the coat, and then work it into the skin. It's up to you. Use only enough elbow grease to work the shampoo in – you're not waxing the car. Then, make another bucket of shampoo solution and pour a small bit over the mane, then scrub like you're at your hairstylist's. With the rest of the bucket, place your horse's tail inside the water and swish it around. Then pour the last bit over the top of the tail and lather up.

■ **Have the shampoo,** *sponge, and bucket of water ready before you start.*

Rinse and (you're all) set

Next, comes the big rinse. Start with your horse's neck and rinse the soap out of his mane. Work over his back so that the soap runs down and off. Then rinse his belly and legs. You can check for suds by running your hand through the hair and seeing if bubbles pop up. If so, continue rinsing.

There are almost as many different equine shampoos and conditioners as you have at your local salon. Pick according to your need among color enhancing, whitening, conditioning, antibacterial, antifungal, insect repelling, and even sun-damage repair varieties.

Finally, do his face. Most horses object to being squirted in the face with a heavy stream of water. Turn your hose to its finest mist and hold it over the horse's head. If he cannot stand for the water to hit him, use a damp sponge. Add conditioner to his mane and tail, then rinse. Use your sweat scraper to pull all of the water out of his coat, and put the cooler on to make him dry quicker. Once he's fairly dry, run a brush over his coat to smooth it out. Too much bathing can lead to a dull coat and even cause some skin problems, so, between baths, give your horse a water-only rinse to remove sweat.

■ **You might want** *to give your horse a bath as often as you have one, but too much bathing strips the coat of its oils.*

173

Once-over for good health

GROOMING OR BATHING your horse allows you to check him out nose to tail and take stock of his general condition. Aside from the obvious nicks and scratches, you will be able to spot the beginnings of fungus or insect infestations and even be able to tell if your horse is sore by watching his body language. If you can detect any swelling or heat early on, it can save you and your horse a lot of grief down the road. As you groom, check for lost shoes, bites, swollen legs, ticks, skin conditions, and symptoms of sickness.

Special care for winter

When the cold months approach, you'll need to adjust your grooming routine to meet the changing climate. During the winter, horses grow a thick, hairy coat, which protects them in moderately cold weather as long as they have shelter from wind and rain.

A lot of horses are ridden during the winter. During these workouts, horses sweat under all that winter fur. It takes horses a longer time to cool off and dry out after their winter rides.

Many people body-clip their horses to keep them from overheating under their winter fur. A clipped horse relies on the added warmth and protection from a blanket, so you can't just throw his blanket on whenever you feel like it. If you are not able to stick to a blanketing routine, it's better to leave your horse with his entire winter coat intact.

BLANKETS

Place the blanket over the horse's neck and withers, then slide it onto his back. The straps under the belly should be snug but not tight. Leg straps should hang with a little bit of slack. Each leg strap should encircle the leg – don't cross them under your horse in a figure eight (he can get hung up in them if you do). Make sure the blanket covers your horse to his tail, but is not so large that it twists. A too-large blanket can cause chafing. A tight blanket will be constricting at the neck and shoulder.

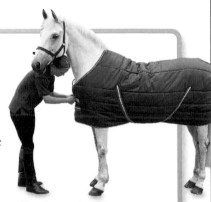

■ **Adjust the chest straps,** *leaving room to slide your hand under the blanket.*

Different types of clips

A horse doing moderate work can sport a partial body clip that allows him to carry most of his coat but reduces the sweaty workouts and long cool-downs. Some people shave the belly and underside of the neck – a strip clip. Some add the lower half of the horse's torso to that – a trace clip. A horse that is clipped so that only the saddle area and legs are left long is sporting a hunter clip. A blanket clip involves clipping hair on the head, neck, shoulders, and belly.

The best time of year to clip is when the coat is nearly full-grown, usually in late October. The coat will grow a bit more, but most owners can get by with just one body clip for the winter. Horses with really thick coats will need to be shaved twice.

INTERNET

www.horse-sense.org

Here, you'll find Jessica Jahiel's Horse Sense Newsletter, which deals with all aspects of horses.

■ **A trace clip** *removes hair from the belly and under the neck.*

■ **A blanket clip** *removes hair from the head, neck, and belly.*

■ **A hunter clip** *leaves hair on the legs and under the saddle.*

A simple summary

✔ Daily grooming involves brushing the coat, combing the tail and mane, and cleaning the feet.

✔ Use grooming and bathing time to check your horse's condition. Don't bath your horse excessively.

✔ A body-clipped horse can either be fully or partially shaved.

✔ Clipped horses will need to be blanketed during the winter. Make sure that your horse's blanket is a comfortable fit.

Chapter 14

First Aid for Equines

AS A HORSE PERSON, it's good to know all you can about the most common ailments that can affect horses. Once you know what they are, there are some simple and practical ways to protect your equine companion against them. By working closely with your veterinarian and by practicing preventative care, you can minimize any risk to your horse. It is also essential that you know how to deal with any emergency you haven't been able to prevent.

In this chapter...
- ✓ Call the doctor!
- ✓ Familiar ailments
- ✓ Common injuries

A LAME HORSE BEING TROTTED UP FOR VET INSPECTION

Call the doctor!

WHEN I BOUGHT MY FIRST HORSE, I went to the library to arm myself with veterinary information. No way was this animal going to get sick on me. I pulled one hefty medical volume off the shelf and gulped. Horses can have so many things go wrong with them. The infectious diseases, the different viruses, the protozoa. It all made my head swim!

The good news is that while there is a host of exotic conditions out there, the chances of your horse becoming afflicted are pretty low. But that's no reason to have a laid-back attitude toward medical situations. Horses do have a way of getting themselves hurt, and even if you provide the most comfortable, protective environment for your horse, she may become ill or injured anyway. The trick is to know the difference between a little bump or bruise and a bona fide emergency. Being prepared for a crisis takes the panic out of any situation, large or small. Not every emergency will be the "quick – grab a towel to soak up the blood" type.

In-depth health check

You've already learned how to take your horse's vital signs, so you should know what her normal pulse, respiration, and temperature are. You can assess her condition further by checking other areas of her body, too. Check for dehydration by lifting her upper lip and pressing your thumb against the gum line, then release. Count how many seconds it takes for the light area you were pressing to turn back to pink. This is called the capillary refill time. Normal is up to 3 seconds. If it takes longer, there could be something wrong with your horse.

A horse's gums should always be a healthy pink color. Any light or gray color indicates a severely sick horse.

You can also check for dehydration by doing a skin-pinch test. Take a pinch of skin in the middle of your horse's neck and hold it for a second or two. A well-hydrated horse's skin will bounce back, but a dehydrated horse's skin will slowly go down.

■ **Check your horse's mouth** *regularly. Gums should be healthy and pink; pale or very red gums mean the horse needs medical attention.*

Checking for swelling

Swelling of the legs could mean a bad strain or even a tear in a tendon or ligament. Hot hooves may indicate laminitis: a dangerous condition which can permanently damage the feet. It's not good, however, if a horse's legs are too cold. Legs should always be somewhat warm, indicating good circulation. If the lower limbs are cold to the touch, even in winter, it could be a sign of advanced endotoxic shock. (This is a potentially fatal condition which develops when toxins from the intestines enter the bloodstream.)

What to do first

How you handle your emergency will make a big difference to your vet's ability to treat your horse and to your horse's recovery. If your horse has a little nick or scrape and he's current on his tetanus shots, you probably don't have to call the vet out. A larger gash or cut may need medical treatment, including stitches.

Salt water is better than plain tap water for treating wounds. The salt helps the tissue resist absorbing the water into its cells, which could lead to edema (fluid retention) and poor blood circulation. Saline solutions merely cleanse and rinse without interfering.

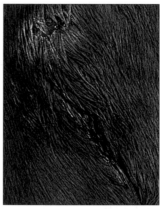

■ **If you are unsure** *how serious a gash or laceration is, seek medical attention.*

Trivia...

Blood makes up almost one fifth of a horse's total weight. A horse can lose a lot of blood – as much as 2 gallons (7.5 liters) – before suffering serious effects. Quick, heavy bleeding is much more dangerous than a slow bleed, even if the horse has been slowly bleeding for a time. Normal clotting time in a horse is about 12 minutes for small veins, with large vessels or arteries taking longer.

Many injuries are not found immediately, so it's important to check your horse regularly. As soon as you discover a wound, try to gently cleanse the area to remove any dirt or contaminants. Sometimes a cut will look superficial, but on closer inspection you'll find that it goes through several layers of tissue. Cleanse the wound with a saline solution. You can use a ready-made product or add a half-tablespoon of salt to one quart of clean water. Irrigate deep cuts using a large syringe (without a needle). This gentle squirting pressure will help wash away dirt that you can't get to.

Bleeding wounds

If your horse has a puncture or gash that just won't stop bleeding, there are ways to minimize the blood loss. Bleeding around the lower leg or hoof may indicate that an artery may have been nicked or even severed. You can recognize artery blood by its bright red colour and the fact that it spurts out with every beat of the pulse.

If you suspect that your horse has cut an artery, it's important to stay calm so that you can be useful to your horse and so you don't panic her. A confused and excited horse can be dangerous, and excessive movement will in any case worsen her condition. Keep your horse confined and quiet, and see if you can have someone hold her while you treat the wound. Ensure that you are not risking your own safety when you make your approach.

After you've placed a towel on a wound, do not prematurely remove it to check if your horse has stopped bleeding. If you do so, the wound won't have a chance to clot. You can help restrict blood to the area by placing ice packs above the wound.

Apply a clean towel directly over the bleeding area, and press down for several minutes. The main purpose of this is to keep pressure over the wound rather than to soak up the blood; just wrapping a towel loosely around the leg won't work. If you don't have a towel or rag, use whatever you can – even the T-shirt on your back. At this point, it's better to have the bleeding stop than to worry about contamination.

■ **Applying a bandage** *keeps pressure on the wound and stops further blood loss.*

After the wound has stopped bleeding, replace your soaked towel with a pressure bandage. Place a nonstick gauze pad over the wound, then wrap with an Ace bandage or self-adhesive stretch bandage material, such as Vetrap®, Elastikon®, or Flexus®. If you think the wound might need stitches, don't apply a spray antiseptic, peroxide, or ointment. These dry out the skin and make stitching more difficult.

Eye injuries

DEFINITION

Conjunctivitis *is an inflammation of the conjunctival membrane, which covers the front of the eyeball and lines the eyelid. It is generally caused by bacteria, pollen, viruses, or parasites getting into the eyes. A fly mask will help to keep these contaminants out.*

If it seems that your horse has suffered an eye injury, there will probably be a yellowish discharge from the corner of the eye, or the eye and surrounding area may be swollen or inflamed. Horses commonly scratch their corneas, although the problem might be caused by *conjunctivitis*.

If it looks like an injury, try to flush the eye out with saline solution used for contact lens storage. By gently squirting the solution into the eye, you may be able to dislodge the debris that could be hurting your horse. You can apply ophthalmologic antibiotic ointment to the eye as long as it is nonsteroidal. Then call your vet for further advice.

Know who to call

Most of the time there won't be any emergency room for horses in your area, so you must select your horse's vet ahead of time. A head wound is no time to introduce yourself to the equine medical community. Keep the number to your vet handy. Program it into your cell phone. Keep it in your wallet. Make sure you always have access to that number.

Be descriptive on the phone

In the event of an urgent situation, first take a moment to compose yourself – don't rush and forget what could be important details. Be prepared to leave a message that is clear and thorough. If you talk to the office or an answering service, find out when your message will be delivered, and when you can expect a call back. Give the following information:

- Who you are, what your horse's name is, and where the horse lives
- What type of injury you believe the horse has sustained, and when it took place
- The phone number at the location
- The phone number where you can be reached (a cell phone is really handy)

If you board at an equestrian center, make sure your contact information is up to date in the office, and put a sign up at your horse's stall with your name and phone number, as well as your vet's and farrier's names and numbers.

When you actually speak to your vet, expand on your description of the situation. Provide additional comments such as the personal details of the horse (age, sex, breed, and any other medical conditions), and say what you believe the horse's mental condition is (dazed, out of it, in shock, aggressive, wild). Any additional details can prepare the vet to act quickly from the moment he or she arrives.

HEALTH INSURANCE FOR HORSES?

Major medical and surgical insurance is often added on to a horse's mortality policy. It is designed to cover surgery and (up to a certain amount) diagnostic tests, nonsurgical illnesses, and certain other medical care that your horse receives from a vet. This type of insurance covers expenses for costly services such as colic surgery but only pays up to policy limits, which might be $5,000. If your expenses exceed the limit, you'll have to pay the rest out of pocket. Not all insurance companies are alike, and it would do you good to research your options before you think about taking out a policy.

First-aid kits

Some people never put a first-aid kit together. For even the laziest people, though, there are kits that are sold pre-stocked. These all-in-one kits can be purchased and packed up on a shelf – out of the way until needed. Make sure you have one.

You'll have to get over any squeamishness if you're a horse owner. Horses seem to get hurt in the most unsightly manner, often when professional medical help is hours away. Just stay calm and try your best to alleviate any pain or dangerous situations. That's half the battle.

It is wise to have a back-up vet selected just in case your own vet is unavailable. Seek the advice of other equestrians in your area for a second doctor. Another thing you really need to think about in advance is teaching your horse to get into a trailer. When it's time for a ride to the hospital, the horse should be able to load quickly and safely.

THE FIRST-AID KIT

To handle any type of medical situation that comes your way, you should be prepared with a first-aid kit. Many of these items can be found at your local drug store, while others are available through your tack shop or even your vet. Keep the following items, along with any emergency contact numbers, in a sealed container. It is a good idea to have a kit in more than one place (for example, the barn and the trailer). If you use any item in your first-aid kit, you should replace it immediately. You'll never know when you might need it again.

- Stethoscope
- Wristwatch
- Rectal thermometer
- Nonsteroidal eye ointment
- Oral syringe
- Pocket knife/multipurpose tool
- Betadine scrub (antiseptic scrub)
- Scissors
- First-aid book
- Disposable razor for shaving hair
- Betadine solution (antiseptic wash)
- Rubbing alcohol
- Wound cream/ointment

- Absorbent cotton
- Roll gauze
- Nonstick gauze dressing (Telfa pad)
- Self-stick elastic bandage (Vetrap)
- Adhesive tape
- Duct tape
- Syringe (without needle)

■ **Safety scissors** *should always be used to cut dressings.*

Familiar ailments

THERE ARE SEVERAL AILMENTS that may affect your horse at some time in her life. Some are extremely common, such as some types of colic, whereas others are thankfully rare. In all cases, you should contact your vet as soon as you notice the symptoms in your horse.

Colic

In a very short time, colic can be life threatening. Abdominal pain and upset in a horse is dangerous because horses are unable to vomit. If a horse has a blockage or twisted intestine, she must have treatment or surgery.

■ **A colicky horse** *should be prevented from rolling as this will increase the risk of her twisting her gut.*

There are four types of colic: Flatulent colic is caused by excess gas in the intestine. Spasmodic colic is caused by intestinal cramps, due to stress or drinking cold water. Impaction colic is a blockage in the intestine. Peritonitis colic occurs when part of the intestine ruptures or twists and dies off.

■ **Providing a thick bed** *is important for sick horses. Extra attention should be paid to keeping the stall clean and dry.*

If your horse is rolling or attempting to roll, pawing the ground, breaking into sweaty patches, standing with her hind legs outstretched, or looking at her belly, she may be colicky. Your vet will medicate your horse to relax the spasms and make her feel more comfortable, and will administer mineral oil through a stomach tube to help move any blockages.

Strangles

This disease affecting the respiratory tract is spread through contact with affected horses and equipment. It's usually not fatal, although it can permanently damage the lungs. Coughing, fever, weepy eyes and nose, loss of appetite, and swollen lymph nodes under the chin can indicate strangles. Left for too long, the abscesses that then develop in the lymph tissue will eventually burst through the skin and release pus. The vet will isolate your horse and administer penicillin.

Laminitis

This painful disease, also called founder, can be devastating to the horse's ability to work and perform, and sometimes just to walk. It occurs when an upset in the horse's metabolic, endocrine, or digestive system (such as rich food, too much water after a workout, or a bad infection) causes toxins to be released into the blood supply. The inner structures of the hoof capsule become inflamed and in serious cases detach from the hoof wall.

Laminitis is the second leading cause of death (on the disease list) of horses, with colic being the number one cause.

Signs of laminitis include shifting weight; reluctance to walk; rocking back on the heels; very hot front feet; and a bounding pulse behind the pastern. If your vet determines that your horse has laminitis, he or she will move the horse to a well-bedded stall; remove all feed; put the horse on a strict diet; administer pain-killing medication; and arrange for special shoeing if this is possible. Some horses recover after a mild bout, but others have permanently deformed feet and must be destroyed.

Tying up

This disease, also known as Monday morning disease or, most correctly, azoturia, attacks the horse's muscles. It often occurs when a horse is fed grain during her inactive days, and then works hard. As a result, toxic amounts of nitrogen waste build up in the tissues, leading to muscle breakdown and kidney failure. Cover your horse's hindquarters with a light blanket and keep her still and quiet until the vet arrives.

Do not cool off a horse that is tying up by hosing down her muscles. It will result in extreme cramping and even colic. Blood vessels will constrict and keep in all that nitrogen waste that needs to be flushed from deep muscle tissues.

Signs of tying up include anxiety, apparent pain, sweating, then uncoordination and extreme stiffness after a short workout. The best way to prevent tying up syndrome is to warm up your horse gradually, and then cool her down the same way. Cutting back on her grain ration (if she's not doing hard work) is prudent advice. To treat this condition, your vet will administer an anti-inflammatory drug and perhaps a tranquilizer to enhance blood supply to muscles; fluids may also be administered to maintain kidney function.

Flu

Equine influenza is a contagious condition affecting the horse's upper and lower respiratory tracts. Signs include sneezing, fever, runny nose, cough, appetite loss, or muscle stiffness. As with a human flu, there's not really any treatment from the doctor. The horse just has to rest to get better, with careful nursing from her owner.

Common injuries

THERE ARE SEVERAL TYPES of injury that can cause a horse to become lame, be in pain, or both. The horse's legs and feet tend to be most vulnerable to sudden injury. As always, prevention is better than cure, and making sure your horse is properly shod and stabled is an essential part of this. Injuries are still likely to occur, however – often in the most unpredictable manner – and you should know how to handle them correctly.

INTERNET

www.thehorse.com

This site is a companion to the print edition of The Horse magazine, and has up-to-date medical information in an easy-to-understand format.

Strains and sprains

A pulled ligament or tendon, usually caused by a bad step or even a fall, is a soft tissue injury. These are painful for the horse, and she might show it by not bearing weight on the affected leg. Don't attempt to move the horse too much or you might cause more damage. Place ice packs on the leg or hose it with cold water to reduce swelling and prevent further injury, then call your veterinarian for advice on how to proceed.

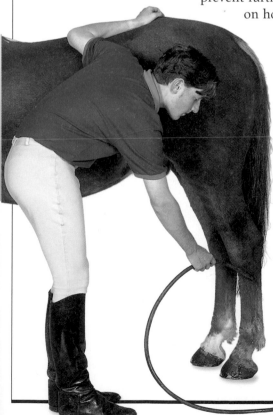

Bone injuries

Bone fractures are not the most common injuries, but they do happen. If it looks like your horse has broken a bone, perhaps in a severe fall, you probably won't have it confirmed until the vet arrives. Keep the horse as still and quiet as possible and phone the vet at once.

The vast majority of horses will suffer some form of lameness at some time in their lives. The causes are many and varied, and symptoms may range from mild stiffness to severe pain.

■ **Cold water hosing** *reduces inflammation of the muscles, preventing further damage and pain. This is sometimes followed by cold bandaging.*

Foot injuries

Horses can easily step on wire, glass, nails, or other debris, which can puncture the sole of the hoof. It is best not to pull the foreign object out, however, because your vet will need to see how deep the object has penetrated before he or she flushes the wound out.

If your horse accidentally pulls off her shoe, it might not seem like a big emergency, but it can turn into one. A pulled shoe might yank off a portion of the hoof. Sometimes a shoe that is barely hanging by one nail might actually puncture the foot with a different nail. Such a wound is likely to get infected. Tetanus is often caused by contact with nails, so make sure your horse is vaccinated. Cuts or scrapes to the heels of the forefeet are often caused by overreaching – when the toe of a horse's hind foot catches or scrapes the heel of the fore. This is most likely to occur when the horse is moving at speed in muddy conditions. Overreach boots, which cover the hoof, can help to prevent this type of injury.

BANDAGING YOUR HORSE'S FOOT

The foot is awkward to bandage, but in some situations it is necessary to keep a wound clean and prevent further infection. It is most commonly done to secure a poultice, which is used to draw out infection from puncture wounds.

1 **Apply poultice**

Ready-made poultice material (Animalintex) should be soaked in warm (not hot) water and placed over the sole.

2 **Fix with bandage**

Fix the poultice in place with self-stick elastic bandage. Secure the outer edges before bandaging across the sole.

3 **Finish off**

Continue to bandage until the poultice is well covered. It is a good idea then to protect the bandage with a medicine boot.

Cuts and bruises

These will be the most obvious injuries, and they can take various forms. An abrasion is a scrape or graze. Abrasions are too often caused by ill-fitting or dirty tack; in such cases they are most likely to occur in the saddle area and under the girth. A laceration is a tear. Some lacerations are superficial, while others go through many layers of tissue. Other types of open wound include incisions, which are clean cuts or slices into the flesh, and puncture wounds, which are deep holes in the flesh caused by nails or similar long objects. Bruises differ from the above in that the skin is not broken although the soft tissue beneath the skin is damaged.

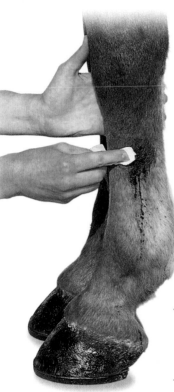

Many cuts and bruises can be prevented if your horse is wearing protective leg bandages or boots during exercise, especially when jumping or trail riding.

■ **Small wounds** *are not necessarily less significant than larger ones. Small puncture wounds can harbor infection well below the skin's surface, and yet they are easily missed by the less than vigilant horse owner.*

A simple summary

✔ Learn how to recognize the difference between a first-aid situation and an emergency.

✔ Keep your veterinarian's contact number at hand at all times. If your horse is boarding, make sure the barn office also has it.

✔ Keep a clear head and give your veterinarian detailed information when phoning in a crisis.

✔ Familiarize yourself with the common horse diseases and their symptoms.

✔ Horses can injure themselves in different ways. Check your horse regularly so that you can take prompt action.

✔ Build a first-aid kit and keep it well stocked. Replace any items that you use.

Chapter 15

Special Attention

T RADITIONAL MEDICINE FROM YOUR VETERINARIAN is one way to keep your horse healthy and content. But there are also complementary treatments and nontraditional holistic therapies that can keep him going strong. Some of these are now accepted by regular Western culture, while others are still new, unconventional methods for care. Some owners love to use a combination of several new therapies, embracing the weird and the wonderful, while others might only consider the most conservative option. Work with your vet to see which alternative treatments, if any, will benefit your horse.

In this chapter...

✓ **Chiropractic and massage**

✓ **Dentistry**

✓ **Natural herbs and more**

✓ **Therapy options**

A HEALTHY HORSE HAS FLEXIBILITY IN HIS NECK AND SPINE

Chiropractic and massage

SOME INJURIES AND LAMENESS are easy to spot. You see your horse limp out of his stall, and you know, basically, where the pain is coming from. But other signs that all is not fine with your horse can be easily missed, until one day you come to ride and he just says "no more."

Trivia...

Does your horse really have back pain? Think: "teeth, feet, seat." If a horse has a toothache or pain in his mouth, he will carry his head and neck differently, which can cause him to hollow his back and not travel freely. Or he could have a foot imbalance or pain in his hooves caused by improper shoeing, affecting how he trots and how he uses his back. Finally, it could be the seat: an ill-fitting saddle would hurt the horse's back.

For some horses (and their owners), chiropractic care is the answer to their troubles. The horse doesn't need an attitude adjustment, he needs a body adjustment. Equine chiropractic does just that, concentrating on the manipulation of the horse's spine, vertebrae, and other joints to reestablish free movement.

Your horse's aching back

Sometimes the vertebrae get "stuck" or limited in their range of motion. When this happens, the muscles surrounding the stuck vertebrae compensate by working harder, and eventually they can become tight, sore, or even spasmodic. When a certain vertebra is misaligned, stuck, or moving improperly, it is called a subluxation. This results in a horse which has little flexibility in his spine and becomes resistant, stiff, and unable to perform his work properly. He will most likely develop a sensitivity to touch and show discomfort when you saddle or ride him.

The horse has 31 vertebrae in his spine, and his spinal column has nearly 200 joints. The spinal cord passes through each vertebra. A network of nerves branches off the spinal cord and exits between each pair of vertebra, traveling and sending messages to the body's muscles and organs. Numerous muscles are attached to the vertebrae, enabling the spinal column to flex and bend.

There are many situations in a horse's life that can cause a subluxation, and they don't always have to be traumatic, such as a fall or getting cast in the stall. Subluxation can be caused by several little stresses that, over time, might build into something painful. When you notice that there is a problem, you should always consult your vet for a thorough examination. That way, you can be sure you know the real culprit to your horse's pain. Your vet may even refer you to a qualified chiropractor, saving you the trouble of searching for one on your own.

The chiropractic visit

Each chiropractor may have a different way of approaching exams and making adjustments. But during a typical exam, the doctor makes the horse walk a straight line then a circle to observe how the spine and pelvis are moving. Then, the doctor checks acupuncture points with his or her fingers to feel the tone of the muscle and how the horse reacts to being prodded (any flinching away from light touches indicates a problem). Palpating the horse's body, the chiropractor will check for motion and where there should be motion to see if all vertebrae are moving with each other. Some chiropractors massage the horse first as part of treating the horse's soft tissue. Then they perform the bone adjustments. This should take just about a ½-hour. After finding any joints that need manipulation, the doctor uses a quick thrust of one or both hands, in a sort of sideways push, to restore normal motion.

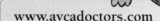

Don't take the doctor's word that he or she is a qualified equine chiropractor. Some might not have formal training. Make sure the doctor who works with your horse is accredited with the American Veterinary Chiropractic Association, as only veterinarians and human chiropractors are accepted into the AVCA's extensive 150-hour training course.

INTERNET

www.avcadoctors.com

Use the AVCA Doctors' web site to search for an AVCA vet in your area.

■ **The first stage** *of the chiropractor's assessment of your horse will involve watching the horse move around in the arena to judge the function of the spine and pelvis.*

The equine masseuse

In addition to chiropractic care, many horse owners have found that their mounts benefit from sports massage therapy. Massage has been used on humans and other animals for centuries, with documented use going back to ancient cultures. As an alternative therapy, it complements traditional Western medicine because it is noninvasive. Massage increases blood supply, which actually nourishes muscles as well as flushing out any built-up toxins. It relaxes tight, tense muscles and can even help heal soft tissues. Massage therapy can allow horses to have a better range of motion (for instance, in jumping).

During massage, endorphins – the body's natural painkillers – are released and help to alleviate the horse's pain.

Similar to massage and chiropractic, equine acupressure is another noninvasive therapy, meaning it doesn't penetrate the horse's skin like acupuncture does. It stimulates specific energy points in the horse's body that have been proven effective in maintaining and restoring vitality and strength in the body. These meridian points, as they are called, have been studied and charted by the Chinese for over 3,000 years. In recent times, through the use of electromagnetic research, the location of these points has been confirmed, and more widespread use of this therapy has resulted in better health for horses (and people).

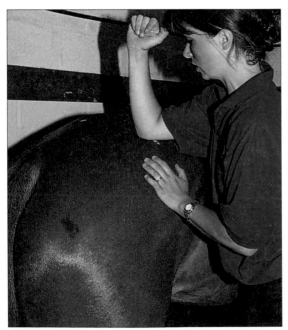

■ **Massage treatment** *relieves cramping and knots, and can help to reduce any swelling.*

Choosing the right remedy

To determine whether your horse might need alternative therapy, you should have your horse seen by your regular vet for a thorough exam. But you can give your vet the heads up early by reviewing your horse's current performance and alerting the vet to any problems you see. Here is a list of symptoms that might mean that your horse could use a therapy such as chiropractic, massage, or acupressure:

- Behavioral changes
- Obscure lameness
- Unusual shoe wear (such as the toe has been dragged)
- Head tilting
- Abnormal posture when standing
- Resistance to bend, or shorter or longer strides
- Cannot jump or pick up leads

Dentistry

JUST LIKE YOU, your horse must visit the dentist. But, his checkup is not designed to see if he's cavity free or if his teeth are pearly white. It's to see how efficiently he's chewing.

Why examine teeth?

A horse's molar teeth grow constantly. When a horse eats, his jaw's grinding motion, combined with the forage he eats, helps wear down his teeth. When the teeth wear down evenly, it helps the horse to break down the food most efficiently. So it's important that his teeth are in a good state. The sooner you can catch a dental condition, the more comfortable your horse will be carrying his bit and listening to your rein communication.

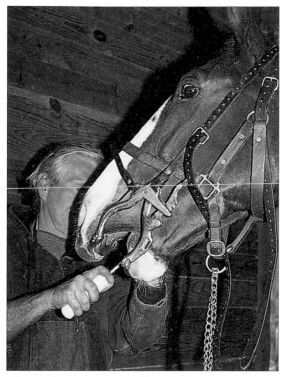

■ **Dental treatment** *usually includes rasping off any sharp edges, which can affect the horse's chewing.*

Make dental health checkups a part of your horse's routine twice a year. All licensed veterinarians have a degree in dentistry, but there are also equine dentists who are not veterinarians. Many of them work in tandem with a vet.

Most horses don't have a perfect bite. Instead, over time, the horse gets little sharp points, "ramps," and angles, which can lead to jaw problems and food-digestion troubles.

The dental exam is much different from ours. A horse usually won't hold his mouth open for the procedure, so a special dental speculum is often used to help him open wide and say "ah." Your vet will check the upper and lower molars to see if there are points, called hooks, or uneven surfaces. The most common procedure to eliminate these hooks is called floating, where the vet inserts small files on the end of thin rods into the horse's mouth, and rasps down the sharp points to give the horse an even chewing surface. This procedure has to be carried out on a regular basis for ***parrot-mouthed*** horses and older horses.

> **DEFINITION**
>
> A **parrot-mouthed** horse *has an overbite, and in some extreme cases looks like he has bucked teeth. This condition is inherited.*

Natural herbs and more

SINCE ANCIENT TIMES, plants have been used for medicinal purposes. Even today, many of our drugs are derived from herbs. From garlic to witch hazel, herbs are said to help horses with common ailments and even behavioral problems. They have been formulated to boost immune systems (helpful when traveling from place to place), soothe irritated soft tissue, reduce pain and swelling in joints, and stimulate the circulatory system.

GARLIC

Other herbs are designed to help calm nervous horses, perk up lazy horses, and, believe it or not, get rid of mare PMS. Even racehorse trainers have said that some herbs can be used in place of Lasix, a drug used for horses with bleeding lungs. Some people turn to herbal remedies because of concerns about the high incidence of ulcers that may be caused by feeding synthetic additives or medications. With natural herbal products, many owners feel more confident about the long-term well-being of their horses.

Don't use herbal remedies prior to a show. Many herbal blends designed to strengthen and calm the nervous system contain valerian, which may register when horses are tested for banned substances under current horse show rulings.

There are many herbal blends available through tack shops and catalogs that offer ingredients that are safe and tested to maintain quality standards. For the lay person, it's a good idea to rely on these rather than concoct your own homemade remedies. While herbs are natural, they can also be pretty potent. A trained herbalist knows which herbs to combine to offer the best solution to your problem. You should also check with your vet that you have diagnosed your horse's condition correctly and that it is safe to use herbal remedies in place of regular medication.

■ **Witch hazel** *can be used as a muscle liniment, a coat cleanser, and even as a natural insect repellent.*

All animals are individual and have different needs. Some will respond better to faster acting herbal liquids, while others to the gentle, long-term benefits of pure dried herbs.

Supplement smart

Your local drug store will have rows and rows of vitamins, minerals, and supplements. It's no surprise that horses have nearly the same number of supplements available for them. Whether your horse is an athlete, an old timer, or young and growing, he might benefit from extras in his diet. Your vet will be able to evaluate the quality of hay that is available in your area and determine if supplementation is necessary. Based on your horse's age, general health, and his workload, the vet will make suggestions concerning supplemental vitamins. See Chapter 12 for information on vitamins and minerals.

There is no regulatory body for equine supplements, and they can vary in the quality and effectiveness of ingredients. Read as much as you can on a particular product to determine if your horse will benefit from its use.

INTERNET

www.dropinbucket.com

This is one of many web sites offering alternative remedies online. There is also information on how to find a holistic practitioner for your horse in your area.

There are supplements that are designed with a certain task in mind: some improve hoof condition, some help put weight on a slender horse, some aid in improving coat condition, and some can prevent certain types of colic, such as sand colic. There are other supplements called nutraceuticals. These have more medical properties. They get their ingredients from synthetic sources as well as unusual sources, such as bovine tracheal cartilage, perna mussel shells, shark cartilage, and even seaweed.

The bottom line for you is to determine whether your horse needs a supplement in the first place. If you're interested in enhancing his performance, or maybe preventing a certain condition, one or more specific supplements may have a place in your feed room. But if you decide to go that route, remember that, because these products are not regulated, it would be wise to do a little homework before scooping them into your horse's feed bucket.

■ **Feed supplements** *containing vitamins, minerals, and other dietary additions come in both dry and liquid forms.*

Homeopathic options

Homeopathy is becoming a more recognized and respected branch of nontraditional medicine. It was developed in the 1800s by Samuel Hahnemann, a physician and researcher. Homeopathy is based on "like is cured by like." For instance, for a patient who had a terrible fever, Hahnemann would use an herb – in very diluted form – that would cause feverish symptoms in a well person.

Homeopathy is based on the premise that its treatments stimulate the body to heal itself, and that it works with the body's natural forces. The remedies are prepared in a way so that they are nontoxic. Homeopathic remedies are generally not designed to be given continually over extended periods of time, so once desired results are obtained, the remedy is decreased or stopped altogether.

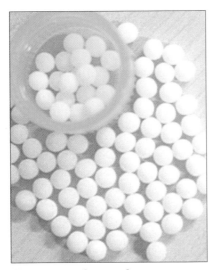

■ **Homeopathic medicines** *can be given to the horse in miniature pill form along with a treat or in its regular feed.*

How homeopathy is used

Homeopathy has been used to treat colic, lameness, skin disorders, and behavioral problems. A tiny dose (usually in the form of drops or miniature pellets) is given orally. Remedies are created by making serial dilutions alternating with violent shaking, called succussion. Succussion was thought by Hahnemann to bring out the medicinal properties of the substances.

Sometimes the substance is diluted by as much as 10,000 times – meaning that there's very little of the original substance remaining in the final solution. This has the advantage that side effects that come with regular doses of medicines will not be a problem. However, it also makes it hard to understand how the substance can benefit the horse either. In fact, there hasn't yet been any research that scientifically proves that homeopathy works, although answers regarding its effectiveness will come as more research is done.

Herbals and homeopathy are not one and the same. While they may sometimes use the same plants, herbals are often aimed at soothing the symptoms of the illness, while homeopathic remedies are about getting the immune system to tackle the cause.

Be very careful about giving any sort of treatment to your horse without consulting a veterinarian first. In some countries, you can face prosecution if you fail to get proper treatment for an animal in your care. Only a qualified veterinarian should attempt to diagnose an animal's condition.

Therapy options

IT'S HARD TO SAY WHETHER human athletes benefit from research gleaned from the equine athlete or whether it's the other way around. In any event, what's good for human competitors is also good for our horses.

Heat therapy

One way to help the body's repair process is to use heat therapy. While debate exists as to exactly when heat should be applied following an injury, warmth does have many benefits. Once initial swelling has subsided, heat therapy increases blood flow to the injured area, which carries oxygen and nutrients to promote healing and decrease pain. Heat is also an effective way to relax muscles and joints, especially in horses suffering from arthritis. Used before exercise, it can increase flexibility in the joints.

Heat therapy should only be used later on in the healing process. Do not apply heat immediately after an injury as this will make any inflammation worse. If you are unsure, check with your veterinarian first.

Heat can be applied with a warm hose or a hot cloth, but today you can also deliver therapy in the form of gel packs, which go up to about 170° F (77° C) instantly. Hydrotherapy machines are also available that deliver both heat and massaging movements to injured areas. Some heat packs combine herbs and essential oils to provide your horse with soothing aromatherapy, too.

■ **Heat massage treatment** *involves applying heat via pads attached to various muscle groups on the horse's body. This treatment is effective in alleviating muscle strain.*

Cold therapy

One of the most basic, and yet most beneficial therapies for your horse's hard-working legs is cold. Cold therapy helps decrease blood flow and swelling, and it reduces pain. Your horse doesn't even need to be injured to benefit from cold therapy. While you should definitely apply cold whenever you feel heat or swelling in an area, many riders also use cold therapy as a preventative measure after a hard workout.

To maximize the effectiveness of cold therapy, limit cooling sessions to no more than 15 to 20 minutes every 2 hours. More than that and tissues can be damaged. Too much cold can slow down the healing process.

■ **Cold water** *is applied by hose to the legs to relieve any bruising, or swelling.*

There are a number of options to choose from, including affordable attachments that turn a regular hose into a hydrotherapy machine, with pulsating water that can be sprayed on the affected area. Cold boots or cold wraps, which are either placed in your freezer or have ice added to them, are also popular.

Light and sound

Treatment using radiation of light is called light therapy. Visible red light penetrates tissue close to the surface and can be used to treat cuts and skin infections. Infrared light reaches deeper tissue, such as bones, joints, and deep muscle. Light therapy can increase circulation by encouraging the formation of new capillaries, which in turn speeds up the healing process by carrying oxygen and nutrients to an injury site. It also increases the production of collagen, an essential protein for repairing damaged tissue.

Light therapy stimulates the release of adenosine triphosphate (ATP). An increase in ATP allows cells to accept nutrients faster and dispose of waste products, increasing cell energy level.

■ **Mobile laser therapy units** *enable the veterinarian to apply light radiation directly to the site of the horse's injury.*

Low level lasers with adjustable frequencies have been created for home use. Handheld units are used in horses to promote wound healing, reduce pain, treat trauma, discourage **proud flesh**, decrease postoperative swelling, and reduce arthritis. The latest battery operated units are even able to detect acupunture points and apply laser light to these automatically.

> **DEFINITION**
>
> **Proud flesh** *is puffy, granular flesh that sticks out from a wound and won't heal. It's similar to scar tissue.*

One of the newest therapies for horses incorporates infrasound (the same type of sound by which whales communicate). This type of sound travels in low-frequency waves which are below human hearing, but which can affect body tissues. Infrasound has been used to treat a broad spectrum of equine problems such as colic, trauma, arthritis, muscle soreness and swelling, and has been an asset in encouraging relaxation.

Magnetic therapy

Magnetic therapy is often the source of heated debate among traditional veterinarians, but other vets may actually recommend it. In really basic terms, when magnets are applied with the proper polarity, intensity, and frequency, they are said to create a magnetic field that penetrates soft tissue and bone. This is supposed to allow increased blood flow to the area, promoting healing and regeneration. While magnetic therapy is not recommended right when the horse injures himself (ice is best during the first 24 to 48 hours), it is used generally to treat such problems as bruises, abscesses, laminitis, and navicular disease, or when increased circulation is essential.

A simple summary

✔ Many holistic and alternative remedies exist for horse owners to select from.

✔ Chiropractic, massage, and acupressure therapies are noninvasive methods for treating unsound or injured horses.

✔ Dental checkups are part of your horse's regular health regimen.

✔ Ask your vet whether your horse can benefit from supplements.

✔ Cold therapy helps injured areas by reducing swelling and soothing pain.

✔ Heat, light, sound, and magnetic therapies all help increase circulation and stimulate the body to heal itself.

PART FOUR

Two Become One

ONE OF THE MOST EXCITING ELEMENTS of being around horses is riding. There are few activities more fulfilling than communicating wordlessly with your horse and having her respond to your cues. With so many different activities to participate in once you have mastered the basics, you may want to expand your horizons and try a variety of riding disciplines before settling on just one.

Chapter 16

Becoming a Better Equestrian

MOST PEOPLE SAY THAT THEY KNOW how to ride a horse. What they really mean is that they know how to sit on one. To really ride, however, is to communicate your instructions to your horse so that she responds when you want her to, and performs what you've asked. Real riders have their share of setbacks and triumphs, from little kids competing with their ponies at their first show, to Olympic champions. While you don't have to set lofty goals for your riding, you should be comfortable in the saddle and able to deal with most situations that trot your way.

In this chapter...

✓ **From passenger to rider**

✓ **Fear busters**

✓ **Moving on up**

YOU CAN PARTICIPATE IN A HOST OF EQUINE ACTIVITIES, INCLUDING RIDING ON VACATION

From passenger to rider

WHAT MAKES A GOOD RIDER? Is it being able to look tall and elegant in the saddle? Is it the skill of the cowboy who leaps aboard his steed and, with a good kick, gallops off into the sunset? Or is it the achievement of competition wins?

■ **A good rider** *knows how to ask the horse effectively to perform certain movements, so that the horse willingly obliges.*

A good rider enhances the horse's performance, rather than detracts from it. Good riders don't interfere with their horses or cause them pain or discomfort.

When people start out riding, they're not much more than passengers. It takes time and coordination to learn how to influence the horse's way of moving. Rudimentary riding skills such as steering, stopping, and going are just the foundation on which to place your other riding building blocks. Your cues (aids) become a broader language that you can use to communicate more complex movements. This enables you to get exactly what you want from your horse.

Riding technique

At the top end of the scale is dressage, which most equestrians would say is the most complex and involved type of riding. The rider sits nearly immobile and gives very subtle cues to the horse. The dressage horse receives many years of thorough training, and she is tuned in to the slightest muscle changes and weight shifts of her rider, and to the barest flicker of pressure on the reins. The rider cues the horse almost imperceptibly, and yet the horse responds by performing complex movements such as changing leads at every stride, pirouetting, trotting in place, and elevated prancing.

Dressage may be considered the most complex form of riding, but reining horses, jumping horses, and even horses used for cattle sorting all need to be trained beyond the basic cues.

A well-trained horse

The reason some horses are so well mannered and easy to ride while others seem to be headstrong or stubborn is usually due to a combination of lack of training for the horse and poor riding by the rider. You tell can a well-trained horse from the way she travels around the arena. For example, she will have her head slightly tilted to the inside instead of gazing outside the ring and disregarding her rider. She will accept light tension on the reins by bringing her head down instead of flinging it up sky-high like a giraffe (a high-headed horse can ignore her rider's rein aids). When the rider lightly pulls on the reins (or simply closes the hands like squeezing a sponge), the horse will immediately halt. When asked, the horse quietly steps into the canter, moving in a controlled fashion; she doesn't trot faster and faster until she finally breaks into a canter. She can also do more than just go forward; she can also back up in a straight line or move laterally, performing sideways movements.

Advanced aids

Western and English riders use aids differently. Generally, for basic arena and trail riding, it's essential to know more than just "kick and go." Your legs provide energy to the horse. Not only do you squeeze with your lower legs or give a little kick with your heels to go, but you can also get your horse to move in other ways. Use leg pressure against one side, from heel and calf, to make a horse move away from the pressure.

■ **Use pressure** *from your lower legs to get the horse to move in the direction you want.*

This will result in a sideways movement for the horse, such as a *side-pass* or a *leg yield*. If you place your inside leg at the girth and your outside leg slightly behind the girth, this will result in a horse moving with a slight bend – a flex that is desirable while riding in an arena.

*A **side-pass** is like a side step. The horse crosses the right feet in front of the left while moving sideways rather than forward. In a **leg yield**, the horse moves both forward and sideways, eventually moving across the arena in a diagonal line.*

Contact is a friendly connection between you and your horse via the bit and rein. You always want to be in communication with your horse, so hold the reins until you can feel the slack taken up completely. Your leg helps to "push him into the contact."

You can help your horse bend by placing a little tension on the inside rein. Good riders never let the reins just flop along. They must be kind to the horse's mouth but also effective. Hold the reins so that there is contact with the horse's mouth.

Your first fall

It's going to happen sooner or later. All riders fall off their horses, and it can be a scary experience. Admittedly, most folks who experience a gentle fall often relay the story as if they'd come off a bronco at the National Finals Rodeo, but that's because it's so unexpected. Understand, however, that falling is a normal part of learning, just like when you were learning to ride a bike. And take heart in the fact that the better rider you become, the better chance you have of staying in the saddle!

So let's say that you're out riding and your horse sees something out of the corner of her eye that startles her. She reacts by spooking, and you're caught a bit off balance. In a split second, you realize that you're not going to be able to stay on. If you do feel you're coming off, your best bet is to simply let go. If you struggle to stay on, you could put yourself in harm's way by pulling and twisting to regain your seat.

Experts have conflicting opinions about the proper way to fall off. Some say that you should fall loose because, if you tense up and try to break your fall, you might end up breaking a limb. Others say you should pull yourself in as tight as you can, so that an arm or leg doesn't end up underneath the horse's feet. The truth is, it's hard to perfect your fall when you've never had one, and it's REALLY hard to be thinking about your form when you have no time to prepare.

When you fall, do not hold on to your reins; you could damage your arms and shoulders trying to hang on. You could also be dragged and possibly trampled if you don't let go. Kick yourself free from the stirrups, try to push away from the saddle, and let go of the reins.

Fear busters

I'VE MET A COUPLE OF EQUESTRIANS who love being with their horses. They groom them to shiny perfection, lavish affection, and dole out treats for their equine charges. Yet, when it comes to swinging in the saddle, they have a terrible sense of dread. What is it about riding that can be frightening to some, yet still not deter people from being with horses?

Nearly every rider at one time in his or her life has been scared. There are different reasons for being afraid. Some riders only fear certain things: windy days; their horse's fast canter; or the possibility the horse will bolt, buck, or rear. Other riders become uneasy after they've experienced a fall, and often riders who are pushed too hard by their instructors begin to dread the saddle. If you start becoming afraid of riding, don't beat yourself up about it. Anxiety about riding is real and can set you back in subtle or serious ways.

The effect of fear

Riders transmit their fear to horses through their body language. You might think this is ridiculous, but your horse can feel your muscles tense, your breathing change, your body stiffen, and your posture alter.

Some horses are more easygoing than others. But because horses are prey animals and used to living in herds, your fears may trigger a horse's natural instinct for flight, resulting in your horse shying, running away, balking, or ditching you.

If you feel tense or anxious about riding, this can affect your progress as a rider. Some riders tense up and get stiff through the back and seat, or become rigid in the arms, hands, and legs. Other riders do exactly the opposite by reverting to zero communication with their horse – loose reins, no leg. Others still opt for a combination of the two.

■ **The tension or anxiety** *you feel can be communicated to your horse, making her less responsive to your aids.*

Identifying the cause

The first step to overcoming your fear is to acknowledge the reasons. To get back in control, many psychologists recommend that you get to the root of your fear. You may discover that you are afraid of being physically hurt. After all, a fall several feet can result in bumps and bruises, but it can also cause broken bones or worse. You may fear being embarrassed by your horse or your lack of knowledge. Some riders report that their instructors move too quickly for their comfort level – what we call overfacing the rider. Other people fear competing at a show.

> ### Trivia...
> Some of the top riders play a mental "video tape" in their minds of their ideal performance. This technique puts them in a positive frame of mind, making them more likely to win.

After identifying your fear, try to discover the cause. Did you have a frightening experience when you fell off your horse and got the wind knocked out of you? Did seeing a friend get seriously injured after a fall make you frightened to ride? If your fear stems from physical pain, you should work toward improving your riding in an area where you feel safe – for example, a small riding ring instead of the large community arena.

Watch other more experienced, successful riders to see how they handle their horses. You can learn a lot by watching good riders and using them as a mental picture for your own riding.

Expand your knowledge base to help improve your riding. Read books and watch videos. Perhaps listen to a sports psychology audiotape to help you understand how to conquer your fear. It's also important to have an instructor who is supportive of you. Your teacher shouldn't badger you into riding beyond your current capability.

Self-confidence boosters

If it's your horse that is scaring you, you're not alone. Many people get into a situation where their horses are too much for them. Take a break from her and see if one of your friends will let you ride his or her more sedate horse for a while. Riding a mild-mannered mount will help you to increase your confidence and better your riding skills.

■ **Riding in a group** *will help to boost your confidence, especially if others in the group are experienced.*

Building your self-esteem

You can build up your self-esteem by logging in as much riding time as possible. Green riders are generally more timid and cautious – even apprehensive. But as the green rider gets more experience – especially positive experience – confidence, as well as knowledge, grows. If you believe that you just don't have that much experience, but you still have the guts and desire to stick it out, frequent successful rides will raise your comfort level as well as your skill.

Set reasonable goals so that you can meet them comfortably. It doesn't do you much good to tell yourself that you have to be ready to compete in the show finals if you aren't quite ready for that level of riding. Take, instead, a realistic approach, and set your goals to be able to walk, trot, and then canter on the correct lead. When you accomplish this, you will be that much closer to conquering your fear or anxiety.

Thinking positively

Be positive about your sessions on horseback, and keep a perspective about your riding. The world won't end if you mess up in a lesson or at a show. You'll nearly always get another chance to try again! But if you're still having a tough time dealing with fear after you try a few methods to conquer it, talk with a sports psychologist who understands the unique relationship riders share with their horses. It can help you get back in the saddle with a smile.

RELAXATION TECHNIQUES

Mental relaxation techniques, such as deep breathing and meditation, will counteract the stresses of riding and help you to control your fear. Try taking up Yoga, Tai Chi or Pilates: the exercises will improve your posture and muscle tone as well as focus your mind. You can also try using visualization techniques to boost your self-confidence. Picture the perfect ride: an easy walk, a smooth trot, and a flowing canter. Imagine your horse halting at your command and cantering off at the touch of your leg.

■ **Practicing relaxation** *techniques will help to calm nerves and relax tension in the mind and body.*

Riding friends

Nothing enhances a riding relationship like having barn buddies. Riding with a friend is not only good for social reasons, but it's also safer. If you were riding alone and something happened, there would be no one to come to your aid or summon help.

Equestrians are wonderfully social. Find chat groups online through various equine bulletin boards, and see if you can meet up with other horse men or women in your area.

If you have your horses on your own property, it might be difficult to meet other equestrians. In rural areas, your neighbors are not exactly a stone's throw away, so you might have to ride to a community arena to find others. Alternatively, your riding instructor might know someone looking for a buddy.

REASONS FOR HAVING A RIDING BUDDY

Having a friend to go riding with can help give you confidence and make you safer in several ways:

1. Your buddy can trade off setting up jumps or trail obstacles during practice

2. Tack and riding clothes exchanges are instantly made more convenient

3. You'll have a person to split a big sack of carrots with before it goes bad

4. You'll have someone to compare notes with at shows and other horsey events

5. Trail rides are safer and more enjoyable

6. You'll be able to give someone else pointers on their horsemanship for a change

7. Trailering fees to shows can be split in two

8. No one will gossip about you at the barn in your friend's presence

9. Lifting bales of hay is no longer backbreaking

10. Lifelong friendships can be made

Moving on up

A RIDER ISN'T MADE overnight. It is a lifelong quest for most riders to become the best that they can, and the learning process is never-ending. There will always be more you can achieve.

■ **Health and vitality** *are essential prerequisites for an able rider and a responsive horse. Make sure you are both keeping fit and well.*

The fit horse

A horse in a fit condition will be able to cope with longer rides, more intense training, and the stresses of traveling and competing. A horse that is a little run down, out of shape, or undernourished will not be able to stand up to the rigors of extended exercise. She will also be less able to fight off illness.

As you increase demands on your horse, don't forget to support her with the energy resources that she needs to draw from. Correct nutrition improves a horse's well-being as well as helping her body and mind function.

Although your horse won't need the carefully devised diet of a racehorse, she will still need the right energy-boosting foods. (Of course, it is important that you don't over feed her on days when she is not exercising.) You may also decide to add supplements to her feed to keep her immune system in good shape.

Fitness indicators

You can tell if your hose is in good condition by observing and feeling her body. Her neck should be firm and well developed but not **cresty**. She should have muscle definition in the haunches. There should be no channel running down her spine, nor should her hipbones jut out or her flanks be hollowed. You should be able to feel her ribs, but not actually see them, when prodding her sides.

The key to getting your horse fit is to keep sessions on the short side at first and then build upon them daily. Don't push her too hard right away or she could sustain an injury. Warm her up sufficiently before you start any real work by trotting for about 5 minutes on a loose rein. In between sessions, give her walk breaks before loping off again.

> **DEFINITION**
>
> A **cresty** neck is the top arch of the neck exaggerated by extra fat deposits and muscle. Stallions often have these thick, curved necks.

The fit equestrian

There's a misconception that all you have to do to ride is sit there and let the horse do the work. Remember the first times you dismounted and noticed how sore you were? That's because you use all kinds of muscles not only to help you cue the horse correctly, but also to help you balance yourself properly during your ride. Riding doesn't require brute strength, but it does require you to think of yourself as an athlete. Unfortunately, unless you have a string of horses to ride every single day, you're going to need to find an additional type of exercise to help you keep up with riding's physical demands. Sore muscles can give you a satisfied feeling after a workout. But riding can also take its toll on you as well. If you're out of shape, it's going to make you feel exhausted even after just a few minutes of trotting. If you're over your ideal weight or the basic couch potato, you'll feel like you need to find a place to lie down and rest after a strenuous ride.

*B*UILDING *STRENGTH*

Different areas of your body need to be fit and toned so that you can cue your horse properly.

- **Arms and shoulders:** Your arms should be toned and supple so that you can guide your horse without hanging on her mouth for support. You should also have enough strength to stop a runaway horse
- **Legs:** Your legs should be very strong because they are your anchor in the saddle. Your thigh and calf muscles combine to tell your horse to go forward, to move right or left, or to help you rebalance
- **Back and stomach:** Strong lower back muscles definitely help protect you from a backache as well as help you absorb the horse's movement and maintain your upright posture

■ **Regular weight training** *and resistance exercises, in addition to your riding sessions, can help you to stay effective in the saddle.*

Increasing your stamina

To increase your overall endurance, add another sport to your training program. A routine with jogging, bicycling, or swimming helps strengthen your cardiovascular system as well as tone muscles. If you have access to a pool, swimming is particularly good for increasing your heart rate and lung capacity without putting any extra stress on your joints. Doing any extra exercise at least twice a week, combined with your riding time, can turn you into a fit athlete.

If you can't get out of the house to exercise, you can still get an effective workout with a fitness video, step routine, or a set of floor exercises.

Obviously, the more time you spend in the saddle, the more comfortable and effective you'll be as a rider. Practice makes perfect!

■ **Select a form of exercise** *that you find interesting and challenging so you won't lose your enthusiasm for it.*

A simple summary

✔ Fine-tuning your aids will help direct your horse to perform more advanced requests.

✔ Falling off a horse is a natural part of learning to ride.

✔ Riding can cause anxiety at one time or another, but there are methods to conquer fear if you identify and address it properly.

✔ Riding with a companion will help to give you confidence in your riding and is wise for both companionship and safety reasons.

✔ There are two athletes involved in a successful riding partnership, so make sure that both you and your horse are physically fit to perform.

Chapter 17

You Show Off!

AFTER ALL THOSE RIDING LESSONS – those hours logged in the saddle honing your skills – are your only rewards aching muscles and a sore bottom? Of course not! You can find your prize in the form of a horse show ribbon. Competing at a horse show not only tests your riding talent against others, it also provides affirmation from another professional – a judge – that you're on the right track. So if you're willing to test your mettle for a medal (or rosette), you can come home not only with an award, but also with a definite sense of accomplishment.

In this chapter...

✓ **The horse show**

✓ **Are you ready to compete?**

✓ **Choose your class**

✓ **Off to the show**

WINNING A ROSETTE IS A HUGE ACHIEVEMENT FOR BOTH OF YOU

The horse show

IF YOU'VE BEEN PRACTICING your riding for some time and feel a competitive spirit, a horse show is a great place to be. As a participant, you have the opportunity to measure all that you've learned over the previous months. It's exciting and rewarding (and even a little nerve-racking, for some.)

Horse shows are divided into classes. There are classes for different abilities, age groups, and riding styles. There is usually just one judge who presides over the arena. He or she watches either from the outside in a booth or from the middle of the arena, as the horses and riders perform. From the criteria of the class, the judge selects the individuals who best meet the ideal.

Judges will look at how both the horse and rider are turned out as well as at how they perform.

■ **Hunters-over-fences** *is one of the many types of show class that riders can compete in.*

RIBBONS

Ribbons are awarded for different placings. Most shows give out ribbons up to fifth place, while others go all the way up to tenth place. Each ribbon has a color that corresponds with its place:

- First: Blue
- Second: Red
- Third: Yellow
- Fourth: White
- Fifth: Pink

- Sixth: Green
- Seventh: Purple
- Eighth: Brown
- Ninth: Dark Gray
- Tenth: Light Blue

- Championship: Blue, red, and yellow
- Reserve championship: Red, white, and yellow

Are you ready to compete?

COMPETITION IS NOT AS EASY as it looks. It may seem that all you have to do is turn up, go around an arena for a few minutes, and then the judge, seeing how wonderful you and your horse are, gives you first place. But there's a lot more to it than that. First off, your horse might be a little apprehensive once you get him in different surroundings.

Second, you will probably be distracted by the strange show ring yourself. There's a lot of commotion at a horse show, and factors such as traveling, unfamiliar show grounds, and different arena footing, not to mention show-day jitters, will affect your performance. The key is to select a show that is appropriate for your current level of riding. To start with, many trainers suggest entering classes that are slightly below your current level, since riders often go on "auto pilot" and don't ride as effectively as if they were at home.

DEFINITION

*When a judge **pins** a class, he or she is assigning places to the top few competitors – picking out the winners in order.*

Types of shows

At the entry level of competition are schooling shows. These competitions have been developed for novice riders. They feature the same types of classes as regular shows but are geared toward the beginner. The judge is prepared to see a few mistakes and botched rides – even a few falls. Sometimes, the judge takes time to speak to each rider just before the class is ***pinned*** in order to offer friendly and constructive criticism.

Local shows, 4-H shows, open shows, or unrated shows are also good competitions to look out for when you're starting out. All of these shows are based more on fun and learning than on cutthroat competition. Rated shows are tougher. They are assigned a letter rating according to their level of difficulty. A C-level show is lower than a B-level. Often, C-Level is held for just one day and offers classes geared more for novice riders. At a B-show, the competition is stiffer, the horses more experienced, and the judging more nitpicky, but these shows still allow ample room for learning. B-shows are often held over two days, usually on a weekend.

Rated shows are assigned their rating by the United States Equestrian Association (USEA) and are sanctioned and governed by this organization.

The crème-de-la-crème are the A-shows. The riders – who hold membership to the USEA – are skilled; the horses are groomed to within an inch of their lives; and the tack is expensive and immaculate. The riding apparel is the finest; the judging is critical; and the horses are extremely schooled and mannered. A-shows do offer classes for novice riders, but they are in a different league to schooling shows.

What to wear for English riding

Like most sports, riding does have its own uniform. At schooling or local shows, you can get away with putting together an affordable outfit before taking the plunge and splurging on the latest, most expensive styles seen at rated shows.

English show apparel includes the hunt coat, shirt, breeches, boots, and helmet (called a hat in Britain). The hunt coat should be dark such as navy blue or hunter green. Newer, trendier colors include various shades of brown, olive, and charcoal black. They feature two vents that drape across the back of the saddle gracefully, and four buttons up the front. The sleeves are long so, when your arms are in riding position, your wrists are covered.

The riding shirt is occasionally referred to as a ratcatcher. Where this name came from is somewhat of a mystery, but nowadays most savvy riders just ask for a show-shirt at the tack store.

The riding shirt is one item of clothing where the hunt-seat rider can show a little more flair. Show shirts come in a lot of colors, from plain white to bold stripes and patterns. Riding shirts for women come with a matching detachable band at the throat called a choker (often monogrammed with the rider's initials). Men wear cotton dress shirts with a button-down collar and a conservative tie.

■ **Show classes** *in England vary from their American counterparts in attire and tack requirements.*

English boots are always black and tall, fitting snugly along the calf and coming up to the back of the leg so that they crease ever so slightly at the back when the leg is bent. Hunt seat riders wear field-style boots, which lace up at the top of the foot.

Breeches are available in many different colors, but for the show ring, you should select a light color. The most prevalent color seen in the ring is khaki, although various versions of beige are also suitable.

If you have a schooling helmet and are riding at your first show, you can get by with placing a black cover over it. However, anyone who is serious about showing should wear black velvet. Show rules require junior riders to wear a safety helmet with a harness and a chin strap. As a final touch, add black gloves. Jewelry should be kept to a minimum and hair should be neat and kept above the collar (that means pin your hair under your helmet or put it in a net and clip).

What to wear for western riding

Western riders have more leeway in what they choose for their riding apparel. Riders can opt for colors and styles that complement their own particular style and their horse's coat color. At small schooling shows, you'll see a lot of western riders going casual, with crisp jeans, a long-sleeved western shirt, boots, belt, and western hat. While most riding clothes can be bought off the rack for smaller shows, at the upper end of the scale, it's custom made all the way.

INTERNET

www.ryegate.com

The American Hunter and Jumper Foundation's web site is dedicated to promoting this branch of English riding with its own shows and championship.

Although western riding apparel is much more casual in style than its English counterpart, you will still need to make sure that your riding clothes look immaculate whenever you take part in a show.

For men, simplicity is the name of the game. Well-starched shirts are worn in earthy colors, jewel tones, or plaids. Women, however, usually get more of a kick out of putting together something snazzy. For many years, cropped jackets and vests worn with tuxedo shirts were the favored uniform for rail classes. Anything with glitter and spangles to catch the judge's eye was worn. Today, vests are still popular, but now they are usually paired with bodysuit-style turtlenecks – and while there's still a bit of glitter to capture the judge's attention, it's all done in moderation.

As far as western pants are concerned, the men tend to wear jeans, usually in blue, black, or a neutral earth tone. Women have the same choices or they wear show pants, which are similar to a polyester trouser. These show pants give the rider a sleek look underneath matching chaps.

Western hats

Your hat should be one of the items you spend the most money on. An ill fitting or cheap hat will scream "amateur." Basically, you want a hat that is shaped along the crown (the top part where your head goes) and brim. The shape varies by riding discipline and where you live. Fur *felt* hats in light colors with names such as silverbelly, sand, and buckskin are popular, but you can never go wrong with black. Finely woven straw hats (not the kind you see at the fair for 5 bucks) are also popular summer show hats. Hat quality is measured by a series of Xs. Most rabbit felt hats are either 3X or 5X, while the beaver fur blends tend to be 10X or 20X. Pure beaver fur hats can bear the symbols 100X and upward.

Besides your hat, chaps are another item where quality shows. Chaps, made of suede or smooth leather, need to match the rest of your outfit and fit properly. They must ride high at the waist, be snug through the leg, and be cut long enough to drape across the top of your boots and cover your heel. The front should not gape or form a pouch.

CHAPS AND HAT

Western accessories

Rules regarding women's neckwear have relaxed, so many wear beautiful silver accents at the throat, instead of a tie. Jewelry can be pronounced, but tasteful. Belts with a silver trophy buckle finish off the outfit (you can buy a silver buckle if you haven't won one yet). Hair should be neat and stylish, with no hint of a rodeo queen 'do. If you're competing in showmanship, you'll sport a longer blazer style jacket and show pants. Horsemanship classes have bodysuit-style blouses that are the same color as the rest of the outfit. Now that you're all dressed up, you'll need somewhere to go!

■ **The correct riding clothes** *are designed for comfort and practicality as well as style. Always take the time to make sure your clothing and equipment are up to scratch.*

Choose your class

*FIND THE SHOW that's right for you by searching for one with the help of a knowledgeable horse friend who can tell you what level is best for your first outing. Your best bet is to start with a schooling show. You can find one in your area by checking the bulletin boards at the tack store, the classifieds in your local horse newspapers, or by calling community equestrian centers. Once you find a show, call for more information and ask for a show **premium**.*

DEFINITION

*A show **premium** gives you any pertinent information on the show, including a list of all the classes, starting times, parking and stabling availability, and the schedule of fees. It may also be called a prize list.*

Trivia...

Showing originated in medieval Europe, when horses were put up for sale at trade fairs.

When you look over the show premium, pick out some classes that sound interesting to you. Classes vary from show to show, and from one part of the country to another. A show that has western and English events running on the same day will have a more all-purpose feel to it than a hunt-seat or western-only show. Here are the types of classes you might come across as well as an explanation of what will be expected from you. Remember to choose a type of class that suits the riding you are accustomed to doing at home.

English classes

In hunt-seat equitation, your ability to control and show off your horse is being judged. You will show at the walk, trot, and canter in both directions and then line up. Occasionally at larger shows, the judge may ask for a collected trot (smaller strides but with the same cadence as the regular trot) or ask that you ride without your stirrups.

In the hunters-under-saddle class, the horse is judged on his manners, obedience, and responsiveness. The winning horse moves freely on a light contact with the rider's hand at the walk, trot, and canter in both directions. In hunters-over-fences, the horse is judged on his jumping style, pace (which should be even), and manners, together with his way of moving over the course of at least eight fences. There is no "rail work" and each competitor is judged alone in the ring. In the hunter-hack class, the horse is judged along with other competitors at a walk, trot, and canter, then each rider must complete a course of two fences and may be asked to gallop and halt individually.

The English pleasure class is developed more for breeds such as Morgans and Arabians shown in full bridles and flat "Lane fox" saddles. The horse is judged on manners, quality, performance, presence, and apparent ability to give a good pleasure ride. English country pleasure is a variation of the English pleasure class, and is designed for gaited horses such as Saddlebreds and National Show Horses.

Western classes

Western classes call for horses with easy dispositions. In western pleasure, the horse is judged at a flat-footed four-beat walk; free-moving, easy-riding two-beat jog; and a three-beat lope both ways of the ring, on a reasonably loose rein without undue restraint. The judge may call for extended gaits.

In the trail class, riders must demonstrate how quickly and easily their horse can negotiate the sorts of obstacles found out on the trail. The horse is required to work over and through obstacles: negotiating a gate; carrying objects; riding through water, over logs, or simulated brush; riding down into and up out of a ditch without lunging or jumping; crossing a bridge; backing through obstacles; side-passing, mounting, and dismounting from either side; and more.

INTERNET

www.nsba.com

The National Snaffle Bit Association promotes western pleasure horses ridden, trained, and shown in snaffles.

The western riding contest is designed to assess the skills and characteristics of a horse performing in a simulated ranch situation. Horses should be sensible, well-mannered, and free-and-easy moving, and tasks should be completed with reasonable speed. They are judged on the riding qualities of their gaits, flying changes of lead, response to rider, manners, and disposition over a prescribed looping pattern.

Rated shows follow the USEA rules. Breed shows put on by their governing association also have their own rulebooks. Open shows often use USEA guidelines, but they can make amendments themselves since they're not sanctioned.

The horsemanship class is judged on the correctness of the rider's seat, hands, and feet; the finesse in riding; and the strength of lines and angles as the competitor rides a series of maneuvers in a 30- to 60-second pattern devised by the judge and posted on the day of the event. Judges can ask for circles, spins, and more.

■ **Walking through a gate** *is one of the skills demonstrated in western trail-class competitions.*

Off to the show

IT'S NEARLY SHOW DAY! Now that you know what classes you're in, all you need to do is get ready. The day before, you'll need to gussy up your horse to his finest. Since you're riding at a smaller show for the first time, you won't have to go the whole nine yards of braiding mane and tail (hunt seat) or banding the mane (western). But you should make his appearance as slick as possible.

First, you'll be giving him a trim with electric clippers on various areas of his body. If you're unsteady or inexperienced, have a knowledgeable friend help you. Start at the muzzle, and shave off all the long whiskers. Take the longer hairs that run from underneath his jaw down to his chin as well.

Always use the right sized clipper blade. The higher the blade number, the closer the shave. A number 10 blade is good for most trimming.

■ **Clipper blades** *should be cleaned and oiled after each use.*

Next comes his bridlepath. This is where the mane grows behind his ears on his neck. The top part of the bridle, the crownpiece, lies in this spot. Here, the mane shouldn't be longer than 2 inches (5 cm), just so that the bridle lies flat. The edges of your horse's ears should also be trimmed to provide a neat appearance. All of the fuzzy hair along the outside edge should be whisked away. Most show horses at the higher rated shows have all of their hair removed from the inside of their ears.

Inside hair protects a horse's ears from insects. Do not remove this hair or your horse will have no protection. If you do shave the inside of the ears, place a fly net over them when your horse is not being ridden.

Then, go to his feet and trim the long hair that grows at his fetlocks. It's okay to shave in the direction of the hair, since the shaving will blend better. Make sure the mane is pulled to a show length (see Chapter 13) before you move to the wash rack. Then, shampoo your horse's coat, and condition his mane and tail. Make sure that he dries completely, and, if you have a clean horse sheet (that lightweight blanket), place it on him. Now put him back in his stall.

A lot of horses roll after they have a bath – seemingly trying to undo all your wonderful efforts. Make sure your horse's stall is free of manure before setting him loose.

Final preparation

Lastly, it's time for the final prep. Get all your tack and supplies together for the next day. Clean your tack thoroughly by using leather cleaner, then follow up with a leather conditioner. Each product has its own instructions on the bottle, can, or box, so follow them carefully for lustrous leather. Check that the protective clothing your horse will wear in the trailer is ready.

Pack what you need in the trailer or truck judiciously so that you won't be dashing around the show grounds desperately searching for a forgotten item. Load all your feed, tack and equipment, grooming kit, and personal items. Then get some rest. It's show day tomorrow.

INTERNET

www.asha.net

The American Saddlebred Horse Association promotes the breed as well as competitions for saddlebreds.

SHOW DAY CHECKLIST

Rider Equipment

- Belt
- Boots
- Chaps
- Gloves
- Hair accessories/net
- Hat or helmet
- Jeans or breeches
- Mirror and brush
- Money
- Safety pins
- Shirt
- Top or jacket

Tack & Equipment

- Bridle
- Extra lead rope
- Extra towels
- Fly spray
- Girth
- Grooming kit (brushes, hoof pick, mane and tail brush)

- Hay net and hay
- Longe line and longe whip
- Manure fork/ muck bucket
- Water bucket
- Sheen spray
- Saddle pad
- Saddle

■ **You'll need** *to bring a lot of supplies with you, but don't take your entire tack room.*

Preparing for your class

You are one of the first people to arrive at the show grounds. Park in designated areas only, and ask anyone who looks official (walkie-talkies are a giveaway) where to rest the trailer. If you're tying up your horse next to someone else's, give your neighbor plenty of room. Sign in for your classes, pay your fees, and pick up your show number. The judge will identify you by a number worn on your back or on your saddle blanket.

233

SHOW NUMBER

DEFINITION

*The **in-gate** is the entrance (and often the exit) to the show arena.*

If your classes are in the afternoon, chill out for a bit, but if you're in the fifth class of the day, start grooming and tacking up. Head for the warm-up ring, and try to get your horse steady and responding to your cues. Keep track of what is happening. Don't leave it till the last minute to get to the ring: Be near the ***in-gate*** by the end of the class prior to yours.

Now the moment of truth, where all your hard work pays off. Enter the arena, look around to see how many other riders are in the class, and space yourself as evenly as possible. You're not officially judged until the announcer says so – try to select a place where you're not going to be blocked in by anyone else.

If you get bunched in behind a rider, look for a place to pass without impacting the other riders.

When the class begins, follow the instructions of the announcer for gait or directional changes. For classes where you're the only one in the ring, you'll have the judge's full attention. Put your skills to the test with a smile, look up, and focus on displaying your best horsemanship. Ride your course to the best of your ability and give your horse a pat at the end of your round.

■ **Your horse will appreciate** *the chance to familiarize himself with the strange sights and sounds of the show arena.*

Mind your manners

The show arena is a place where you can realize your dreams, but you can also be caught in a nightmare. Show etiquette and good sportsmanship are the signs of a seasoned show rider. Don't try to bend the rules or you'll not only anger fellow participants, but you'll look inexperienced.

More often than not, the warm-up ring is the source of many riders' headaches. Often they're full of distracted participants, or rushed coaches trying to give last minute instructions. Remember that, like driving, it's left shoulder to left shoulder when passing a horse going in the other direction. Keep an eye out for little kids, other green riders, or fractious horses. Call out any special position you need in the arena: "rail!" if you need to remind someone of your direction; or "head's up" on a set of warm-up fences.

Give a clear berth to horses with red ribbons in their tails (it mean's he's a kicker), and allow space in between horses in case you need to maneuver quickly. If someone falls off, halt your horse until the horse has been caught and the rider gets up (or has someone attending to him or her).

■ **Keep your commands** *calm and clear. When you're in the class, don't look out for the judge and then harshly correct your horse afterward just because you're out of his or her sight.*

Good sportsmanship

If you get the blue, don't do the end-zone dance. Instead, accept your first with graciousness, and thank your equine partner for his good performance. If you don't get the blue, and were expecting to do better, don't cuss under your breath or blame your horse. Instead, evaluate what made the winning ride, and try to emulate that in your next class. Judges do remember those riders who punish their horses outside of the arena. They also recall the temper tantrums of ill-mannered competitors who throw lesser ribbons in the trash. Equally, judges remember the rider who enthusiastically accepts that pink ribbon and praises the horse for his hard work.

You might not be aware of it, but often judges are still evaluating you, even when the class is pinned and the riders have left the arena.

After the event

Your day is over. Pack up quietly so you don't distract other competitors. Deposit any manure or trash in the proper places. Pull away from the show grounds slowly, so you don't spook horses or make clouds of dust. As you drive home, you can recall the day's events with satisfaction and contentment.

A simple summary

✓ A horse show is a great opportunity to measure and assess all that you've learned over the previous months.

✓ The correct show apparel, your basic uniform for the sport, should be conservative for English and complementary to your horse for western.

✓ Select the classes that best suit your riding level and current riding style.

✓ Preparation for a show day includes special show grooming, tack cleaning, and packing equipment.

✓ Follow show etiquette so that you and your fellow competitors have a positive show experience.

✓ Judges remember good sportsmanship as well as they remember ill-tempered competitors. Make sure you control your emotions.

Chapter 18

Other Events

While competing at a horse show is fun for many riders, it's not for everyone. If you're seeking new exploits outside of the arena, there are still many different ways for you to participate in competitive events and fun activities. Some of these equine endeavors have been around for decades, while others are just becoming hot right now. For the adventurous, the sky's the limit.

In this chapter...

✓ **Organized trail rides**

✓ **Learning adventures**

✓ **Riding at home and abroad**

✓ **Interesting sports**

✓ **Play days**

TAKE IN THE SPECTACULAR SCENERY ON YOUR TRAIL RIDES

Organized trail rides

I AM AN ARENA RIDER, BORN AND BRED. So when the opportunity comes to take my flighty show horse out on the trail, I look at it as more of a chore than an adventure. But one day, my endurance-racing friend invited me to participate in an endurance ride. It completely changed my outlook on riding in the great wide open.

Organized trail rides are appealing to many different types of riders – depending on the event. Some events are based on whoever gets to the finish line first, while others emphasize equitation and horsemanship.

Endurance riding

This is essentially cross-country horse racing. At entry level, there are limited distance rides of around 25 to 30 miles (40 to 48 km) long. Most of the main competitions, however, are 50 miles (80 km) or more. The endurance elite cover 100 miles (160 km) within 24 hours. Multi-day rides cover 50 to 60 miles (80 to 96 km) per day, up to five days in a row.

Vet checks throughout the event ensure that horses are not over-stressed. If a horse's vital signs do not return to a resting baseline fast enough, the horse is held back until they do. If she does not recover to the vet's satisfaction or is unsound, she is pulled from the race.

The first horse to get across the finish line wins – unless she finishes in poor condition.

Endurance riding offers a coveted "best conditioned" award for the horse with the highest marks through the vet stations – and she may or may not have been the race's winner.

■ **In endurance riding,** *horses can be disqualified for crossing the finish line in poor condition. This is to discourage riders from pushing the horses too hard.*

Is endurance riding for you?

First off, think about how your horse will cope. Arabians are the reigning kings of endurance rides, since they have evolved over centuries to be excellent distance horses and have exceptionally efficient metabolisms. But other breeds or breed crosses do well too – even mules have shown up first at the finish line. No matter what breed of horse, the endurance candidate has to have good, sound feet and legs, as well as resilience, stamina, and a positive outlook on the trail.

A horse that gets into a lather the moment her feet touch the trail might be too high strung for this type of competition. Your horse needs a "steady-Eddie" attitude to be able to remain unruffled in the midst of the starting-line commotion and the chaotic vet stops along the way.

Endurance riders are also a unique breed. Since most events are held in remote areas, an enjoyment of camping is a must. Stamina is important for the riders, since they spend a lot of time in the saddle – hours at a stretch. Definitely outdoorsy people, they like a good laugh, a horse with personality, and a challenge. Endurance riders also know their horses backwards and forwards. They are constantly monitoring their horse's vital signs and soundness so they know at any moment if their horse is feeling up to snuff or not.

Endurance is a very social sport. Participants know each other from previous races, and there is a true camaraderie on the trail. An added bonus is that it lends itself well to family participation, as junior riders can accompany adults, and your nonhorsey friends can work as your "pit crew" at the vet checks.

While many of the top riders have a certain strategy and science to their game, most of the "amateur" riders use the philosophy "to finish is to win." There's a sense of accomplishment knowing that you and your horse are conditioned well enough to tackle dozens of miles on the trail successfully.

Competitive trail rides

If you'd like more discipline to your regular trail ride, you might try competitive trail riding (CTR). This sport is a blend of equitation, horsemanship skills, and trail manners. Like endurance riding, CTR takes place on trails of up to 50 miles (80 km) in length. Beginner rides usually start at 15 miles (24 km), and the average ride is 35 miles (56 km). But, unlike endurance riding, the first horse across the finish line isn't always the winner. From the time you arrive at the camp until the ride finishes, you're being judged.

INTERNET

www.aerc.org

The American Endurance Ride Conference is the official sanctioning body for equine endurance rides in the United States and Canada. This web site gives news, information, competition dates, and rankings of competitors, as well as help for newcomers.

Trail-riding evaluation

In competitive trail riding, you're scored on everything from your equitation to how well your tack fits and how obediently your horse navigates the trail.

There are different divisions for various abilities in CTR. Novice is ridden mostly at a walk. Competitive Pleasure features 20 to 30 percent trotting. The Open division requires the rider to tackle the course mostly at a working trot throughout.

Your camp set-up will be evaluated, so you should not only be tidy, but you should also look after your horse properly, with correctly tied hay-nets, filled water buckets, safety knots, and the like.

Trivia...

The Western States Trail Foundation sponsors the Tevis Cup, one of the most famous American endurance races. Horses must cover 100 grueling miles (160 km) of rocky trails and hills in one day, beginning just after 5:00 a.m. The event is held late July or early August on the weekend closest to a full moon to allow riders to have their night ride illuminated.

Before the ride, staff will go over the trail maps, point out any amendments to the map or any difficulties you might encounter, and answer your questions. Once the ride starts, various staff members will be checking on you. You are not allowed to ride in groups, since you're evaluated at obstacles individually. You'll acquire points with each judged obstacle completed. The veterinary staff will check your horse's pulse and respiration (if it does not meet the criteria, you could lose points or be disqualified). The competition doesn't end just because you've completed the course, either. Back at camp, you'll still be judged on how you take care of your horse: how you cool him down, put up his tack – you get the point. You're finally done after the last vet inspection, when all the points are tallied up and a winner awarded.

The basic requirements

Arabians may be endurance champs, but nearly any well-conditioned, sound horse can compete in CTR. A winning horse has to be good-natured, willing to listen to his rider, and responsive to all requests. There will be plenty of challenges, both natural and human made, so the horse has to be accustomed to a variety of situations such as walking through water, going through gates, and dealing with obstacles. Sound conformation is still important, but it's not crucial like it is for endurance.

Is competitive trail riding for you? If you enjoy displaying your best horsemanship, dealing with details, and you don't mind being under the judge's watchful eye, you'll do well. CTR is ideal for those who like to get away from civilization, but not too far; and for those who like a good challenge but also like the finer points of riding.

INTERNET

www.natrc.org

The North American Trail Ride Conference (NATRC) is one of a number of competitive trail ride organizations in the United States. This web site gives all kinds of helpful advice on getting started in competitive trail.

Learning adventures

IF YOU'RE ENJOYING your lessons a great deal, perhaps you'd just like to continue your horsey education. Today's rider has a host of learning adventures at their disposal, with education vacations springing up all over the world. Anyone who loves horses and wants to improve their skills can participate. You can travel across the nation or to the other side of the world and ride a host of differently trained horses – maybe even some that are very advanced – and learn from internationally renowned instructors.

■ **Education vacations** *can be pretty intense, but they do provide exceptional training opportunities.*

Some schooling opportunities include better barrel racing with the nation's foremost trainer; dressage instruction coupled with sports psychology; John Lyons certification program for those interested in learning natural horsemanship; and cross-country jumping in Ireland. You can even go to cowboy school to learn what it's like on a cattle ranch (complete with learning to lasso and other cowboy skills).

If you are not particularly interested in learning new skills or improving your riding, don't book an educational riding trip. These trips are run by experts in the field and operate differently than most dude ranches or resort vacations. You will find them hard work.

These intensive learning programs are similar to going away to camp. While they may have the trappings of a regular vacation, education vacations emphasize riding instruction. Management will take riders on a case-by-case basis and class sizes will be limited. You'll be expected to work at your studies. Anyone not in good physical condition should probably stay home. You'll need to bring correct riding attire and be prepared to have intensive sessions, but you can expect to have a positive training experience. Once you return home, you can enjoy showing off your newfound skills.

Riding at home and abroad

LET'S SAY YOU'D JUST LIKE to get away and not have such a concentrated educational encounter. There are still many chances for you to enjoy a trip that involves riding. Ranch-based vacations and trail tours are definitely the way to go if you're looking for fun in the saddle.

Prices vary, so do your homework. Obviously, camping in the United States is going to be less pricey than a week in the wilds of Ireland.

On a ranch vacation, you can round up cattle, rope and brand, or participate in other working ranch operations. Both working ranches and dude ranches can turn you from a city slicker into a real cowhand. Most dude ranches have more luxurious accommodations than a working ranch, and these also offer activities for nonhorsey family members. At either locale, you'll have the opportunity to do scenic trail rides daily on horses of various abilities.

HORSE VACATIONS

I strongly recommend that you go through an established booking agent. This can be a full-service travel agency specializing in horse vacations, or it can be an organization that has tested these trips for you. Booking agents help you coordinate your holiday, and you'll have the assurance that they've successfully sent many others to these fine destinations. Here are the top agencies in North America:

- Equitour Fits – Worldwide riding holidays, (800) 545-0019; e-mail equitour@wyoming.com
- Cross Country International Equestrian Vacations, (800) 828-8768; e-mail xcintl@aol.com
- Hidden Trails, (604) 323-1141; e-mail vacations@hiddentrails.com

■ **Relaxed trail riding** *is a great way to explore the country as well as practice your riding skills.*

Unlike ranch vacations, trail tours are offered the world over. On a trail tour, plan to spend a lot of time in the saddle with spectacular countryside as your backdrop. Trail tours usually move from one set point to another and may provide lodging along the way. These rides range in length from a weekend to a few weeks. Some trips involve packing into the outback, while others will have your luggage and belongings schlepped to you the next stay. While some might have you camping under the stars, others may offer luxury accommodations so that you can slip into a warm bath after 8 hours in the saddle. Either way, you're sure to get to know your fellow riders and make some friends along the way.

Interesting sports

UP AND COMING SPORTS that once had only a smattering of devoted followers are gaining popularity as more folks get involved. Some of these sports may seem rather specialized, but they are open to all ages and abilities.

Vaulting

If you've ever dreamed of being Nadia or Olga, you'll love vaulting because it is basically gymnastics performed on the back of a horse. Vaulting involves three individuals: the vaulter (or team of vaulters), the horse, and a person who longes the horse in a circle. The longeur has control of the horse, so the vaulter can be free to perform a variety of movements as the horse canters along. Most riding disciplines showcase the performance of the horse, but in vaulting, the horse acts as the stabilizing force and underlying impulse of the vaulter's artistic performance.

Vaulting goes back to Roman times and to the Bull Dancers of ancient Crete. Today's gymnastic event using the vault evolved from the equine version.

Indoor polo

Polo is considered one of the oldest team sports in the world, and can be traced back to Asian nomadic warriors over 2,000 years ago. It used to be considered only as a game for the wealthy, since a whole string of ponies was needed to complete a game. But then arena polo came along, making the game more widely accessible. Arena polo was designed to be played in a smaller, enclosed venue. The dimensions of the playing area are the same as in grass polo, but in feet instead of yards. Only one horse is needed for each player and only three players, rather than four, are on the field for each team. With some adaptation, arena polo follows the same rules of grass polo.

Play days

SOMETIMES IT'S JUST NICE TO PLAY – and that is what play days were invented for. Play days are similar to games you'd play at a company picnic (except you're on horses). They involve contests – usually done at speed – and, while they're geared for kids, some play days are also for the kid at heart. You'll see plenty of silly races and games, as well as the events featured at a **gymkhana**.

DEFINITION

Gymkhana (*pronounced jim-ká-nah*) *originates in India and means "games on horseback." These competitive mounted games are usually timed, and they can either be for individuals or teams.*

At a play day, you'll see a whole range of different speed events, such as barrel racing, keyhole racing, flag racing, and stake racing. Each event involves a starting line, a task (such as looping around the barrels, dashing through poles, or carrying a stake from one bucket to another), and a finish line.

■ **Play days involve a huge variety** *of horseback games and competitions for all ages and abilities. Not only are they great fun, they also help riders develop important skills.*

Everyone's a winner

The great thing about play days is that there's no judge, no favorite, no prejudice – just the one who comes in with the fastest time wins. Then there are other contests of "skill", such as the egg-and-spoon. Like the one at family outings, you need to keep your egg on the spoon no matter what gait the announcer calls for. Laughs and spilled yokes make this and similar events a refreshing change from plodding around an arena.

Play days and gymkhanas might be hard to find in certain areas. If this is the case, why not organize your own event with your friends? To get a start on how to set up an equestrian event, the American Quarter Horse association can provide rules for a variety of timed events. The good folks at the AQHA can be reached at (806) 376-4811; www.aqha.org.

Trivia...

In England, a major competition for under 15 year olds, known as the Prince Philip Cup, is held anually. Team members require great skill and agility to complete a series of high speed mounted games.

Play days are fun days out and don't have the same competitive edge as more formal riding competitions. If you are just starting out on the competition circuit, play days may be the best way for you to gain experience and confidence in your ability to perform in front of a crowd. They are also a great way of introducing your horse to the excitement of the competition atmosphere.

Even if your horse isn't appropriate for showing, you can take part in gymkhana events, as horses are not judged on appearance.

A simple summary

✓ Endurance rides pit stamina and strategy against a grueling long-distance course. The horse must not be over-exerted to win, or she may be disqualified.

✓ Competitive trail rides emphasize equitation and horsemanship over speed and strength.

✓ Riding vacations – both at home and abroad – can expand your horizons and improve your skills.

✓ Up and coming sports are a pleasant alternative to the basic riding disciplines, while play days provide a fun way to compete.

PART FIVE

Harmonious Fellowship

YOUR HORSE CAN BE a willing partner, but sometimes he might need a little help understanding exactly what you want him to do. Consistent training will help iron out most of the problem situations you might encounter. Make sure to break things down in steps that your horse understands, and you will enjoy a more successful relationship.

Chapter 19

You're in Charge

OKAY, WE HAVE TO ADMIT IT. Our horses are not perfect. They don't always behave as we'd like or follow our commands exactly to the letter. But if you wanted to ride a machine that did everything you asked, you'd be on a motorcycle. A 1,200-1b (540-kg) animal that wants to push you around, however, is not only a bully, he's also dangerous. That's why all horses – young and old – must receive solid training so that they don't take advantage of you. If you're consistent with your training, you'll ultimately have a fine, upstanding citizen of the equine community.

In this chapter...

✓ **Be the boss, not bossy**

✓ **Tackling training questions**

✓ **What is a vice?**

Be the boss, not bossy

"YOU GOTTA SHOW 'EM WHO'S BOSS," the old cowboy snarls. In the old days, people were pretty tough on horses. They'd let them grow up with hardly any human contact, and then bring them into a corral and break them. A horse would be roughly saddled and a rider would climb aboard and hang on through the bucks and leaps. The term breaking was used because it was thought that the only way to take a horse from the wild to the saddle was to break his spirit.

Today, most horses are not trained to carry a rider this way. Horses are started under saddle, not broken. But while the training method is not nearly as aggressive or extreme as it once was, the message still is clear: we're the teachers and horses are the students. If a horse gets good grades, there won't be any remedial classes for him to take.

Horses are incredibly large and powerful animals. If they want to, they can definitely throw their weight around (just look at the bareback bronc events at the rodeo.) Some crafty equines will try to "test" you by throwing a little challenge in here and there to see if they can be the boss. You just have to reiterate your position as the herd leader.

How to correct, not punish

When a horse misbehaves, it's not the same as the cat clawing the furniture or the dog peeing on the rug. You have to figure out how to a) let a mischievous or untrained horse know he's done wrong, and b) show him how to do it the right way. Horses learn best through consistency. If you're a little lax in your instructions or late on your correction, it will take your horse a lot longer to grasp the concepts.

Horses respond to rewards. As a trainer, you have to reward the slightest positive attempt your horse makes with a pat or through your voice. Some trainers use food rewards – even from the saddle – but most praise

■ **Giving your horse a food reward** *immediately after he performs a desired behavior will encourage him to keep that habit.*

can be done without treats. Punishment is not an effective training method. There is about a 3-second window during which you can let a horse know that he did wrong – after that, he cannot associate a harsh discipline with the misbehavior. So doing silly things such as tying your horse up for an hour to let him "think about what he's done" simply doesn't work.

Horses learn by repetition. They perform their tasks better once they become familiar with what you're asking them to do. Repeating exercises regularly helps to consolidate their lessons.

Whips and spurs are considered artificial aids, rather than instruments of punishment, because they are not designed to mete out reprimands. They are designed to reinforce your natural aids (seat, leg, voice, and hand).

Think like your horse

We need to understand the pecking order society of horses to know how to act around them and how to train them properly. When we have problems with horses it's because we assume that our relationship with our horses is an equal partnership – it's not. The rules of the herd are that there is a dominant member. For safety's sake, you need to make sure that the dominant one in the partnership is you.

■ **Herd animals** *such as horses establish a strict order of dominance within their numbers. Your horse needs to understand that he is below you in the hierarchy.*

Communicating with horses

If you ever watch two horses together, you'll see they "speak" to each other with subtle and not so subtle body language. By learning to use this language yourself, you can make use of their signals when interacting with horses and get the results you want. For instance, horses use a dominance display to get a subordinate horse to back down. If you take on this dominant posture by standing tall and moving swiftly into the horse's personal space near his shoulders, he should immediately become submissive. If he doesn't, you'll have to follow up as a dominant horse would – with a physical reprimand that is given out swift and strong, but without anger. Then go back as you were, without dwelling on the incident.

Getting your message across

Horses see situations as black and white. That is why you need to be extremely clear in your instructions so that your horse understands what you are after. For example, say you want to get your horse to trot. Yet when you squeeze with your legs, nothing happens. Do you just keep squeezing? No, not only because you are desensitizing him to your leg aids, but he may not have understood what that first squeeze meant. Instead, give the horse a good thump with your leg to tell him, "Hey! Wake up! I'm up here and I want you to go." The horse will probably be startled and react by trotting off. By instantly praising him for his response, the horse knows that was what you wanted. Then you would slow the horse down to a walk, and ask again with a slight squeeze of leg. Now he's awake and anticipating something, and most likely he will trot off, doing exactly what you want. Again, you'd reward him to reinforce the good behavior.

Horses learn when you make the right thing easy and the wrong thing difficult. Let's say you have a horse that doesn't stop when you say, "Whoa." When he ignores you, use an exercise that instead puts him on a circle for several revolutions, making him work a little harder for disregarding your easier request. The horse will quickly learn that it is easier for him to respond to the "Whoa" request than to have an even harder task given to him.

THE IDEAL HORSE

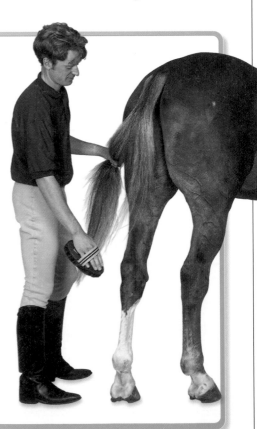

Saddle manners:

- Stands quietly for mounting
- Moves off with regular, even steps
- Does not exhibit nervousness on the trail
- Moves off of your leg aids easily
- Picks up correct leads when asked
- Stops on a dime
- Does not show signs of mean temper

Ground manners:

- Enjoys being groomed without fidgeting
- Can be tied anywhere
- Picks up hooves for picking and shoeing
- Lets you clip and handle his ears
- Is not upset by tacking up

■ **A well-trained horse** *will stand calmly while you groom him, without fidgeting or pawing the ground.*

Tackling training questions

BOOKS, MAGAZINES, VIDEOS, and seminars abound with training suggestions from the cowboy way to new age natural horsemanship. Nearly all riders face a training issue in their lives, from horses that won't stand tied to horses that won't pick up their leads properly. Other horses might have nasty ground manners but are very well behaved when you ride them. The goal for all horse owners is to have a horse that is trained to be a good partner.

Remember that if you bought your horse a few years into his life, you will not know if he had any bad training experiences as a foal.

Not every training method works on every horse – just like not every teaching method gets through to every member of the class. Just seek the right combination of lessons that matches your horse's learning ability and be assertive, but not aggressive. Frightening your horse will not make the situation any better.

When to call a pro

There are some training issues that can be easily handled at home with the help of those training resources mentioned above. But some problems need to be addressed by a professional. How do you know when to call a real trainer? Use this handy checklist:

- When the horse seems to be getting worse, not better, from your efforts
- When you become more anxious about riding your horse
- When other habits begin to spring up, for example, aggressiveness
- When you acquire a green horse
- When you hit a plateau and cannot get past it with your horse

If you've ever watched a trainer who turns a horse from an unmanageable to a well-mannered mount, you might think that he or she has some magical powers that you don't possess. But it's really a case where the trainer understands the horse's learning processes and can better anticipate when the horse is going to test him or her. Horses who need training often are fine with experienced riders, but they "get away" with bad behavior when with a novice. Some of the more common training issues are shying, jigging, kicking, biting, bucking, and rearing. We owe it to our horses to give them the best training possible. A well-mannered horse is a joy for everyone to ride, while a bossy, obstinate animal is a liability to you and to others.

INTERNET

www.johnlyons.com

This web site is dedicated to the teachings of "America's most trusted horseman," John Lyons. Over the years, Lyons has developed his natural horsemanship into a training philosophy every horse owner can use.

Shying

Shying is when a horse is startled and leaps, twists, or bolts away from the source of his fear. By nature, horses can be quite timid, and their senses are developed to protect them from any bogeyman they find in their environment. They are built to run first, ask questions later. Therefore, the terrible monster they see in the grass might have just been a plastic bag on the ground, a bird fluttering by, a change in the position of an arena jump, or even a car backfiring. Some horses shy very quickly and violently, and these are the ones that riders find most unsettling. Since a horse shies most often because something unfamiliar scares him, you can make a spooky horse a little more confident by introducing unfamiliar objects in a safe setting. This gives him a chance to learn that unusual things can still be harmless.

A horse with a wandering eye and a wandering mind has a lot more opportunity to run into things that frighten him. Try to keep your horse's mind focused on what you are asking him to do.

Scary objects become less scary when they become familiar. Keep riding back and forth until your horse doesn't show as much interest in the scary object, then continue on. If he is frightened and won't go past an object, circle and try to approach it at a trot. He'll probably stop and try to turn or get far away. Keep pushing him forward with your legs, sit back and down in the saddle, and keep your reins even. If he obliges and goes by (even rushed) praise him for having the courage to go forward.

Shying can be caused by poor vision. If a horse cannot see an object until he is right on top of it, he will usually overreact. If you have a horse that consistently spooks, have your vet check his eyesight.

As a horse becomes accustomed to a variety of situations, he'll be less prone to shy. That's why you see young horses react to everything, while their unflappable older friends placidly ignore would-be monsters.

Jigging

Jigging is a term used for a horse that refuses to walk freely, but instead gets wound up and trots in mincing steps no matter how hard the rider tries to get him to walk. Jigging is a sign of nervousness, excitement, anticipation, or impatience. Some horses develop this problem on the trail, which makes it difficult to enjoy a leisurely ride. *Barn-sour* horses often jig all the way home. This habit means that the horse will have to be retrained to relax both physically and mentally.

> **DEFINITION**
>
> **Barn-sour** *describes a horse that won't leave his stable. Symptoms range from lackluster performance to refusing to be ridden.*

Curing a jigging horse can be a difficult process for a novice to undertake since it may require the rider to sit on a horse that puts up a fuss. Some trainers suggest introducing impromptu schooling sessions on the trail, where the horse is ridden in tight circles any time he starts to jig. Others suggest that, instead of immediately putting the horse away when returning to the barn, the rider continues the ride back at the stable or ties the horse to stand quietly before putting him in his stall. By not rewarding the jigging behavior, the trainer hopes to eliminate it.

A biting horse *lays his ears back and bites anyone who handles him. This aggressive behavior can be difficult to correct. Try being very firm and say "no" each time he does it.*

Kicking and biting

Kicking and biting are signs of aggression. Aggressive horses see that we are lower on the totem pole than they are, and they let us know when they disagree with our wants or actions. A horse that kicks out is voicing his displeasure that we are in what he considers his space or that we are giving him a task to do. A biting horse is also letting us know, in no uncertain terms, that we are doing something that he does not approve of. An aggressive horse uses these behaviors to try to chase us off, just as he would in a herd situation.

While these behaviors might need to be handled by a professional, you certainly don't want to be in harm's way in the meantime. Aggressive horses often try to kick when you are trying to get them out of their stalls. If your horse has developed this habit, you need to make sure you can get the horse to face you before entering the stall.

Do not stand behind a horse that has the potential to kick. Horses kick straight out and back, so if you are working around the horse, stay close to his flank at his side. The closer you stand to him, the less velocity he can get in his kick, and the less damage it will do to you.

Horses usually give you fair warning that they are going to bite or kick. Look for the swishing tail of an angry kicker or the pinned back ears of a would-be biter. By reading your horse's body language, you can often head him off at the pass. A firm "no" coupled with a smack with the flat of your hand can often remind the horse of his status and put you back on top as the dominant partner.

243

Bucking and rearing

One of the scariest things a rider can experience is a horse that bucks or rears. Not only is the horse refusing to do as he is told, he may even want you off his back. A buck involves an action from the horse where he humps his back, leaps forward, and kicks out with his hind legs. It is usually done because he is showing his displeasure. Some horses buck through sheer exuberance, however, such as show jumping horses who like to throw in a little extra kick after they jump a big fence. Other horses buck due to pent-up energy that they are trying to release.

Trivia...

Bucking broncos are not wild horses, but problem horses that didn't make it as regular mounts. They are made to buck through the use of a bucking strap – a leather strap that is tightened across the horse's flank and genitals to irritate him into bucking.

Some horses buck due to pain. Your saddle may not fit your horse correctly, and every time you sit in it, you might be digging into his back uncomfortably. If your horse has a bucking habit, feel his back for areas of soreness. Have the vet check him if you find he's extra touchy along his spine.

You can usually solve bucking problems yourself by giving your horse more exercise so that he isn't so fresh and feisty when you take him out for a ride. Also, ride assertively with firm rein contact so that he cannot get his head down to buck. A rearing horse, however, is extremely dangerous and you should summon a professional to deal with him. This horse refuses to obey your requests to go. Instead, he stands on his hind legs and rears up. If the behavior escalates, he may flip over backwards on you. A rearing horse must be taught that he has to go forward, no matter what.

■ **Seek professional help** *to deal with a rearing horse as this is a difficult habit to cure. Reasons for rearing may be that the horse is frightened or in pain.*

What is a vice?

CAN HORSES GET STRESSED OUT? The answer is yes. Stressed horses are almost always the product of a confined artificial environment. A lack of mental or physical stimulation can also result in a horse showing signs of stress. Horses manifest stress in different ways, from being hyperactive, to refusing to eat, to creating undesirable outlets for their nervous energy.

Compulsive behaviors, known as vices, are a sure sign that your horse is not adjusting to his environment or daily schedule. Cribbing, weaving, stall walking, and wind sucking are warning signs that all is not well in your horse's world.

Weaving

A repetitive side to side rocking motion, where the horse shifts his weight from one front foot to the other, is known as weaving. Usually done in the same spot in a stall, this activity can wear a trench in the stall floor over time. Weaving can cause uneven wear on horseshoes and will often make a horse's shoulder and neck muscles ache. Stalled horses are usually the only horses that weave – you'll rarely see this vice in pastured horses.

Stall walking

This vice is similar to weaving, although a horse has very little room in which to do it. Most stall walkers will encircle their stall continually in the same direction until they have a path cut. A horse that is usually in a paddock with other horses may pace his stall from nervousness of being alone.

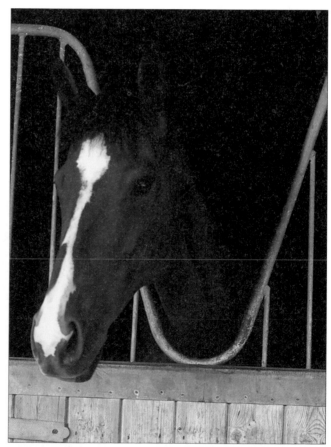

■ **Fitting an antiweave grille** *may stop your horse from weaving, or may just push him further back in the stall, where he can continue to weave.*

Wind sucking

A horse is said to be wind sucking when he bites down on a fence post, tree branch, or any horizontal surface; leans back; and sucks in air in rhythmic gulps. This action releases endorphins in the brain that gives the horse a kind of "high." Once this habit is acquired, it is nearly impossible to break. There are collars and restraint devices on the market that are supposed to inhibit wind sucking, but if these devices are then removed, the horse goes right back to the behavior.

Cribbing

Cribbing is the destructive consumption of wood, which results in chewed fence rails and occasional digestive distress – even colic. Generally, it is prompted by boredom, although some horses seem to develop a genuine taste for lumber, chewing away in pastures and paddocks.

Cribbing can often be prevented by painting your horse's favorite chewing surfaces with a special substance that tastes unpleasant. Occasionally the vice can be a sign of a metabolic problem caused by poor nutrition, so it is worth checking with your veterinarian that your horse is getting a balanced diet. He needs a certain amount of roughage, and you should also provide him with a free-choice mineral block to lick. Regular deworming programs are also a must, as parasite infestations can cause nutritional deficiencies.

■ **A metal strip** *fitted to the stall door may prevent cribbing but your horse may then move on to wind sucking, which is very hard to stop.*

Preventing vices

Behavioral problems and stall vices can be due to a number of factors, including fear, nervousness, or pain. Since vices are such abnormal behaviors, you need to get at the root of the problem to have any success in eliminating them. It is worth remembering that horses have not evolved to live in the closed environments we keep them in. In the wild, food and water would not be put in front of a horse in a prepared form, and much of his day would be spent grazing. In his natural habitat he would have vast amounts of land to cover in any one day, providing him with both physical exercise and mental stimulation. There would also be dozens of other horses to interact with.

Vices are the horse's reaction to being confined and, ultimately, bored. The best way to prevent a horse from developing a vice is to keep him fully occupied both physically and mentally. Here's a few tips for preventing boredom (if you run out of ideas, your local trainer might be able to give some helpful advice):

- Give your horse plenty of exercise
- Move your horse to a stall where he can see or interact with other horses
- Get your horse a companion – even a barn cat or a rooster will do
- Put a toy up in your horse's stall, such as a large ball or cone to toss around
- Split up his meals, so that he can munch on hay throughout the day
- Install metal mirrors at eye level in your horse's stall
- Place objects like tires on the floor of the stall to prevent stall walking – your horse will have to pay attention to where they are and step around them

A simple summary

✔ Let your horse know that you are the dominant individual in your partnership.

✔ Horses learn through consistency, repetition, and reward, not through fear and punishment.

✔ Professionals understand the learning process and know when a horse is testing them.

✔ Common misbehaviors, such as shying and jigging, can often be corrected by owners, while horses that bite, kick, buck, or rear are often best left to the professionals.

✔ Horses that have vices are manifesting their stress by creating strange behaviors as an outlet for their anxiety.

Chapter 20

Parenthood

I T CROSSES NEARLY EVERY MARE OWNER'S MIND – wouldn't it be great to have a baby? Foals are adorable creatures, and breeding your own horse sounds like a good idea if you want to create the horse of your dreams. But breeding and raising a colt or filly is a big undertaking and plenty of preparation, research, and prenatal care must take place before the baby is born. So think about all the benefits and drawbacks to breeding your mare – it is a big responsibility, and a lifetime of commitment.

In this chapter...

✓ **The baby question**

✓ **Pregnant mare care**

✓ **The birth process**

✓ **Growing up**

A MARE LICKS HER NEWBORN FOAL TO STIMULATE ITS CIRCULATION

The baby question

BREEDING YOUR OWN MARE certainly sounds like a wonderful idea. You get to create a new life and have your horse's genes passed along to another generation. Some people dream of breeding the perfect baby that will take them to the top shows, since breeding is cheaper than purchasing a trained show horse.

But there's a lot to think about before checking out the ads for stallions. First, you have to consider whether your mare is appropriate for motherhood. A horse with bad conformation or a poor disposition will most likely pass these faults to her young. Unless you would be truly happy with a younger version of your horse, you should pass on breeding her.

Should your mare be a good candidate, you'll next have to select a sire. This takes some research, since the stallion not only needs to have a proven performance record and pedigree that appeals to you, but he should also have traits that complement your mare's. And don't just go by the price of the stallion's stud fee or the fact that he's located on a nearby farm. Cutting corners can bring disappointing results.

You'll also have to take into account where you will raise the foal. Do you have room on your property to keep another horse? If you board your horse, would the stable allow you to raise a baby there? Do you have enough in your budget to board your foal at a farm where he has room to grow?

The stallion's temperament is very important. While studs are often dominant creatures and need to be handled by experienced breeders, a stud that is too aggressive or ill tempered can pass these traits along to his offspring.

Finally, how patient are you? It takes at least 3 years for a foal to mature enough to be ridden. Three years is a long time to wait. If you're not the one to do the training, you'll have to include a trainer's expenses to start your youngster under saddle. It may turn out that your affordable solution to having a show prospect is just as pricey as buying a horse that is already trained and ready to go.

■ **Take a look at the existing offspring** *of the stallion so you can be aware of any undesirable behavioral traits.*

The mating season

A mare carries her foal for 11 months. Most mares are bred in late spring so that their foals will be on the ground in early spring the following year, after the frost. Mares begin to go into *season* as early as February, and can cycle all through summer and even into early winter. Estrus starts when a fertile egg is released from the ovary. It occurs about every 4 weeks. Being in season can affect the mare's personality. She may become more temperamental when ridden or may exhibit a wilful attitude while in her stable. A mare in heat urinates frequently and turns her rear to other horses, especially in the presence of an interested gelding.

DEFINITION

Being in **season** *is the term for estrus, a mare's heat cycle. A mare usually experiences heat cycles starting in the spring. The cycles last anywhere from 2 to 10 days, during which the mare will be at the optimum time to breed.*

Selecting the stallion

Once you have decided to breed your mare, the next step is to select the right stallion. If your mare is purebred, you might want to breed to a specific breed – or you might want to breed for height, or performance, or even color.

You can find a stallion through various breed association magazines, as well as directories, breeding farm listings, and Internet sites. You might also contact your veterinarian or local trainer for advice. There are millions of stallions worldwide and you should consider as many as possible when picking your mare's mate. Stallion ads are made to sell the stallion's services. In this sort of advertisement, you'll see the stud posed and shiny, with a description that makes him sound like the world's most accomplished horse. But no matter how good he sounds, choose the stallion that is the best match for your mare.

■ **Promotional pictures** *are used to advertise stallions. This is from the royal stables, Abu Dhabi.*

Make a list of the things you really like about your mare and the things that you wish you could change. Using your list, search for a stallion with attributes to balance your mare's positive characteristics and with traits that can help correct her faults.

When selecting the ideal stallion, keep in mind these five elements: conformation; gaits and movement; attitude; performance ability; and mature offspring. Then, think of adding your mare into the equation and you'll know if the stallion is the right match for her.

Consider what you want to achieve with your foal, what you want her to ultimately do, and how you want her to behave and look. Will the stallion you have selected provide the traits you seek? Finally, you can finish your evaluation and make your decision.

The courtship

Horses used to be bred only through the method of "live cover," which meant that the stallion was present to impregnate the mare. Today, horse owners can have their mares artificially inseminated with frozen semen, which provides much more opportunity to select the ideal mate for your mare, no matter where the stallion lives. If you are going to have your horse bred the traditional way, you'll contact the farm where the stallion is located, and arrange to have your mare delivered to the farm around the week when she goes into season. She will stay on the premises until she is bred.

Sometimes a teasing gelding will be used to determine whether a mare is ready for mating. The mare's reaction to the teaser's presence will indicate whether it is time to bring the stallion to her.

INTERNET

www.stallionfinder.com

If you are in the market for Quarter Horse, Paint, Thoroughbred or Appaloosa sires, then Stallion Finder is a good place to start. The site also has its own newsletter as well as links to other resources for breeders.

The stallion is the only horse that will actually cover, or mount, the mare. When it is time for the mare to be bred, she will be placed in breeding hobbles, which fit on her back legs and prevent her from kicking and injuring the stallion. The stallion will be led out and will mount the mare. The entire act of copulation takes only a minute or two. Once the stallion has ejaculated, he will be removed and the mare will have the hobbles taken off and she'll be put away. To ensure that the mare becomes pregnant, most stallions will cover the mare more than once during her heat cycle.

If your stallion is across the country, his semen can be delivered to you for your veterinarian to artificially inseminate your mare. Semen is shipped via express delivery in a large blue thermos-type container. Your vet will choose the time when the mare is ovulating to perform the insemination procedure.

Pregnant mare care

THE MOST IMPORTANT THING you can do for your pregnant mare is to give her correct prenatal care. You can ensure a healthy pregnancy and a robust foal by following a program of good nutrition, deworming, and vaccinations. Alert your vet at the slightest sign of trouble.

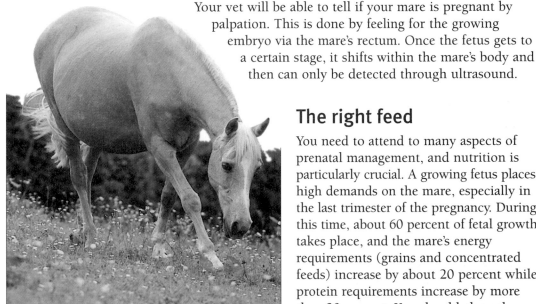
■ **During pregnancy,** *your mare needs to have the right balance of nutrients to sustain the fetus.*

Your vet will be able to tell if your mare is pregnant by palpation. This is done by feeling for the growing embryo via the mare's rectum. Once the fetus gets to a certain stage, it shifts within the mare's body and then can only be detected through ultrasound.

The right feed

You need to attend to many aspects of prenatal management, and nutrition is particularly crucial. A growing fetus places high demands on the mare, especially in the last trimester of the pregnancy. During this time, about 60 percent of fetal growth takes place, and the mare's energy requirements (grains and concentrated feeds) increase by about 20 percent while protein requirements increase by more than 30 percent. You should also ask your veterinarian whether she needs a special vitamin supplement.

As the foal grows larger, the mare doesn't have as much capacity to digest large concentrated meals. By the time she's ready to foal, she should be eating 70 percent forage so that her nutritional needs are met without overloading her digestive system.

Use caution when changing anything in your mare's diet – even when you're just switching hay. Any change might alter the amount of phosphorus to unhealthy levels.

Throughout your mare's pregnancy, your vet needs to check her periodically. Mares should be up to date on their vaccines, as foals get protection from the antibodies in their mother's milk. They should also be placed on a regular deworming program. Internal parasites take their toll on a mare's health, and can also harm the growing fetus.

The birth process

AS THE MARE GETS TO THE END of her pregnancy, you need to make certain preparations in time for the birth. The mare will need a comfortable space in which to give birth, and you will need to provide constant attention.

Preparations

Your mare should have a large stall since she will need room to give birth and the foal will be living in there as well. Nearer the due date, the bedding should be switched to straw because wood shavings can block the tiny nasal passages of the newborn.

Mares – particularly *maiden mares* – can be unpredictable. Even if you know the exact due date, your mare might foal a week early or even a couple of weeks past that date. Undoubtedly, you will want to be there to witness the event and to help out, but there are plenty of stories of owners who stand vigil night after night, only to doze off and wake to a little filly or colt standing by her side. You might want to invest in a closed-circuit television system to monitor your mare in her stall.

DEFINITION

*A **maiden mare** is a mare that has never given birth to a foal before. The due date is unpredictable.*

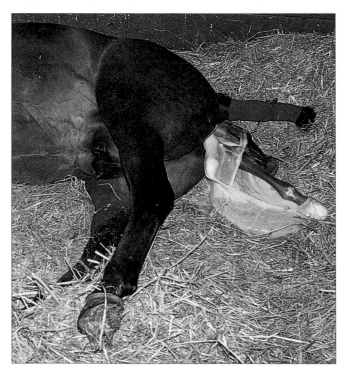

Going into labor

Once your mare gets close to foaling, there are specific signs that the birth is imminent. One is that her tail head will drop, and the area of her haunches directly in front will become loose and spongy. Her teats will wax up, meaning that the mare's first milk will leak out in droplets. Her vulva will also begin to relax in preparation for the foal's birth. When your mare is going into labor, she is likely to lie down.

■ **The front feet** *of the foal, along with the nose, emerge first with the amniotic sac. The mare's tail should be bandaged to keep it out of the way.*

The birth

The front feet of the foal emerge first with the amniotic sac. The mare will push hard to deliver the shoulders, and her whole body will tighten to push out the widest part of the foal. If you are assisting in the birth, you should remove the membrane over the foal's nose so she can begin breathing air. You can also aid the mare by supporting the baby. Once the foal is mostly out, it is time for a rest. The foal will still have the amniotic sac around its lower body with its back legs still inside the mare. The umbilicus will still be attached, providing the last needed nutrients to the foal. It will eventually break, and the mare will expel the placenta.

A breach birth, where the foal is positioned improperly and cannot travel through the birth canal, is life threatening for both mare and foal. Do not try to pull the foal out – call your vet immediately.

The foal is helpless right at birth but will try to make her various body parts work. She gains strength with every minute and attempts to stand by rolling on her chest. After a 30 minute struggle, she will finally rise, balancing precariously on her stiltlike legs. Within an hour, she will be suckling her mother for her first meal.

■ **Mom will take time to bond with her newborn** *through smelling and licking. Your mare will continue licking the foal in the hours after birth to clean her and help her circulation.*

Growing up

*YOUR FOAL'S EDUCATION begins right at birth. The mother begins to teach her baby how to behave. The foal can also be **imprinted** soon after she is born. This will teach her to accept training and handling later in her life.*

A foal grows strong within her first few days and will gambol and play and do all those cute things babies do. Within a week to 10 days, she can be taught to wear a halter, which is sometimes called a foal slip.

Young foals should not be led just by their halters; their necks are still fragile, and you could cause serious injury. Instead, a lead rope should be placed behind a foal's rump, over her back, and then around her front chest, in a figure 8 pattern. You can control her better and more safely this way.

■ **A newborn foal** *will spend the first few weeks of her life staying close by her mother's side. She will rely on her mother for food and protection.*

At about 6 weeks of age, the foal will begin trying to eat solid foods. Within about 3 months, she'll be accustomed to eating on her own, although she will still feed off of her mother.

Foals are usually weaned at around 4 to 6 months. Weaning can be traumatic for foals, and some people prefer to do it gradually by taking the mare away for short periods of time and then bringing her back. Then, the separation sessions become longer and longer until they are permanent.

Foals must be fed correctly, or they can develop growth-related soundness problems. And while very young foals are adorable and friendly, they can quickly become bossy, obstinate creatures that bite and kick. Once they're weaned, their antics can get worse as they challenge you for dominance.

A weaned foal should be kept out of earshot of her mother. If she can hear her mother's whinnies and vice versa, it can make the separation process more unpleasant for both the foal and the mother.

Trivia...

The growth plates on a horse's leg bone do not close entirely until the youngster is at least 2 years old. Race horses often "break down" because their legs are not fully developed when they begin training and racing.

Many foals are turned out for their first 2 years without having much training. During this time, a foal's bones are growing strong and fusing properly. To begin training would put a lot of stress on her growing frame and could cause irreparable damage if she hurts herself.

Enlist the help of a knowledgeable horse person if you run into any trouble while looking after your new foal. There is help on hand either from your veterinarian or branches of breed societies. By handling your foal correctly during the first 2 years of her life, you can better ensure that her saddle training will go smoothly.

A simple summary

✓ If you want to breed your mare, you have to determine whether her genes or temperament are ideal to be passed along.

✓ Consider a potential stallion's conformation, movement, temperament, performance, and existing offspring.

✓ Your pregnant mare should receive proper nutrition, vaccination, and deworming.

✓ The birth of a foal can be hard to predict; some mares deliver up to 2 weeks after the due date.

✓ You need to be ready to provide special care to your mare and new foal after the birth.

✓ A foal begins to be weaned at between the ages of 4 to 6 months, after which time she will be permanently separated from her mother.

Chapter 21

The Golden Years

THANKS TO SCIENCE AND RESEARCH, horses are living longer than ever. New developments in pharmaceuticals have helped the older horse thrive into his 20s and beyond. You can help your aged horse live a useful life by learning what his special needs are as a senior citizen, and then the two of you can have more twilight rides in the sunset years.

In this chapter...

✓ **Growing older**

✓ **Elderly ailments**

✓ **Out to pasture**

✓ **How to let go**

✓ **Special horses**

YOUR HORSE WILL NEED SPECIAL CARE AS HE GETS OLDER

Growing older

DEALING WITH OLD AGE is a sad but inevitable part of being a horse owner. That doesn't mean, however, that your last few years together can't be every bit as rewarding as the earlier years.

How old is old?

It used to be that a horse was considered old by the time he reached his twelfth birthday. Today, however, we consider a 12-year-old horse to be at his peak. As far as competition horses go, many are at the height of their careers in their teens.

Some horses remain active well into their 20s, and you'll even hear tales of 20-something champion horses that are still competing at an international level. But, just like older people, the older horse needs special care to help him remain healthy. Every horse is different and you'll need to cater for your horse's particular needs.

■ **Signs of old age** *will gradually become more visible, particularly around the horse's eyes and muzzle.*

Physical characteristics

When is a horse considered old? It depends on the individual as well as what type of life he has led. If a horse is handled and cared for properly when he is young, he will undoubtedly be in better condition as an older horse than one who didn't have such a good start. Like people, a hard life as a youngster affects a horse's adult years.

In dealing with the older horse, it's important to pay attention to the signs of ageing. If your horse has been in your life for years, you may not notice the gradual changes.

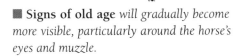

You can tell your horse is getting older by obvious physical changes. One of the most apparent is a swayed back. In addition, he will eat the same amount as before but will not be able to utilize his feed as well, possibly resulting in some weight loss. He might also lose muscle tone. With each winter, his coat will grow in longer and thicker, and each spring, it will take him longer to shed out properly. You might see gray hair appear, especially around the eyes, muzzle, and ears. His pasterns on his hind legs (the bones just below his ankles) will begin to slope more. His incisor teeth will become elongated. And older horses often have a droopy lower lip.

Elderly ailments

AS A HORSE GETS OLDER, he experiences his share of aches and pains as his body changes. Poor conformation, poor nutrition, hard use, injury, obesity, or improper hoof care can increase problems for the aging equine. Here are some of the ailments that afflict the older horse.

Trivia...

The expression "long in the tooth," meaning "old," comes straight from the horse's mouth. In elderly horses, the gums tend to recede which makes the teeth appear longer than they are.

Teeth

Since your older horse may have problems digesting his food and utilizing the nutrients it contains, make sure that his teeth are well maintained. Sometimes a horse's teeth are too worn to chew hay and grain correctly. Unevenly worn teeth can develop sharp points, which can make eating painful for a horse. If your horse has a tooth or gum infection he may not eat at all.

When a horse gets very old, he may start losing his teeth. When this happens, the tooth opposite the missing one doesn't get worn down evenly because there is nothing for it to grind against.

If your horse is having trouble chewing because of teeth loss, you may want to give him a hand by creating a mash of his feed. Alfalfa pellets and complete feeds can be soaked in water and broken down into a gruel.

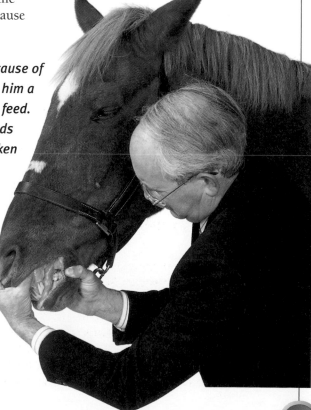

One sign that your horse has dental problems is the dropping of most of his feed on the floor as he eats. You may need to put him on a special diet to prevent him losing weight.

■ **Have your vet check** *your horse regularly and float his teeth (file them with a dental rasp) to remove any uneven points.*

Arthritis

Nearly all older horses are plagued by arthritic conditions to some degree. You can keep your horse comfortable by using a nonsteroidal anti-inflammatory such as phenylbutazone, or by using joint supplements or injections.

It is a good idea to give your older horse medication as sparingly as possible – when he is having a bad arthritis day, for instance. Regularly medicating the older horse may lead to stomach ulcers.

INTERNET

www.horsecentric.com

This site provides both the novice horse person and the expert general information on care, feeding, grooming, and older horse care, among other equine-related topics.

Don't let your horse get out of shape. Regular exercise increases mobility and helps to keep the horse supple. He should have enough room to roam around freely, so that he can keep joints moving on his own.

■ **Even older and arthritic horses** *still need regular exercise and access to outside space to keep them feeling healthy and happy. The more mobile your horse is, the more supple his joints will be.*

Hormonal imbalances

Problems with hormone imbalances are common to the aged equine. These imbalances stem from a deterioration or disease of the endocrine system and may result in the development of Cushing's disease, Addison's disease, or pituitary adenoma. Your vet should check your horse for endocrine function if he seems to get weak or if he sweats excessively, is constantly thirsty, or grows a long hair coat that he cannot shed. If he has a drastic personality change or seems lethargic, let your vet know this as well. These are classic signs of hormonal imbalances.

■ **If your older horse grows** *a thick, curly coat that refuses to shed out even in warmer months, suspect Cushing's disease. This condition also causes a pot-bellied appearance and weight loss elsewhere on the body.*

Weight problems

Nutrition is important to the care of an older horse, so adjust your horse's diet to meet his needs. Be sure he does not get too much protein. Anything over 10 percent protein may put extra strain on his liver and kidneys.

While some older horses lose weight, it is more dangerous for them to be overweight. Excess weight places strain on muscular and skeletal structures, and makes the horse more susceptible to conditions such as laminitis and the development of fatty tumors. Make sure you are not providing your horse with more energy than he can work off.

An underweight horse should be fed foods that are energy dense so that he can get as many calories as possible. You can add extra fat to your horse's diet by simply adding vegetable oil to his regular feed ration.

If your older horse is having problems keeping his weight up, he may benefit from a probiotic, a supplement that contains healthy microflora to help him digest his food better. Many senior feeds have this as an extra ingredient added in.

If you notice that your horse is continuing to gain weight regardless of how much you are feeding him, he may have a thyroid problem. This condition is treatable, so seek advice from your veterinarian. Remember to make any changes or additions to your horse's diet gradually so that he doesn't develop colic.

Out to pasture

YOUR HORSE CAN GIVE YOU MANY YEARS of service and pleasure. And no doubt you'll want to do what is best for your older horse by considering all kinds of options for his senior years. One option is retirement. Most people think older horses should be put out to pasture, but for some, this might not be the best option for body or mind. Many older horses still do well with light exercise to keep their muscles toned, their joints lubricated, and their minds active.

You might consider allowing an older child to ride and care for your horse part time. This will not only give the horse something to do, but the child will also benefit from a placid-natured equine. The child's light weight will not cause stress on the horse's ageing bone structure.

If your horse has lost a lot of muscle over his back, use extra saddle pads to make him more comfortable. Also, a liniment rubdown can soothe his tired muscles after a workout.

■ **Companionship** *will keep older horses happy and alert, and prevent them from feeling lonely if retirement really is the best option.*

While workouts for older horses are beneficial, they shouldn't be too strenuous. Keep the sessions brief and not too difficult. Once riding is no longer possible for your older horse, remember that you can still *pony* him on trail rides.

If you do decide to retire your horse, you might consider making him a companion to another horse. Companionship is important to all horses, and especially to retired horses, who have few other distractions. What you do for your horse in his last years is repayment for all he has done for you during his prime.

DEFINITION

*To **pony** a horse is to lead him alongside a rider who is mounted on another horse. Using this method, two horses can be exercised at the same time.*

How to let go

WHEN A HORSE GETS OLD, he has the same problems that geriatric humans have. He may develop a cranky personality or even exhibit senile behavior. His attention span may become shorter, and he may not be able to react as quickly to situations as he did in the past.

There will come a time, however, when all of your best efforts to manage your horse's ageing processes cannot protect his health and well-being. He will have all but stopped eating, he will take no interest in you or his other companions, and he will be in pain whenever he tries to move about. When this happens, it is time to let your old friend go.

Although death is part of life, it's a really sad time for a horse owner. But having a veterinarian send your horse to his final rest is the most humane way to give him a fitting end to his life – quickly and painlessly. While this is a sad time in our relationship with our horses – and one of the most difficult decisions to make – it is one of the kindest things we can do for them.

What the end is like

Death is different for animals than it is for us humans. Their reality is different from our own. They live very much in the present, without a concept of the future. Although it is very hard for us to deal with, we must always put the horse first.

Death to a horse is simply an end. He doesn't have lost dreams or sadness – just a very dignified acceptance. Veterinarians have reported that a peacefulness comes over a horse at the moment of passing.

In the United States, horses are humanely euthanized, or put down, by administering a massive overdose of a barbiturate drug that acts on the central nervous system. The barbiturate travels within a heartbeat to the horse's brain to depress its functions. The horse first loses consciousness. The parts of the brain that control breathing and heartbeat are more protected, and as a result it may take another few minutes for those functions to cease. But it is important to remember that the horse is unconscious and can't feel any pain. In Europe, the usual method in which a horse is euthanized is by shooting with a humane-killer gun to the head. Death is instantaneous.

Euthanasia is not always a quiet event. When a horse is given the initial drug to end his life, he falls to the ground awkwardly and may groan. Take advice from your vet before deciding to be present during the procedure.

Practical decisions

Euthanasia is one of the most difficult decisions to make. If your inner voice tells you that euthanasia is the best decision, yet you just can't seem to let go, ask yourself why. You might be trying to put off the pain of losing your best friend. You might be feeling like you could have done more for him. You might even hope that natural death will take place first so you won't have to make that hard decision yourself. The main thing is to be honest with yourself. Put aside your own feelings to do what is best for the horse who has done so much for you.

Grieving is normal

It is never easy to put a horse down. You might feel overwhelming sadness, anger, and depression – which are all normal. If friends or relatives don't understand why you are so upset, don't feel that there is something wrong with you. Your horse was a special friend who you lost, and it's natural for you to grieve and mourn his passing.

There are books devoted to the loss of a pet that can help you through your grief. Even speaking to other horse owners who have had to go through the same experience can be comforting.

There are no wrong answers in the decision-making process you had to go through, so don't feel guilty. Euthanasia is an extremely tough decision to make, and you did as best as humanly possible by him.

Your horse lives on

You can pay tribute to your horse in different ways. Arranging favorite photographs into a collage or writing a journal about the good times that you shared can help you cope with his loss better. Some horse owners like to publicly make a memorial to their horses in local magazines by taking out space for a photo and perhaps a poem or story. Others make donations to an equine rescue group or research foundation for a fitting memorial.

INTERNET

www.petloss.com

There are several sites offering support and advice to bereaved horse owners. This web site offers personal support, advice, and poetry. It also has a "Monday Night Pet Loss Candlelight Ceremony" to pay tribute to deceased animals.

It is said that time heals all wounds, and no doubt this is true with the passing of your equine friend. It may take some time to get over the loss, but remember that your grief is a reflection of how much he meant to you. You were lucky to have such a special relationship for the time that you shared together. What you are left with is a wealth of wonderful memories to help you adapt to life without him.

Special horses

IT'S A FACT THAT HORSES touch our lives so strongly that we become attached. They are altruistic creatures that want to please and work with us – giving us a glimpse into unselfishness that we should try to emulate.

Some equines have special jobs that heal troubled people. These horses – often in their senior years – are therapeutic riding horses. Through these special riding programs, disabled children have become strong. Kids with learning disabilities have gained confidence and knowledge. Some with psychological troubles have even gone on to have breakthroughs.

Special horses don't just help children; they touch troubled adults as well. Various programs at correctional facilities throughout North America are now beginning to use horses not only in vocational training, but also to heal those whom the system has forgotten.

■ **The horse is a friend,** *partner, companion, soul mate, and healer. We are better people for being involved with horses.*

A simple summary

✔ Many horses remain active well into their 20s, but like people, the older horse needs special care to help him remain healthy.

✔ Older horses exhibit several signs of ageing, including loss of muscle tone, teeth deterioration, gray hair, a long coat, and a droopy lower lip.

✔ The older horse has several ailments that can debilitate him.

✔ Horses live in the present, and therefore do not fear death the way humans do.

✔ You can pay tribute to your horse after he passes to preserve and honor his memory.

A Simple Glossary

Aids Cues to communicate with a horse. *See also* Artificial aids and Natural aids.

Artificial aids Human-made devices that are designed to help reinforce natural aids. These include spurs, whips, and martingales. Artificial aids should never replace the natural aids, and they should never be used to punish a horse. *See also* Aids and Natural aids.

Backing a horse A phrase used to describe the first time a horse is trained to carry a rider. It refers to the fact that a horse has items (a saddle and, later, a person) placed on his back.

Barn sour A term used for a horse that doesn't want to leave his stable. This behavior is manifested by a poor attitude toward work or obstinate manners under saddle. It is usually caused by too much repetition in a horse's life.

Box stall A space inside a barn in which to keep a horse when he is not working (and when he does not live in a pasture). Usually stalls have dimensions of 12 feet by 12 feet (3.6 m by 3.6 m).

Broodmare A mare that is used for breeding. She should be in good reproductive health and have desirable traits to pass along to her offspring.

Cantle The C-shaped back of the saddle that rises up to cradle the rider's seat. An important part of the saddle, the cantle (along with the pommel) keeps the rider secure in his or her seat.

Cast A cast horse is one that is lying on the ground and finds that he cannot get into a position to get up because he's too close to a stable wall or fence. A cast horse is trapped until someone intervenes.

Chaps Leather or suede protective pants that fit over the front of regular riding pants for western riding.

Coldblooded A term used to describe horses that are not related to Thoroughbred or purebred lines. Coldblooded horses include heavy and draft breeds.

Conjunctivitis An infection of the conjunctival membrane, which covers the front of the eyeball and lines the eyelid. It is generally caused by bacteria, pollen, viruses, or parasites getting into the eyes.

Contact The light but firm connection that a rider has from his or her hands through the reins to the bit, so that he or she can guide and direct the horse.

Cooler A large, absorbent blanket that drapes from the horse's ears down to his knees and over his tail. It is used to help cool down a horse gradually after a sweaty workout. Conversely, the warmer wool and synthetic versions can trap body heat and are used to keep the horse warm.

Cresty A neck where the top arch is exaggerated by extra fat deposits and muscle. Stallions often have these thick, curved necks.

Donkey A domestic ass, that is strong, reliable, and surefooted. *See also* Mule.

Draft horse A breed of horse that was developed for its strength in order to pull a vehicle. Usually associated with heavy breeds, such as the Shire.

Dressage A complex riding discipline. The horse is trained to respond instantly to the subtlest of cues to perform a series of complicated movements.

Farrier An individual who shoes horses. A farrier may also be a blacksmith, since both work over a forge and fashion items from metal. Some blacksmiths, however, have never made horseshoes.

Felt A hard, durable fabric manufactured from loose clumps of rabbit or beaver fur. Most low-cost western riding hats are made of commercial rabbit-fur felt.

Floating A process used by a horse dentist to eliminate any rough or uneven surfaces in a horse's teeth.

Freeze branding A method of identification whereby a freezing-cold iron is used to mark the horse's skin. The hair grows back white.

Frog The V-shaped pad inside a horse's hoof that acts like a shock absorber for the foot.

Furlong A unit of distance that is equal to 220 yards (200 m). There are 8 furlongs in a mile.

Gait There are several horse gaits: The walk is a 4-beat gait; the trot is a 2-beat gait; and the canter is a 3-beat gait.

Gaited Horses that exhibit paces different from the normal walk, trot, and canter. Gaited horses demonstrate tendencies to perform these unique paces naturally, but training brings their gaits out to the fullest.

Ground manners The horse's conduct while you are grooming, bathing, or saddling up.

Gut The horse's digestive tract. The horse's stomach is small, but the intestines are large – nearly 100 feet (91 m) in length – so the horse's body is always digesting food.

Gymkhana From the East Indian word for "games on horseback," these competitive mounted games can be either for individuals or teams.

Hand The unit used when describing the height of a horse, equivalent to 4 inches (10 cm). It originally referred to the width of a hand placed horizontally with the thumb held flat.

Hotblooded A term used to describe horses that are descended from Thoroughbred and purebred lines, such as the Arabian.

Imprinting A method of exposing a newborn foal to various stimuli and situations within the first few hours after birth.

In-Gate The entrance (and often the exit) to a show arena.

Leg yield A sideways dressage movement. The horse moves both forward and sideways, ending up moving across the arena in a diagonal manner. *See also* Side-pass.

Longeing A type of exercise where the horse makes a circle around his handler via an extra-long lead that is attached to the horse's bridle and halter. This allows the horse to be exercised and controlled from a distance.

Maiden mare A mare that has never given birth to a foal before. The delivery date can be harder to predict in a maiden mare.

Manners under saddle The pleasant behavior and willingness a horse displays while being ridden.

Martingale A series of leather straps that attach to a horse's bridle and affix to the saddle's girth to make the horse keep his head down. This artificial aid is called a tie-down in western riding.

Mineral block A block containing salts and trace minerals that are otherwise missing from a horse's diet. The horse licks the block to ingest the minerals.

Mounting block A square step or block on the ground that makes it easier for a rider to climb aboard a horse. Using a block helps relieve stress on the horse's back caused by the rider pulling up from the ground.

Mule A hybrid offspring of a male horse crossed with a female donkey. A mule is usually sterile and cannot reproduce. *See also* Donkey.

Natural aids The cues a rider uses to direct a horse, using the legs, hands, balance (also known as the seat), and voice. *See also* Aids and Artificial aids.

On the bit A horse that is responding to the rider's hand and leg aids, and is moving forward in a balanced, willing manner, carrying his head and body without resistance.

Pacer A horse that is taught a human-made gait that differs from trotting. During the trot, a horse travels in a 2-beat gait with legs moving in diagonal pairs. At the **pace**, the legs move on horizontal pairs. The front and back legs reach forward at the same time with the help of guides, called hobbles, around the top of the legs.

Parrot mouthed A horse that has an overbite, and in some extreme cases, looks like he has bucked teeth. Sometimes this condition, which is inherited, can interfere with eating and wearing a bit.

Pinning the class When a judge assigns places to the top competitors – picking out the winners in order.

Ponying When an unridden horse is led alongside a rider who is mounted on another horse. Using this method, two horses can be exercised at once.

Pommel An important part of the saddle. The pommel is the "head" of the saddle, placed directly in front of the rider. Along with the cantle, it keeps the rider secure in the seat of the saddle.

Premium A show program that gives pertinent information on the competition, including a list of classes, starting time, parking and stabling availability, and the schedule of fees. It may also be called a prize list.

Proud flesh Puffy, granular flesh that sticks out from a wound and does not heal. It is similar to scar tissue.

Pulling a mane A process of thinning and evening out the length of mane hairs to make the mane more regular and smooth.

Run-in shed A three-sided shelter with a roof on the top. It gets its name because a lot of horse owners build them in large pastures, so that the horse can shelter during inclement weather.

Saddleseat A type of riding that originated in the American South, developing out of the desire to have horses travel smoothly over country lanes. The rider sits in a very flat saddle in the middle of the horse's back (instead of up nearer the shoulder, as in most riding styles). This frees up the saddleseat horse's front end to show off his gaits.

Scurf The equivalent of horse dandruff. It is the combination of dirt and skin particles.

Season Being in season is the term for estrus, the mare's heat cycle. A mare usually experiences heat cycles starting in the spring. The cycles last anywhere from 2 to 10 days during which the mare will be at the optimum time to breed.

Shod The process of having a horse's feet trimmed and shoes nailed on.

Shying The action of a horse when he sees a frightening object and has an extremely quick reaction to step sideways. Leaping and running off can accompany this sideways step.

Side-Pass A side-pass is like a side step. The horse crosses the right feet in front of the left while moving sideways rather than forward. *See also* Leg yield.

Signalment The term for using the horse's natural markings for identification. A standard series of numbers and letters corresponds to each mark, giving the horse a code that can be recorded on his papers. Every breed registry utilizes signalment, recording a physical description of the animals registered with them.

Slicked out A horse that has fully shed his winter coat, revealing the short, shiny new hair underneath.

Spooky A horse that is easily startled by things in his environment and overreacts by bolting, shying, or whirling around.

Stallion A male horse that has not been castrated.

Standing a stallion When a breeder offers the stud services of his stallion to mare owners for a fee. Stallion owners earn their living by having their horses impregnate other people's mares.

Trot When a horse trots, her legs move in diagonal pairs in a 2-beat gait.

Turn-Out The leisure time that a horse gets to spend in a small pasture, paddock, or arena by himself. You should turn out your horse for the benefit of his physical and mental health.

Vice A bad habit that a horse can develop – often through boredom or by copying other horses. This includes chewing up fences, pacing, or kicking in his stall. These habits can be very difficult to change.

Breeds of Horses From Around the World

Asia/Africa

Akhal Teke
Arabian
Barb
Przewalski Horse

Europe

Andalusian
Belgian Warmblood
Danish Warmblood
Dutch Warmblood
Friesian
Gelderlander
Groningen
Halflinger
Hanoverian
Holsteiner
Icelandic
Lipizzaner
Lusitano
Norwegian Fjord
Oldenburg
Percheron
Spanish-Norman
Swedish Gotland
Swedish Warmblood
Shagya Arabian
Trakehner

Great Britain and Ireland

Cleveland Bay
Clydesdale
Connemara
Dales
Dartmoor
Exmoor
Fell
Hackney
Highland Pony
Irish Draft
New Forest Pony
Shetland Pony
Shire
Suffolk
Thoroughbred
Welsh Cob
Welsh Pony

South/Central America

Azteca
Criollo
Mangalara Marchador
Paso Fino
Peruvian Paso

United States

American Cream Draft
   Horse
American Paint Horse
American Quarter Horse
American Saddlebred
American White & Cream
Appaloosa
Bashkir Curly
Champagne Horse
Colorado Ranger Horse
Miniature Horse
Missouri Fox Trotter
Morab
Morgan
Mustang
Pony of the Americas
Racking Horse
Rocky Mountain Horse
Standardbred
Tennessee Walking Horse
Thoroughbred (*see also*
   Great Britain)

Other Resources

Educational Organizations

American Association for Horsemanship Safety, Inc.
P.O. Drawer 39
Fentress, TX 78622-0039
USA
512-488-2220
www.law.utexas.edu

American Association of Riding Schools
8375 Coldwater Rd.
Davison, MI 48423-8966
USA
810-653-1440
www.ucanride.com

American Riding Instructors Association
28801 Trenton Ct.
Bonita Springs, FL 34134-3337
USA
941-948-3232
www.riding-instructor.com

American Youth Horse Council
4093 Iron Works Pkwy.
Lexington, KY 40511
USA
800-TRY-AYHC
www.ayhc.org

Canadian Pony Club
C.P.C National Office
Box 127
Baldur, MB R0K 0B0
CANADA
www.canadianponyclub.org

Canadian 4-H Council
930 Carling Avenue
Building #26
Ottawa, ON K1A 0C6
CANADA
www.4-h-canada.ca

Certified Horsemanship Association (CHA)
5318 Old Bullard Rd.
Tyler, TX 75703-3612
USA
www.cha-ahse.org

National 4-H Council
7100 Connecticut Ave.
Chevy Chase, MD 20815-49999
USA
301-961-2959

Legislative/Government Sources

The American Horse Council
1700 K Street, N.W., Suite 300
Washington, D.C. 20006-3805
USA
202-296-4031
www.horsecouncil.org

U.S. Department of Agriculture
Animal and Plant Health
Inspection Services
Administration Building
1400 Independence Ave., SW
Washington, D.C. 20250
USA
www.aphis.usda.gov

Equine Trainers and Clinicians

Clinton Anderson
DownUnder Horsemanship
Equi-Management Group
RR 4 Box 1775
Marble Hill, MO 63764
USA
573-238-4005

John Lyons
John Lyons Symposiums, Inc.
PO Box 479
Parachute, CO 81635
USA
970-285-9797
www.johnlyons.com

Ken McNabb
Ken McNabb Apprenticeships
P.O. Box 2350
Cody, WY 82414
USA
307-645-3149
www.kenmcnabb.com

Lynn Salvatori Palm
Royal Palm Ranch, Ltd.
P.O. Box 197
Bessemer, MI 49911
USA
906-932-0770
http://www.lynnpalm.com

Pat Parelli/Linda Parelli
Natural HorseManShip
463 Turner Drive, Suite 101
Durango, CO 81301
USA
888-293-4287
www.parellicollection.com

Equine Welfare Organizations

American Horse Protection Association
1000 29th St. N.W., #T-100
Washington, D.C. 20007-3820
USA
202-965-0500

Canadian Federation of Humane Societies
102-30 Concourse Gate
Nepean, ON K2E 7V7
USA
(613) 224-8072
www.cfhs.ca

Equine Protection Network, Inc.
P.O. Box 232
Friedensburg, PA 17933
USA
570-345-644
http://equineprotectionnetwork.com

Hooved Animal Humane Society
10804 McConnell Rd.
P.O. Box 400
Woodstock, IL 60098
USA
815-337-5563
www.hahs.org

International League for the Protection of Horses
Anne Colvin House
Snetterton
Norfolk NR16 2LR
ENGLAND
011-44-1953-498-682
www.ilph.org

Redwings Horse Sanctuary
P.O. Box 222705
Carmel, CA 93922-2705
USA
831-624-8464

Veterinary and Health Care Organizations

American Association of Equine Practitioners
4075 Iron Works Pkwy
Lexington, KY 40511-8434
USA
859-233-0147
www.aaep.org

American Holistic Veterinary Medical Association
2214 Old Edmorton Rd.
Bel Air, MD 21015
USA
410-569-0795
www.altvetmed.com

American Veterinary Medical Association
1931 N. Meacham Rd., #100
Schaumburg, IL 60173-4360
USA
800-248-2862
www.avma.org

Animal Chiropractic Center
623 Main St.
Hillsdale, IL 61257
USA
309-658-2920
www.animalchiropractic.org

Canadian Veterinary Medical Association
339 Booth Street
Ottawa, ON K1R 7K1
CANADA
(613) 236-1162
www.cvma-acmv.org

Morris Animal Foundation
45 Inverness Dr. E.
Englewood, CO 80112-5480
USA
800-243-2345
www.morrisanimalfoundation.org

Horse Sport Organizations

American Driving Society
P.O. Box 160
Metamora, MI 48455-0160
USA
810-664-8666

American Endurance Ride Conference
11960 Heritage Oak Place, Suite 9
Auburn, CA 95603
USA
530-823-2260
www.aerc.org

American Hunter and Jumper Foundation
335 Lancaster St.
P.O. Box 369
West Boylston, MA 01583
USA
508-835-8813
www.ryegate.com/AHJF/ahjf.htm

American Vaulting Association
642 Alford Place
Bainbridge Island, WA 98110-3657
USA
206-780-9353
www.americanvaulting.org

Canadian Equestrian Federation
& Equestrian Team
National Office
2460 Lancaster Road
Ottawa, ON K1B 4S5
CANADA
1-866-282-8395
www.equinecanada.ca

Canadian Sport Horse Association
  P.O Box 1625
  Holland Landing, ON L9N 1P2
  CANADA
  (905) 830-9288
  www.canadian-sport-horse.org

Canadian Trotting Association
and Standard Bred Society
  2150 Meadowvale Blvd.
  Mississauga, ON L5N 6R6
  CANADA
  (905) 858-3060
  www.standardbredcanada.ca

Federation Equestre International
  Avenue Mon-Repos 24
  P.O. Box 157
  CH-1000 Lausanne 5
  SWITZERLAND
  011-41-21-310-47-47
  www.horsesport.org

National Barrel Horse Association
  725 Broad St.
  P.O. Box 1988
  Augusta, GA 30903-1988
  USA
  706-722-7223
  www.nbha.com

National Cutting Horse Association
  4704 Hwy. 377 S.
  Fort Worth, TX 76116-8805
  USA
  817-244-6188
  www.nchacutting.com

National Horse Show Commission
  P.O. Box 167
  Shelbyville, TN 3716
  USA
  931-684-9506

National Reining Horse Association
  3000 N.W. 10th Street
  Oklahoma City, OK 73107
  USA
  405-946-7400
  www.nrha.com

North American Riding for the Handicapped
Association
  P.O. Box 33150
  Denver, CO 80233
  USA
  303-452-1212
  www.narha.org

United States Combined Training Association
  525 Old Waterford Rd., NW
  Leesburg, VA 20176-2050
  USA
  703-779-0440
  www.eventingusa.com

United States of America Equestrian
  4047 Iron Works Pkwy
  Lexington, KY 40511
  USA
  859-258-2472
  www.ahsa.org

United States Dressage Federation
  P.O. Box 6669
  Lincoln, NE 68506-0669
  USA
  402-434-8550
  www.usdf.org

United States Equestrian Team
  Pottersville Rd.
  Gladstone, NJ 07934
  USA
  908-234-1251
  www.uset.org

Horse Publications

Chronicle of the Horse
P.O. Box 46
Middleburg, VA 20018
USA
540-687-6341
www.chronofhorse.com

Dressage Today
656 Quince Orchard Rd., #600
Gaithersburg, MD 20878-1472
USA
301-977-3900

Equus
656 Quince Orchard Rd., #600
Gaithersburg, MD 20878-1472
USA
301-977-3900

Horse & Rider
P.O. Box 404
Golden, CO 80401
USA
303-278-1010

Horse Illustrated
P.O. Box 6050
Mission Viejo, CA 92690
USA
949-855-8822
www.horseillustratedmagazine.com

HorseLife Magazine
Equine Canada/Canada Hippique
2460 Lancaster Road
Suite 200
Ottawa, ON K1B 4S5
CANADA
(613) 248-3433

Practical Horseman
P.O. Box 589
Unionville, PA 19375
USA
610-380-8977

Saddle & Bridle
375 Jackson Ave.
St. Louis, MO 63130-4243
USA
314-725-9115

Thoroughbred Times
P.O. Box 8237
496 Southland Dr.
Lexington, KY 40533-8237
USA
www.thoroughbredtimes.com

Western Horseman
P.O. Box 7980
Colorado Springs, CO 80933-7980
USA
www.westernhorseman.com

Young Rider
P.O. Box 8237
496 Southland Dr.
Lexington, KY 40533-8237
USA
www.youngrider.com

Books

Centered Riding, Sally Swift, Trafalgar Square, Vermont, 1985

The Complete Horse Care Manual, Colin Vogel, DK Publishing Inc., New York, 1995

Dressage by the Letter, A Guide for the Novice, Moira C. Harris. Hungry Minds Inc., New York, 1997

Grooming to Win: How to Groom, Trim, Braid, and Prepare Your Horse for Show, Susan E. Harris, Hungry Minds Inc., New York, 1991

Horse Handling & Grooming, Cherry Hill, Storey Communications, Vermont, 1997

The Horseman's Spanish/English Dictionary, Maria Belknap, Breakthrough Publications, New York, 1996

Hunter Seat Equitation, George Morris, Doubleday, New York, 1990

My Horses, My Teachers, Alois Podhajsky, Trafalgar Square, Vermont, 1997

Riding for the Rest of Us: A Practical Guide for Adult Riders, Jessica Jahiel, Hungry Minds Inc., New York, 1996

Saddleseat Equitation, Helen K. Crabtree, Doubleday, New York, 1982

That Winning Feeling!, Jane Savoie, Trafalgar Square, Vermont, 1992

The Ultimate Horse Book, Elwyn Hartley Edwards, DK Publishing Inc., New York, 1991

The United States Pony Club Manual of Horsemanship: Basics for Beginners/D Level, Susan Harris, Hungry Minds Inc., New York, 1994

Western Riding, Charlene Strickland, Storey Communications, Vermont, 1995

Horses on the Web

NO MATTER WHAT horse breed you love or what style of riding you're into, there's a web site devoted to it. Literally hundreds of pages are out there that can help expand your equine knowledge, from medical advice to live rider chat rooms, to online tack catalogs. Find out the latest news and information at the click of a mouse with some of the sites listed below:

www.AAEP.org
This is the official site of the American Association of Equine Practitioners, and it can help you find a veterinarian in your area.

www.aavmc.org
This web site for the American Association of Veterinary Medical Colleges provides information on various educational opportunities and requirements for potential vet students.

www.aerc.org
The American Endurance Ride Conference is the official sanctioning body for equine endurance rides in the United States and Canada. This web site gives news, information, competition dates, and rankings of competitors, as well as help for newcomers.

www.ansci.cornell.edu
To see a list of plant species that are of particular concern to horse owners, log onto this Cornell University site. Also, see www.ansci.cornell.edu/plants/toxhorses.html, another page from Cornell University's Animal Science department, which provides a list of plant species that are toxic to horses, including pictures of many of them.

www.ansi.okstate.edu/breeds/HORSES/
Everything you'd like to know about dozens of horse breeds can be found on this web site.

www.aqha.com
Check out the official web site of the American Quarter Horse Association.

www.arabhorse.com
At Arab Horse, you'll find links for everything imaginable for fans of the Arabian.

www.asha.net
This web site for the American Saddlebred Horse Association promotes the breed as well as the competitions available to Saddlebred horses.

www.avcadoctors.com
Use the American Veterinary Chiropractic Association Doctors web site to search for an AVCA vet in your area.

www.bmbtack.com
Looking for gear for your new horse? This is the home site for BMB blankets, sheets, and other tack and supplies made in America.

www.breedersguide.com
Breeder's Guide is a web site that has a directory of stallion services and information for breeders. It is organized by breed and location, with pedigree and performance details.

www.cantra.ca
The Canadian Therapeutic Riding Association promotes riding as a therapeutic and sports activity for children and adults with disabilities.

www.countrysinglesonline.com
Country Singles Online not only provides you with a site where that country guy or girl can lasso your heart; it also has links to all sorts of country lifestyle sites.

www.cybersteed.com

Cybersteed is a web site from Kentucky Equine Research, Inc., which conducts equine nutrition studies and works with nutritionists to provide information on the latest feed advances.

www.cvma-acma.org

The website for the Canadian Veterinary Medical Association provides information on animal care and educational opportunities for potential vet students.

www.devonaire.com

Check out Devon-Aire, a manufacturer that has a great selection of affordable boots, shirts, jackets, breeches, and more.

www.dropinbucket.com

This is one of many web sites offering alternative remedies online. There is also information on how to find a holistic practitioner in your area.

www.equestrian.org

The American Horse Shows Association provides a calendar of competitions on its web site.

www.equinecanada.ca

The Canadian Equestrian Federation site is great for information on horses and equestrian sports in Canada.

www.equi-sense.com

Equi Sense has all kinds of horse health information, including feeding horses safely, types of horse feed, and equine nutrition.

www.erc.on.ca

Here's an interesting site that includes a Safety Around Horses fact sheet from the Equine Research Center at Guelph, in Canada.

www.erc.on.ca/poison.htm

This web site from the Horse Council of British Columbia, Canada, offers answers to frequently asked questions about poisonous plants.

www.foragetesting.org

Got some hay that you want to know more about? This web site for the National Forage Testing Association can provide you with names of certified test labs in your area.

www.gprix.com

Grand Prix Equestrian Products is an online catalog that features all types of grooming equipment and other horse products.

www.haynet.net

This site has everything under the sun that has to do with horses, plus links to a host of other sites. It works as a portal to other pages around the world.

www.horsecentric.com

Horse Centric provides to both the novice horse person and the expert general information on care, feeding, grooming, and older horse care, among other equine-related topics.

www.horsecity.com

This award-winning site brings you news and information on all horse topics and is updated daily.

www.horseforsale.com

This web site features classified listings and ads for hundreds of horses for sale.

www.horsesincanada.com

Provides information on horses and equipment for sales and lists equine events and equine services.

www.horse-sense.org

On this site, you'll find Jessica Jahiel's Horse Sense Newsletter, which deals with all aspects of horses, their management, riding, and training.

www.horseshoes.net/school and www.horseshoes.com/okstate

The Oklahoma Horseshoeing School and the Oklahoma State Horseshoeing School both offer vocational programs for prospective blacksmiths.

www.horsestudies.com

Equine Body Works Inc. provides information on educational opportunities for people wanting to study equine massage in Canada.

www.horsetrailerclassifieds.com

This site features advertisements placed by people selling trailers as well as those who are looking to buy a used trailer.

www.jimbalzotti.com

Jim Balzotti's Guest Ranch Resource is a wonderful web site that serves as a guide to the horseback riding and guest ranch vacation industry. Balzotti also publishes a comprehensive book on choosing your riding holiday.

www.johnlyons.com

This web site is dedicated to the teachings of "America's most trusted horseman," John Lyons. Over the years, Lyons has developed his natural horsemanship into a training philosophy every horse owner can use.

www.millerharness.com

Miller's Harness Company is the world's leading distributor and manufacturer of equestrian apparel and equipment, offering more than 30,000 products.

www.natrc.org

The North American Trail Ride Conference (NATRC) is one of a number of competitive trail ride organizations in the United States. This web site gives all kinds of helpful advice on getting started in competitive trail.

www.newrider.com

New Rider.com is a British-based site with basic information for the beginning rider.

nicholnl.wcp.muohio.edu/DingosBreakfast Club/IQ/EquineSmarts.html

Check out the equine social intelligence test results from the Journal of Animal Science.

www.nsba.com

The National Snaffle Bit Association is dedicated to promoting western pleasure horses ridden, trained, and shown in snaffle bits (as opposed to other types of tack).

www.overnightstabling.com

This is a web site that provides information on purchasing the Nationwide Overnight Stabling Directory and Equestrian Vacation Guide.

www.petloss.com

This web site offers personal support, advice, and poetry. It also has a "Monday Night Pet Loss Candle Light Ceremony" to pay tribute to deceased animals.

www.prairiehorse.com

An excellent site that provides information on breeders, clubs and associations, schools, holidays, and vets across Canada.

www.riding-instructor.com

The American Riding Instructors Association promotes safe riding by certifying competent riding instructors, publishing Riding Instructor magazine, selling horse books, and running seminars.

www.roamingrider.com

This site provides information on holidays with horses in Canada. It lists where to stay in towns across the country from pack trips and residential holidays to trail rides by the hour.

www.ryegate.com

The American Hunter and Jumper Foundation's web site is dedicated to promoting this branch of English riding with its own shows and championship.

www.shamrock.org

This web site is Ireland's official tourist board site. It's a safe bet that Ireland has more riding and educational holidays than any other country, and this site gives you advice on planning a horse vacation in style.

www.stallionfinder.com

If you are in the market for Quarter Horse, Paint,
Thoroughbred, or Appaloosa sires, then Stallion Finder
is a good place to start. The site has its own newsletter
and links to other resources for breeders.

www.thehorse.com

This site is a companion to the print edition of The Horse
magazine, and has up-to-date medical information in an
easy-to-understand format.

www.therighthorse.com

This is a database that matches buyers' wants
with available horses.

www.thoroughbredtimes.com

Thoroughbred Times is a weekly magazine for breeders,
trainers, owners, and enthusiasts of Thoroughbred horse
racing. This web site is a companion to the print
magazine.

www.yourhorseshealth.com

This site can help you locate equine practitioners in
your area if you haven't selected a vet for your horse.

Index

Acknowledgments

Author's acknowledgments
Much appreciation goes to my fellow equestrians who have helped shape this book and have been my instant "focus group" whenever I needed it: Sharon Biggs; Cindy Hale; Pamela Hampton; Lorraine Hollweg; Matt Rayal of Serrano Creek Ranch; Joe and Katie Lifto of Pacific Coast Jumpers; Janice Posnikoff, DVM; and all my equine teachers.

Packager's acknowledgments
Studio Cactus would like to thank Elizabeth Mallard-Shaw for proofreading and editorial consultancy, Dawn Terrey for design assistance, Hilary Bird for the index, and Barry Robson for the dog illustrations.

Picture credits

t = top, b = bottom, c = centre, r = right, l = left

Andrew Macdonald: 145t
Akhil Bahkshi: 48
Andy Crawford and Kit Houghton: 21, 29tr, 41, 45, 93, 97, 99, 106, 107c, 107bl, 113, 115tl, 115c, 119, 120, 121t, 121b, 124, 125, 133l, 134, 136, 140, 142, 144, 145b, 149b, 151, 154, 157, 159, 160, 165, 170, 175, 178, 179, 180, 182, 183, 185, 186, 198t, 198b, 221, 236, 238, 240, 243
Bob Langrish: 16, 33, 36, 58, 65, 81, 88, 90, 128, 131, 148, 158, 166, 176, 188, 191, 192, 193, 197, 212, 214, 216, 218b, 223b, 226, 228, 231, 246, 248, 251, 254, 255, 258, 260, 261, 263, 267
National Archaeological Museum: 14cr
Photodisc: 210, 211
Richard Tibbits: 30t
Stephen Oliver: 31bl (buckskin detail), 118
Studio Cactus: 29bl, 30bl, 46, 92, 133r, 135bl, 168, 169, 173, 195, 200, 203, 205, 220, 223t, 224, 262

Images are used for illustrative purposes only and do not imply endorsement of any product or service.

All other images © Dorling Kindersley
For further information see: www.dkimages.com